Curriculum, Spirituality and Human Rights towards a Just Public Education

# On (De)Coloniality: Curriculum Within and Beyond the West

*Series Editor*

João M. Paraskeva (*School of Education, University of Strathclyde, U.K.*)

VOLUME 5

The titles published in this series are listed at *brill.com/cwbw*

# Curriculum, Spirituality and Human Rights towards a Just Public Education

*By*

Rogério C. Venturini

*To my Friends:*
*Laurence and Sarah*
*I hope you like what*
*you are about to read.*

*Rgr Vrt.*

BRILL

LEIDEN | BOSTON

Cover illustration: iStock.com/liuzishan

All chapters in this book have undergone peer review.

The Library of Congress Cataloging-in-Publication Data is available online at https://catalog.loc.gov

Typeface for the Latin, Greek, and Cyrillic scripts: "Brill". See and download: brill.com/brill-typeface.

ISSN 2666-3775
ISBN 978-90-04-54994-4 (paperback)
ISBN 978-90-04-54995-1 (hardback)
ISBN 978-90-04-54996-8 (e-book)

Copyright 2023 by Koninklijke Brill NV, Leiden, The Netherlands.
Koninklijke Brill NV incorporates the imprints Brill, Brill Nijhoff, Brill Hotei, Brill Schöningh, Brill Fink, Brill mentis, Vandenhoeck & Ruprecht, Böhlau, V&R unipress and Wageningen Academic.
All rights reserved. No part of this publication may be reproduced, translated, stored in a retrieval system, or transmitted in any form or by any means, electronic, mechanical, photocopying, recording or otherwise, without prior written permission from the publisher. Requests for re-use and/or translations must be addressed to Koninklijke Brill NV via brill.com or copyright.com.

This book is printed on acid-free paper and produced in a sustainable manner.

# Advance Praise for
## *Curriculum, Spirituality and Human Rights towards a Just Public Education*

"In *Curriculum, Spirituality and Human Rights towards a Just Public Education*, Rogério Venturini brilliantly questions what a just (or justice-focused) public education could be. In doing so, he challenges far too often neglected and necessary issues about spirituality in education. As Venturini weaves his text we experience a scholarly depth that integrates the need to addend to the neglect of human rights and the centrality of the spiritual. Venturini's takes the reader on a journey that should lead many to fashion variations on a question posed in Todd Price's foreword: "Should there be a place for the spirit in public education?" Of course there should be. After all, there is a spirit in the public; thus, it follows that this spirit should be formative in public education that is truly of, by, and for the public. One cannot depart from this compelling book without reflecting deeply on the need to integrate advocacy for human rights and the deepest spiritual quest within human capacity. To move toward a praxis of such integration Venturini shows that we must draw upon less-tapped literatures. As an exemplary scholar, teacher and pastor, he draws upon a corpus of work that includes substantial emphasis from Santos, Paraskeva, Freire, Anzaldúa, Mignolo, Quijano, Nkrumah, Valenzuela, Darder, hooks, Apple, Giroux, Huebner, Pinar, Palmer, Saltman, Williams, Tillich, and more—providing an original aesthetic of perspectives from the Global South, a diversity of racial and cultural sources, as well as radical Western views of education and spirituality. I urge you to let this book enter your being and inspire your work to evoke spirituality that contributes to human rights and justice throughout the world."
– **William H. Schubert, Professor Emeritus and University Scholar, University of Illinois Chicago**

"Rogério Venturini's book speaks volumes of a "struggle from within" of an organic intellectual from the Global South. It is a deeply personal and moving account of the epistemic and racial injustice he—like so many others—experienced in his childhood in Brazil. The author offers an insightful critical anti-colonial and decolonial analysis of the dominance of Western Eurocentric epistemology that plagued the curriculum and education systems. In doing so, he advocates the itinerant curriculum theory (ICT) as a just way to address the world's different differences and places spirituality as a counter-hegemonic

human rights issue. Despite the dark picture that this book (rightly) paints of the current state of education and curriculum, it offers hope for a better future. As such it is a gem among the critical curriculum literature and definitely worth reading."
– **Maria Erss, Professor of Education Talin University, Estonia**

# Contents

Foreword: Should There Be a Place for the Spirit in Public Education? IX
   *Todd Price*
Preface XVIII
Acknowledgments XX

Introduction: On Curriculum and Spirituality: Itinerant Curriculum Theory and the Struggle for Non-Derivative Curriculum 'Langue' and 'Parole' 1
   *João M. Paraskeva*

1. The Inevitable Unfinished Transcendent 5
2. Towards a *Plus Que Parfait Imparfait* Theory 14
3. 'Conscientização' and 'Consciencism': A Spiritual Call 19
4. Critical Prophetic Pragmatism 25
5. Confronting the 'Chamber of Horrors' 29
6. The Monumentality of a Prosperous Divisive Curriculum Reason 37
7. Itinerant Curriculum Theory: Towards a Non-Derivative Curriculum *'Langue'* and *'Parole'* 45

1 **The Truth about My Schooling: "A Struggle to Fly Inside a Bottle"** 59
   1. Let Me Begin from the Beginning, as "in the Beginning Was the Word" 63
   2. A Subtractive Culture of Learning 69
   3. Contradictory Education 84

2 **Identity Matters: On (Whose) Spirituality!** 94
   1. Introduction 94
   2. Defining Spirituality: A Possible Impossibility? 94
   3. Coherence—*Really*—Matters: "Morality" and "Honesty" 108
   4. Within and beyond Life "as Is" 113
   5. The Ordinary: A Global Context 118
   6. "Consciencism" and "Conscientização": A Spiritual Call 123
   7. Whose Identity! 131

3   A Conservative Neoliberalism or Neoliberal Conservatism?   155
    1   Introduction   155
    2   The Absence of Authentic Leadership: Framing Dropouts   155
    3   On Neoliberalism   164
    4   Everything But Spirituality and the Humanities   171
    5   Reflection on Whose Knowledge!   180

4   Coloniality and the Pedagogies of Neoliberalism   188
    1   On Coloniality   189
    2   A Sociology of Absences   201
    3   The Decolonial Turn: Towards an Itinerant Curriculum Theory   210

5   A Conclusion: Spirituality as a Counter-Hegemonic Human Right   216

    References   221

FOREWORD

# Should There Be a Place for the Spirit in Public Education?

*Todd Price*

It is neither a trivial or insignificant question. In the 1600s, little communities in the New England colonies sought to educate their young in a righteous path and relied on a minister and the King James Bible in that order. Spirituality largely imagined the older, learned man imparting 'the Word' on his flock. Post-revolution, some hundred years later, brought radical changes to a newly federated United States; education was re-imagined as *public,* orientated toward sustainability…of the new Republic. *Public education* would be secular, conceived in common law for the common good, with the creation of a Common Man (although Common Women filled out the teaching corps, see Catherine Beecher) and in a non-sectarian Common School (Horace Mann from the 1830s). Bringing together families and their offspring from different sects (different ethnicities, different classes) required keeping at arms-length religious indoctrination, spiritual orientation, and personal predilection.

Reading, 'riting, and 'rithmetic were part and parcel of the curricula, but additionally was the formation of an American citizen, not a religious acolyte. The Common School's primary purpose was to grow a child into an adult, with the "knowledge of most worth" (Spencer, 1867) based on science, not dogma. This question was/is unpacked by scholars, such as within what Paraskeva (2021a, 2021b) defines as a radical critical river within a generation of utopia.

As the nineteenth century drew on, waves of immigrants necessitated placing children into factory-type schools, and by the turn of the twentieth century, the modern high school took form, sorting future workers (Marjorie Murray notes the concurrent rise of the union movement), managers and business owners (David Tyack and Larry Cuban et al. describe this history) throughout. Religious practices related to non-economic or spiritual growth were relegated to communities of fellowship, largely in gatherings around township churches.

In everyday practice since then, religious church attendance has waxed and waned; spiritual teachings remain the purview of book study groups or more intimate settings.

This is not to say that public schools sat idle. Sans spirituality, schools filled the space with curricula beyond academics; it is in evidence today that teaching practices, curricular materials, and the learning space itself are moving beyond merely the cognitive and more toward (ironically so, since the discarding of religion per se) the beatification of the individual.

In a straightforward example, public schools and school districts are embracing (or some are fighting) socio-emotional learning (SEL), culturally responsive teaching and leading (CRTL), and positive behavior intervention systems (PBIS).

In other words, teaching children how to get along with one another, something that would have been unheard of a few short decades ago, is deemed to be of some 'sort of benefit to the child's soul.' Public education in this 21st century instance, and in so many more ways, is now the site of infusions of the transcendent over the material, meaning that children are being taught to evolve into something more, and not simply that which is measurable in terms of standardized test score (although these indices still carry significant weight in college admissions). Public schools are charged with taking children and refining them, making them lifelong learners, productive workers, and responsible citizens. Why not add to their spiritual maturation development so they emerge as ethical human beings too?

Such is the aspiration I believe Venturini's text strives for. There are challenges in the first instance from the law, and here is how.

To digress for a moment, from Thomas Jefferson's letters in the early 1800s, culminating with the Blaine Amendment (1875) post-Civil War, a wall was gradually established between church and state. This was a forward-thinking, modern move that valorized scientists over sentimentalists and pedagogues over proselytizers. Working its way through the Common School, as mentioned, the era of Horace Mann, evangelicalism was sidelined; religiosity would occasionally show up, but only in a modest form (although to agnostics and atheists, overbearingly so) in the celebration of Christian holidays, in the recitation "one nation under God" during the pledge of allegiance, and the assemblage (and debates from the 1950s forward) of 'prayer in school.'

To date, Supreme Court rulings generally find fault with the exercise, incantation, or expression of any catechism served in the public school.

Nonetheless, battles continue to wax and wane throughout modern society concerning sectarian values of the church(es) and state, often devolving down to simple terms such as the innocuous-sounding 'choice.' In a (re)renewal of the culture wars today, religious zealots seek to forward the innocent-sounding 'choice in education' yet at the same time seek to take away choice from others or to undermine historical, social, or cultural discussions in classrooms (or the classrooms they imagine) that deviate from their own 'choice' of storytelling. Their passion is, too often, a peculiar and narrow notion of consequentiality following "one nation under God."

But all of these interesting examples of the back-and-forth history, what has been termed "the struggle for the American Curriculum" (Kliebard, 1987), only serve to provide a prelude to the thesis of this critical essay. In *Curriculum, Spirituality, and Human Rights towards a Just Public Education*, Rogério Venturini argues not for state-sanctioned religion but rather for a kinder, more reflective pedagogy, a liminal space honoring the dignity of the individual as *homo spiritus*. That man [sic] is more than merely a rational, self-interested being (*homo econimicus*), Venturini feels is worth fighting for. His is a call amidst this separation toward a recognition of the whole person, of respect for that person as a human being, one with a spirit and an entirety. Absent the spiritual, Venturini would explain, is alienation, perhaps in the vein of 'one-dimensional man' (Marcuse, 1964).

Further still is the march toward depersonalization and commodification of human souls, as is characterized in Venturini's vision of 21st century neoliberalism and its felt impression on schools and classrooms. Drawing on Paraskeva (2021b), he frames such depersonalization and commodification within the current absurdism that became normalcy. We live in an era "of absurdism and abnormality. From successive devastating economic and environmental havoc, the war is now facing a pandemic with a lethal footprint throughout the planet" (Paraskeva, 2021b, p. 4). But let's consider Venturini's own text to continue.

### Unfolding and Emerging

Venturini's excerpts provide rich terrain for extrapolation, for meaning-making. The observation appears to me that the spiritual might have started as unknowable and unnamable, but in the curricular and pedagogical work imagined here, it begins to be understood differently. We begin here:

> spirit constitutively refers to who we are, and the sphere where we are is in constant unfolding, enhancing, and enabling mode, our unique inner essence and being that may be linked to a greater good and/or divinity. This relationship makes spiritual 'beings.'

To my reading, this idea of a relationship makes possible an evolution in our conception of the spirit from the primordial thing (think of, for example, the Tao) to a beatific deed (coming into communion with one another, for example). Without any reference, in particular, it is easy to imagine a pre-modern time when conceived is a spirit as an external entity. Over centuries (in the Americas, for another example, access to printed text—the Guttenberg-published bible—meant not only spiritual consciousness-raising but the development of individual literacy. The ability of one to make their own sense of the omnipotent leads to spirituality becoming a process and action, and the development of the notion of an individual being who moves through greater awakening became more explicit and legitimate.

To further this point, I believe the evolution from spirit to spirituality appears in the conception of the idea throughout Venturini's text and in the questions made possible. First are the perennial curriculum questions that Venturini's scholarly work engages with crucial curriculum questions such as 'what knowledge is of most worth?' and 'whose knowledge is of most worth?' But using the spiritual lens, the itinerant curriculum theory, and theorists—championed by João M. Paraskeva (2011)—must wrestle with a more challenging question, namely, 'where are we going…now?' In Paraskeva's (2016, 2021a, 2021b, 2022) proclamation, such 'now' implies a decolonial turn towards a non-derivative non-abyssal theory, one that responds to the world's different and diverse epistemes—a declaration of epistemological independence (Paraskeva, 2016, 2018, 2021a, 2021b, 2022).

To the teaching of Itinerant Curriculum Theory (ICT), the existential is/has a cognitive and empirical referent; we must go beyond the Eurocentric cognitive and empirical (and the critical) and commit to deterritorialize and to de-link from the epistemicidal Eurocentric matrix as Paraskeva (2016, 2017, 2021a, 2021b, 2022) implore, however, and reflect upon during our spiritual journey (as the itinerant traveler tends to do) our presence in the world, and state what we know to be true. This is not a contradiction, and in Chapter 2 Venturini says so when he notes:

> Positivism claims that the only authentic knowledge is scientific knowledge derived from actual sensed experience and the "strict" application of the scientific method as measurable things. However, even ultra-positivist Comte (1822) created the law of three stages, acknowledging that human beings rely on supernatural agencies to explain what they can't explain otherwise.

In acknowledging a material world, Venturini goes on to affirm a role, nonetheless, for spiritual understanding and lauds a common good. In Chapter 2, he draws on Lamont (1990), who, in turn, claims that

> humanism "believes in an ethics or morality that grounds all human values in this-earthly experiences and relationships and that holds as its highest goal the this-worldly happiness, freedom, and progress—economic, cultural, and ethical—of all humankind, irrespective of nation, race, or religion. (p. 13)

In Venturini's terms, consciousness cannot be denied or ignored by any pedagogical and curriculum approach. It is inherent to any individual and part of any human being's temporality. He places spirituality as a significant dynamic within the major struggles against power structures and oppression, such as the civil rights glorious momentum. In doing so, he introduces a new itinerant river in the field, 'blending'—as he argues—Paulo Freire's (1995) well-known frame of 'conscientização' with Kwame Nkrumah's (1964) 'consciencism.' Sentient of the importance of Gloria Anzaldúa, Cornell West, and Michael Dantley matrixes, Venturini advances spirituality as a form of critical consciousness, resistance, and inquiry; he subscribes to the importance of prophetic pragmatism (West, 1988) as part of the human being's 'formas de conocimiento' (Anzaldúa, 2002) (ways of knowing), that needed to be respected within a very concrete temporality (Huebner, 1975). Spirituality is a critical way of existing (Dantley, 2005), the 'courage to be' (Tillich, 1952), which implies a struggle from within (Pinar, 1974). Such cannot be absent (Santos, 2014) in our field.

Even amidst the advent of neoliberalism, I find that schools and communities nonetheless would essentially subscribe, at least in theory and often in practice (classrooms), to 'happiness, freedom, and progress' as laudable goals. Can these goals be achieved without an explicit connection to the spiritual? It is Venturini's take (see Chapter 2) that thinking better is not sufficient:

> The journey to have access to truth, however, is by no means a purely intellectual act. It sometimes requires certain sacrifices, renunciations, and purifications, of which Socrates provides an example. Socrates claimed to have a mission from God to exhort the Athenians, whether they were old or young, to stop taking care of things and instead take care of themselves.

As noted herein, 'to take care of themselves' is highly relevant to the modern era, with programs such as "social-emotional learning" (SEL) in widespread use across the country. Maslow's hierarchy obliquely refers in its highest stage to a 'self-actualization' that, with a little creativity, could be translated into the spiritual relationship Venturini seeks for himself and all of his students. But certainly, in classroom instances, to talk explicitly about the spirit is, in public, secular education, a transgression. Is there another way to honor the whole soul that Venturini sees in each of his pupils?

A different and perhaps most compelling claim of Venturini's is the archetype of 'recognition.' He accurately brings Nancy Fraser into the conversation. It is worthy and timely to delve into more expert scholars in this ultra-modern concept, which is for another study; I much encourage it. Suffice it to state here that Venturini seems to take particular issue more with the contemporary moment that (I would assume) from his vantage point is (a)historical and (a)spiritual, and fixes in time and place identity. In Chapter 3, he draws from an interesting scholar whose work is prefaced on the distinctions attributed to identity but perhaps has second thoughts?

> I want to argue here that we need a way of rethinking the politics of recognition…this means conceptualizing struggles for recognition so that they can be integrated with struggles for redistribution rather than displacing and undermining them. It also means developing an account of recognition that can accommodate the full complexity of social identities instead of one that promotes reification and separatism. (Fraser, 2000, p. 119)

This is a critical point that society in contemporary forms excludes through binary thinking and attempts to erase foundations, or alternatively cements in time foundations that in turn erase or marginalize other stories of recognition, upon which identities are made or are misinformed. Venturini (Chapter 2) is obviously more than a little interested in such matters when he writes that

> we should operate on the principle that individuals identify themselves via already existing terms, and, from there, tend to align themselves with the aims of those terms; further, these same terms also determine how the individual will be identified by society…

Venturini (Chapter 2) insightfully references Kwame Anthony Appiah (2005). Moreover, he scratches the itch, sure to spread in the years ahead amidst the latest round of culture wars:

> Identity thus now depends on whatever the current volatile social culture is presenting as style. The rhetoric of diversity has hybridized new cultural identities, wherein most of us have something in common while we leave behind what we originally were in order to belong or fit in.

But in Chapter 2, Venturini offers a corrective, rejecting, to a large degree, foundationlessness in pursuit of hybridity,

> We cannot move away from the social-cultural piece. Indeed, if we remember that it is the suture that unites culture to unfolding identity, we must recognize that we intrinsically need our communities and societies. Separated, there can be no proper fit, no belonging whatsoever.

Further, Venturini (in Chapter 2) subjects to the analysis of colonial and post-colonial, nation-state, and neoliberal conditions and relates most tellingly given his personal narrative to migration, especially with his reference here:

> The migrations of modern times...the people have taken with them only a part of the total culture...peculiar types of culture-sympathy and culture-clash appear. (Bhabha, 1994, p. 54)

### Identity, Recognition, and the Transcendent

Deeply influenced by Paul Tillich, Dwayne Huebner, and James MacDonald, Venturini takes aim in a crucial part of this essay on identity, recognition (and misrecognition), and life itself; here, I see the connection with my own contribution to Paraskeva's work his "clarion call" for a different difference, for not leaving behind any stone unturned in the quest for a knowledge of *most* worth. In one example, my mentor, Cuban pedagogue Roberto Oscaris, who noted that

> [spiritual] incentives were designed to supplement the material items with social recognition...in the workplace...in the area of residence...in society in general; the workers would be distinguished by wearing small labels, little buttons such as "vanguard workers" and "forefront farmer."

The story still leaves a warm impression upon me of everyone in the new society, a revolutionary one at that, doing their part, and being seen. In sum, and inspired by the clarion call of Paraskeva for a "different difference," I note that,

> Life will save education...life is education. ICT is a poesis that itinerantly throws the subject against the infinitude of representation to grasp the omnitude of the real(ity) and the rational(ity), thus mastering the transcendent. (Price, 2017)

In asserting a spiritual life, Venturini is the same. While he does not take up a battle between church and (neoliberal) state (although he does indeed reduce the school to the condition of late, modern capitalism) rather—and more interestingly so to my rendering—he makes a case for the spiritual education. He claims and (re)claims the spirit as process and places in motion spiritual beings in relationship to a common good. A common good might be a foundation, one essentialism *we* curricularists could all strive for or toward. And for that reason, the following essay is highly worth engaging in and with and wondering about the infinitude for which no amount of exploration can genuinely explain.

Venturini's *Curriculum, Spirituality, and Human Rights towards a Just Public Education* is a timely and priceless volume. In a moment that liberal arts and education are under the gun of market desires, in a moment that neoliberalism became public pedagogy—accountability, meritocracy, de-funding policies, de-skilling of teachers, mechanization of teacher education programs, classroom management, weak unionism or no unionism at all, choice creed, abyssal curriculum forms, curriculum for jobs, among others aspects—it is crucial to place spirituality at the center of our curriculum non-derivative debates; it is essential to fight for a holistic education one that protects the human being in its complex temporality (Huebner, 1975)—as Venturini adamantly advocates. In doing so and drawing on Santos (2015), Venturini challenges the hegemonic normative and celebratory pedagogical praxis of human rights and calls for spirituality as a counter-hegemonic human rights issue that all educators must protect.

## References

Anzaldúa, G. (2002). (Un)natural bridges. (Un)safe places. In G. Anzaldúa & A. Keating (Eds.), *This bridge we call home* (pp. 1–6). Routledge.

Appiah, A. (2005). *The ethics of identity*. Princeton University Press.

Dantley, M. (2005). African American spirituality and Cornell west notions of prophetic pragmatism. *Education Administration Quarterly, 41*(4), 651–674.

Huebner, D. (1975). Curriculum as concern for man's temporality. *Theory into Practice, 6*(4), 172–179.

Kliebard, H. (1995). *The struggle for the American curriculum, 1893–1958*. Routledge.

Macdonald, J. (1974). *Theory as a prayerful act: The collected essays of James B. Macdonald*. P. Lang.

Marcuse, H. (1964). *One dimensional man*. Routledge.

Paraskeva, J. (2011). *Conflicts in curriculum theory: Challenging hegemonic epistemologies* (1st ed.). Palgrave.

Paraskeva, J. (2016). *Curriculum epistemicide: Towards an itinerant curriculum theory*. Routledge/Taylor & Francis.

Paraskeva. J. (2018). *Towards a just curriculum theory: The epistemicide*. Routledge.

Paraskeva, J. (2021a). *Curriculum and the generation of Utopia*. Routledge.

Paraskeva, J. (2021b). Did Covid-19 exist before the scientists? Towards curriculum theory now. *Educational Philosophy and Theory, 54*(2), 158–169. https://doi.org/10.1080/00131857.2021.1888288

Paraskeva, J. (2022). *Conflicts in curriculum theory* (2nd ed.). Palgrave.

Price, T. (2017). Welcome to the new Taylorism! Teacher education meets itinerant curriculum theory. *Journal for the American Association for the Advancement of Curriculum Studies, 12*(1), 1–20.

Santos, B. (2014). *Epistemologies of the south: Justice against epistemicide*. Routledge/Taylor & Francis.

Santos, B. (2015). *If god were a human rights activist: Human rights and the challenge of political theologies*. Stanford University Press.

Spencer, H. (1860). *Education: Intellectual, moral, and physical*. D. Appleton and Company.

Tillich, P. (1952). *The courage to be*. Yale University Press.

West, C. (1988). *Keeping faith: Philosophy and race in America*. Routledge.

# Preface

Although spirituality in education and curriculum is a sensitive topic, it is nonetheless vital to move beyond restrictive religious views of spirituality and to see how it plays a role in all of our lives. Western modernity has created a dangerous cult of totalitarian positivist notions, deploying a praxis of rationality that arrogantly legitimizes only specific epistemological frameworks (Paraskeva, 2011, 2016). In the process, this hegemonic worldview has sidelined any other forms of understanding the self, the other, the word, and the world, while superciliously claiming that Western modern rationality is the only way to comprehend our complex reality. Spirituality is an integral part of human subjectivity and thus Western modernity rationality alone has been insufficient to address or even mitigate the major social issues we are facing in this third phase of capitalism (Arrighi, 2005).

Public institutions, such as schools, have been used to foster this totalitarian positivist cult. These alleged instruments of the public good have imposed a set of concepts and practices that defend and legitimize Western modernity rationality as not just the superior epistemological framework but the only valid one. In a world that is epistemologically diverse, any mode of thought that purports itself to be "the only epistemology" is a eugenic claim (Santos, 2014). I challenge such eugenic claims and call for a public education that is inclusive and genuinely dedicated to the common good. A lethal reign of individualism, competition, ethnic cleansing, poverty, and starvation, along with anti-human immigration and slavery practices, has paved the path to the current neoliberal era.

I argue that in silencing other epistemological forms outside of Western modern rationality, U.S. public education has created an abyssal line (Santos, 2014). I further contend that the need for spirituality in public education is a human rights issue—a matter of social and cognitive justice (Santos, 2014)—a subject that, throughout this book, I intend to dissect down to its bones. Along the way, I will examine identity and spirituality from a personal perspective, through my experiences of (1) being a chaplain dealing with dying patients, (2) losing my brother, (3) observing the death of Geronimo, an itinerant worker, (4) being a private school administrator, and (5) attempting to crossing an abyssal line in moving from Brazil to the United States.

In addition, these five events will help me unravel how (a) the sense of the wonder of life and, the sense of spirituality as an aspect of life should be a capstone within and throughout the schooling process in order to educate students for life, instead of preparing them for future "success"; (b) during critical moments in life, regardless of age, our consciousness puts us up against the wall, thereby stirring questions that bring us to a maturing transcendent aspect of conscientization (Freire's term, explored more in Chapter 2, encompasses action and reflection) of life's value; (c) as dehumanized children of the empire, our identities and life values may be colonized through schooling and social constructivism perpetuating ideas of existence without essence. Through my analysis, I will call for a public education and curriculum that encourages students and educators to engage with spirituality as a powerful tool to overcome imposed, colonized understandings of life and the self. I will frame the pursuit of such strategies as both an act of social justice and a human rights issue.

The very nature of my claim—one effectively silenced in so many sectors of our field—implies different approaches in which the "power of the person" is not sidelined. As a male minority for whom spirituality plays a major role in my own ways of being and thinking and acting, as Smith (2004) would put it, I experience oppression by both dominant and counter-dominant Eurocentric theories and methodologies that systematically dismiss an important component of my identity. Darder (2019) states,

> [I]n many academic settings, doctoral students are infantilized and, more so, if these students are members of indigenous or subaltern communities. This is further intensified if they hail from working class communities of color, where they obviously lack the social and academic pedigree of the elite and privileged student. The deficit lens that has generally accompanied their educational journeys is recognized only too well by those who have traversed the path to a doctoral degree, often as the first in their families to receive an advanced degree of any kind. In this case, perceptions and judgements are tied to stereotypical notions that these students are insufficiently prepared to participate in the ambitious project of critiquing and transforming educational theory. In the process, they were often met with "well-meaning" disrespect and a professional tendency to expertly silence their dissident voices. (pp. 4–5)

I rely on post-abyssal thinking, rather than the modes of thought academia has attempted to impose on me, to understand—and teach how to understand—the importance of spirituality within our schools' curricula. So, I've consciously designed this book to provide an overview of how spirituality, curriculum, and human rights have been dealt with within the educational realm, across all grades and levels, including colleges and universities. As they have for decades, most academics and educators categorically deny the beneficial aspects of spirituality. That denial drove me to establish my own framework—"aja"/conociminento" (Anzaldúa, 2002a, 2002b)—for breaking the silence about the interrelations between cultural relevance, spirituality, and curriculum.

# Acknowledgments

Building a brick wall is always a collaborative process in which, brick by brick, layers are assembled that eventually make up a wall. Although I have long had a deep passion for education in this diverse society, my concerns grow stronger every day as I observe the struggles people are going through just to live a life that makes sense to them. My interests in justice and a better, more fair society are vital to my spiritual commitments. I always want to teach subjects that lean towards cultural relevance, especially in the university setting, where more and more students are expressing significant concerns about the meaning of their lives. I believe that addressing these questions can add equity not just to students' lives but to academics as well.

There are numerous people I would like to thank for participating in this assemblage of ideas. To be sure, my wife Holly and my daughters Gabriela, Sophia, and Bianca have been the reason why I strive to spread ideas for a better and more just society. They have been my motivation, a source of key observations, and a haven where I can always find love and strength without any reservations.

I want to acknowledge my dear professor and friend, Professor João Paraskeva, who has been a central influence in my decision to publish this manuscript. All along the way, he has inspired me and so many others to continue to fight for relevance in the academic sphere, to champion the whole student and education that makes sense—even though the academic world is beyond epistemologically diverse and sometimes controversial. As Zig Ziglar states, "end the day with gratitude," and gratitude will always make me deeply admire and respect Professor Paraskeva on so many levels. I thank my dear colleague Dr. Elizabeth Janson for helping me organize my thoughts, motivating me to express my inner sense of spirituality, and providing editorial enhancement. But the most significant thing I want to thank her for is her friendship and transparency. A special thanks to Professor Kenneth Saltman for his teasing ideas and critical eyes in seeing dominance through policies and capitalism affecting education and our society, and especially for his demonstration of sympathy when I lost my father while a doctoral student. A special thanks to Professors Todd Price and William Schubert for his critical comments and generous foreword and gracious endorsements. My gratitude to John Bennet as well, my publisher at Brill, for his care and support.

Needless to say, I'm grateful to my parents, Geraldo and Antonia, who planted the seed and who, with suffering, struggles, tears, and sacrifice, were able to motivate me to get where I am now. From them I learned, in multiple ways, not only to construct knowledge but to make meaningful sense of life. Finally, I want to thank the one who makes all things possible, my Creator in whom I trust!

INTRODUCTION

# On Curriculum and Spirituality

*Itinerant Curriculum Theory and the Struggle for Non-Derivative Curriculum 'Langue' and 'Parole'*

*João M. Paraskeva*

> Can education be re-imagined?
> HUEBNER (1999a)

∴

Spirituality could very well be defined as one of the contemporary *Freudian* hysterical silences—or marginalizations—that saturate our field—as Murzban Jal (2023) would have put it. It is a socially constructed 'non-existence' (Santos, 2014), particularly and oddly within the current counter-dominant hemisphere of curriculum *langue* and *parole*. This 'invisibility' fertilizes a reductive and inaccurate pedagogical grammar that cannot grasp the inner complexities of the human being and its relationship with the world. As Dwayne Huebner alerts us, the work of the German phenomenologist and existentialist philosopher Martin Heidegger is crucial in our curriculum endeavor as it helps to unpack how "language is our most dangerous possession; it covers or hides at the same time that it uncovers and reveals" (Huebner, 1999a, p. 257). Our language, the language through which we weaved our theoretical labor—or what's left of it—and praxis, the language through which we have unpacked the struggle for the U.S. curriculum fits the—Heidegger's—bill.

Spirituality is a very sensitive and disruptive topic. That 'spirituality is a dimension of human 'personality,' and cognitive matrix' and quite structural on how one reads the world (Hogan, 2009) is quite contentious. However, the idea that "we each have an interior mind and spirit that resides within us and to which we have privilege access hunts and pervades western thinking since the time of Plato and continues to dominate the conceptualizations of spirituality" (Radford, 2006, p. 387). Such idea is exceptionally touchy and divisive though. For some, spirituality is discernible in all aspects of our society (Drazenovich, 2004); it "deals with an unseen reality beyond the material of what one can perceive with the senses" (Jacobs, 2012, p. 239); it deals with the "nature of meaning, an expression of non-materiality in a fundamentally material universe" (Kay, 2003, p. 292). That is, spirituality "refers to human beings' subjective relationship (cognitive, emotional, and intuitive) to what is unknowable about existence, and how a person integrates that relationship into a perspective about the universe, the world, others, self, moral values, and one's sense of meaning" (Senreich, 2013, p. 553). Some detach spirituality from religion. Religion is framed not as metaphysical, but as a social construction (Schilbrack, 2012). That is, "spirituality should be excavated scientifically out of any religious creed" (Hogan, 2009, p. 138). Others place spirituality as a flux of religion—an undividable way of existence. Spirituality has no social validity; it is a reified concept of a reified reality instrumental in producing reified human beings and institutionalized in pluriverse forms of religions—framed in *Marxian* terms, as social opium. Spirituality, in this view, is a reactionary force blocking any struggle toward knowledge freedom and the emancipation of the individual. Walach (2011, p. 18) defines spirituality as a "spiritual experience and as a direct, unmediated experience of an absolute reality that is beyond the experiencing self."

For others, spirituality is framed as "the most powerful and authentic form of agency" (Tario, 2019, p. 182), a form of "critical—pragmatic—consciousness" (Todorova, 2019, p. 223; Nkrumah, 1964; Freire, 1995; Dantley, 2005; West, 1988); spirituality is 'conocimiento.' (Anzaldúa, 2002); an inner "tool or methodology that can enable one to navigate through life after their complete life has been distorted, fragmented and many times destroyed" (Wane, 2019, p. 16). There is "no private inner world of wonder but rather a public world that is internalized" (Radford, 2006, p. 393). Spirituality relates to spaces of authenticity (Tario, 2019). It is thus a form of unmeasurable social capital (Noghiu, 2020) that allows understanding and challenging unjust mechanisms of power, segregation, exploitation, and oppression unleashed by 'greedy materialistic' traditions. Such dualism is recognized by some philosophical materialistic pundits who argue that "there are no mental events without physical ones, bodily or neurologically" (Radford, 2006, pp. 387–388). Some research defines such agency within multiple forms of spiritual activism (Tario, 2019, p. 188). Spirituality is thus lived as a political asset to navigate within the absolutism of 'the physical' and challenge it. Such 'politicality' produced and has been produced a specific "spiritual capital theory through a specific language" (Noghiu, 2020, p. 49). Rogério Venturini's *Curriculum, Spirituality, and Human Rights towards a Just Public Education* places spirituality as intrinsically critical and transformative (Nkrumah, 1964; Freire, 1995; Dantley, 2005; Anzaldúa, 2002), as a perpetual 'possible impossibility.' His rationale complexifies spirituality as social capital, inquiry, and resistance; he frames spirituality as a 'counter-hegemonic human rights issue.'

The battle between imparity and parity of reality/experience *vs.* spirituality is as old as the existence of humanity. The history of such a wrangle is rich and floods the estuary of humanity with endless multifarious debris that our field cannot afford to ignore. The fact that it is a divisive 'dualist' topic—or field—that raises many controversies and might open irreversible pandora boxes cannot be a reason for such dynamic not being discussed, thought about, and addressed by curriculum theorists. Spirituality structures the experiences and nature of millions of human beings (Hogan, 2009; Freire, 1995; Nkrumah, 1964; Dantley, 2005; West, 1988; Anzaldúa, 2002; hooks, 2009).

Despite its centrality in the pre-enlightenment period—in which "curriculum was assumed to be a spiritual journey" (Pinar et al., 1995, p. 74)—and its marked influence on the emergence of the curriculum as a field of study, the truth is that spirituality nowadays does not enjoy the weight and space that it once had in education and curriculum debates—notwithstanding being at the core of major theoretical battles that framed our field historically.

Spirituality is undeniably at the center of one of the most contentious wrangles in our field, opposing the Herbartians and the polemic Report of the Committee of the Fifteen chaired by William Harris (Paraskeva, 2011, 2014, 2022a, 2022b). As I was able to examine in another context (Paraskeva, 2011, p. 31), "in 1895 in Cleveland, the Committee of Fifteen began to face severe criticism, principally about the report that emerged from one of its subcommittees, *The Correlation of Studies in Elementary Education*." This criticism came, in particular, from a group of U.S. educators who, in 1892, had founded the National Herbart Society (Krug, 1969). Harris used the terms 'correlation'—crucial in Herbartian curriculum theory—and 'concentration,' but not in the sense proposed by the *Herbartians*. Harris and 'his report' defended that curriculum implied a "correlation of pupil's course of study with the world in which he lives—his spiritual and natural environment" (Harris, 2022, p. 180), whereas to the Herbartians—such as Charles and Frank McMurry—'correlation' was an umbrella concept that would promote the "interrelationship among the subjects themselves" and not, as mentioned by Harris, an instrument of "correlating the pupil with his spiritual and natural environment" (Kliebard, 1995, p. 16). According to William Harris, curriculum workers and developers should be in tune with the "spiritual aspirations shall be adopted for the conduct of his life" (Harris, 2022, p. 180).

Spirituality was also central in the emergence of the Progressive Education Association championed by progressive pedagogues such as Francis Parker, John Dewey, Jane Addams, and others. One of the aims of the Association was "the freest and fullest development of the individual based upon the scientific study of his mental, physical, spiritual and social characteristics and needs"

(Pinar et al., 1995, p. 110). Spirituality played a significant role in curriculum social meaning (Addams, 2022, p. 419) as it was framed as inherently related to human nature and experience. As Frank McMurry argued, "the most practical knowledge of all, it will be admitted, is a knowledge of human nature—a knowledge that enables one to combine with his fellow men and to share with them the physical and spiritual wealth of the race" (McMurry, 2022, p. 386). Parker (2022) advocated the holistic preparation of the individual and argued that "the battle for the common schools is the battle for human liberty through educational movement committed to 'save the world' through an emphasis on "faith, spirit, open-mindedness, and work" (p. 397).

As the doctrine of scientific management increasingly took root in all spheres of curriculum development, consolidating its dominance as curriculum theory and praxis, a very disparate counter-dominant plethora of intellectuals and movements that fought for a more humanistic and holistic (Chu, 2019) view of the curriculum was also gaining strength. Such a plethora, which crosses endless diverse epistemological rivers—aligned and/or non-aligned with critical, post-structural, post-modern, and feminist excavations—didn't ignore the role of spirituality and moral values as intrinsic dynamics within the struggle for a just curriculum theory and development. I have called such an endless diverse radical critical river 'the generation of utopia' (Paraskeva, 2021a). Particular critical counties of such a generation defined curriculum "as a moral activity and as such it cannot be understood without recourse to, and this must be held accountable, to ethical perspectives and obligations of justice and responsibilities to other persons" (Apple, 1975, p. 89). Other critical axels—arguably more sensible to 'post' impulses—"found congruencies between certain strands of homiletical work and certain strands of the autobiographical, the feminist and the political" (Pinar et al., 1995, p. 637). Spiritual, moral, and ethical values provide authenticity to the curriculum enterprise (Pinar et al., 1995). Debates about curriculum just social meaning were incomprehensible out of spiritual impulses (Pinar et al., 1995). In this view, the search for such authenticity is at the core of George Counts (1932) challenge—'can schools change society'—which implies forcibly to re-think our curriculum, teaching, and supervision incursions; to rethink the very mission of public education, places what I termed elsewhere (Paraskeva, 2022a, 2022b) the Dwayne Huebner's (1999a, p. 402) question right at the epicenter of our theory: "Can education be re-imagined—or not?" I would say, along with Slavoj Žižek (2019), 'yes please' yet not out of non-derivative divisive itinerant approaches, that—among many issues—responds to the world's onto-epistemological differences and diversity.

Rogério Venturuni's *Curriculum, Spirituality, and Human Rights towards a Just Public Education* advocates a re-imagining of schools and curriculum, which implies the reimagination of the unfinished finitude of the human being in their temporality as a spiritual being. In a *Freirean* way, education doesn't change society, education changes people, and people can change society. Advocates of the vital role of spirituality in any curriculum dialogue—which claims to be just—related to the transformation of the individual couldn't marginalize spiritual impulses that populate different forms of agency. Allow me to pause here to clarify one point. By advocating the need for the legitimate presence of spirituality in the non-derivative curricular dialogue, it does not necessarily imply that one agrees—without reticence—with the existence of the spiritual human being or spirituality as a humanoid impulse. It does suggest reading the world and the word in a non-derivative way and perceiving how and why spirituality is a form of critical consciousness (Dantley, 2005), a form of prophetic pragmatism (West, 1988), a form of inquiry (Anzaldúa, 2002) structuring the daily lives of billions of human beings. Our curriculum struggle cannot be just about what we agree on. Our curriculum conversations are not complicated if we—just—engage with the 'identical' (Han, 2018). Our conversation can only be 'just', "if we are willing to be influenced by [the] other" (Alexander, 2003, p. 234). Our curriculum dialogues need to highlight the *Voltairean* principle; that is, while we might disagree or disapprove of what the other says, we need to defend to the death their right to say it. 'Our' dialogues cannot slide into an *agora* of academic tribalism.

## 1 The Inevitable Unfinished Transcendent

Within the tributaries of such a dispersed group of successful utopians—and without minimizing the role of any particular intellectual or group one needs to highlight the journey of scholars such as Dwayne Huebner, James Macdonald, and others that during the second half of the twentieth century fought tenaciously to take the curriculum conversation away from the chains of positivism and the yoke of learning theories (Huebner & Paraskeva, 2022a, 2022b). They did not hide in euphemimisms to smash the absolutism behaviorism and learning theories. In Dwayne Huebner and James Macdonald's terms, the curriculum is a human affair; it was impossible to detach the spiritual dimension from such matters. Both argued for the need to understand the human being as a temporal being. Human experience was not 'atemporal,' or 'ahistorical,' and there were "mind-boggling discrepancies in scientific studies between what is revealed in deep physical laws and how we experienced our everyday lives" (Chu, 2019, p. 115). Temporality framed all human experience with spiritual, moral, and ethical vectors. The curriculum is an intricate—present—environment. Dwayne Huebner (1959, p. 35) states:

> The person is not an isolated entity. He cannot live separated from his environment and has no meaning distinct from his environmental entanglements. He can be discriminated from his environment only because he occupies space in a form that remains relatively constant through time. Physiologically and psychologically, the boundary separating the individual and the environment is not rigid. Changes need only to be introduced in the environment to make apparent that they result in rapid and significant changes in the person.

Such an environment "embodies the dialectical forms valued by society" (Huebner, 1967, p. 177); it

> must include components which will call forth responses from the students [that must] be reactive [and] must provide opportunities for the student to become aware of his temporality, to participate in a history which is one horizon of his present. (Huebner, 1967, p. 177)

Curriculum is perceived as human beings' temporality, as it is related to human experience "which is never fixed, but is always emergent as the past and the future become horizons of the present" (Huebner, 1967, p. 137). The elucidation of the relationship of human being and time, Chu (2019, p. 116) argues,

> not only increases our awareness of the dynamic and emerging nature of human existence and deepens our appreciation of the present which signifies infinite transcendental possibilities but also makes clear the inseparability of human being and the world in which one already finds oneself.

The human experience is intrinsically related to an environment that the human being helps to craft.

> The individual and his environment are vitally related; they are in continuous interaction. As the person grows, his relationships with his environment become broader, and more extensive in scope. The environment presents itself to the individual, and he finds some means of incorporating aspects of that environment. Likewise, the individual acts on the

environment, and again some degree of incorporation occurs whereby the environment is modified to accommodate the individual. (Huebner, 1959, p. 41)

Thus, we are faced with the "curriculum as a form of human praxis, a shaping of a world [which means] that the responsible individuals are engaged in art and politics" (Huebner, 1999c, p. 226); it epitomizes John Dewey's (1916) claim that 'education is not a preparation for life, but it is life itself.' Interfering with the environment and acting on it interferes with people's lives; interfering in people's lives is always a political, spiritual, and moral act. The symbiosis between the individual and the environment is political. The curriculum is thus "inherently political; it always has been, it always will be [since it] implies that someone or some social group has use of power as scarce resources to intervene in the life of others" (Huebner, 1974, p. 1). Using power to intervene in "the life of others is a political act" (Huebner, 1974, p. 1).

Moral and spiritual values, Dwayne Huebner (1999b) argues, have been misplaced. He (1999b, p. 414) adds that our field ignores "that everything that is done in schools and in preparation for school activity is already infused with the spiritual." James Macdonald also expressed frustration in a field saturated with learning theories and behaviorist approaches. In his proclamation, curriculum theorizing is a "challenging undertaking [framed] by the total rational potential of man" (Macdonald, 1967, pp. 166–169). Such 'totality' could not be accurately grasped by ignoring the spiritual and moral dimension of the human being. Curriculum search for meaning wasn't a neutral enterprise. Education and curriculum, James Macdonald (1975, p. 4) alerts, are political, spiritual, moral, and ethical enterprises "rather than simply a set of technical problems to be resolved with a satisfying conceptual scheme." The struggle to situate the human being as a temporal being is a social justice struggle that implies "the constant reevaluation of oneself, one's work, and one's world, hoping that whatever creative talent one possesses will lead toward something better than we may all share" (Macdonald, 1975, p. 4). As Huebner argues,

> everyone experiences and continues to have the possibility of experiencing the transcending of present forms of life, of finding that life is more than is presently known of lived. This is what education is about. Education is only possible because the human being is a being that can transcend itself. (Huebner, 1999f, p. 345)

As the humanistic-holistic view of education gained ground, hostility grew stronger.

Curriculum, however, could not afford to give up on the question of "what it means to be a human being" (Huebner, 1967, p. 135). In Dwayne Huebner and James Macdonald's terms, learning theories irredeemably sunk the field in a swamp of historical abstraction. That is, "it yanked the individual of his/her world and freezes him/her at a stage in his/her biographic evolution" (Huebner, 1967, p. 136). As Chu (2019, p. 103) insightfully argues, Huebner

> illuminates how objectivism, despite no longer being convincing, is institutionalized in our *curriculum* language and practices and in the ways we teach and learn through the power of hidden curriculum rooted in a lack of awareness regarding the ultimate nature of man's existence.

Chu (2019) provides us with a brief but accurate overview of some perspectives regarding spiritual, moral, and ethical perspectives in our field. Chu (2019) places such spiritual, moral, and ethical rivers within a broader context of the humanist holistic education hemisphere. In doing so, the works of John Miller, Parker Palmer, and others are—and accurately so—emphasized. However, notwithstanding the powerful theoretical incursions of the advocates of a humanist-holistic education sensitive to the spiritual, moral, and ethical dimensions of the curriculum (Chu, 2019), it is unquestionable that as we approached the end of the twentieth century and entered the twenty-first century, such a river has lost the flow it once displayed. The spiritual, moral, and ethical dimensions are absent from most of our current curriculum debates. Such a river does not have the centrality it should have in our theoretical incursions.

The spiritual dimensions—when and if they emerge—are chokingly celebratory, pure curriculum folklore, never treated, grasped, or enjoyed as 'one'—and within an—epistemological matrix that reflects a way of human existence, a way of 'being-in-this-world,' one that among other issues, fatally breaks with the dictatorship of what is understood as science, and helps to confront 'technicalities of modern curriculum, which has been shaped over the decades and centuries by a global social engineering mentality' as stressed by Venturini's volume (Chapter 1).

As Chu (2019, p. 19) argues, spirituality "becomes just another set of tools for instrumentalists." Drawing on Tara Fenwick (2001), Chu (2019) stresses how spirituality has been perverted as a "hurry-up-and-feel-good praxis erroneously focusing only on an inner journey of healing, personal piece and exploring the self" (p. 19). Paradoxically, our curriculum conversations are sensitive to mindfulness—a theme that saturates specific zip codes in the field today—yet quite insensible with the path pioneered by intellectuals like Dwayne Huebner, James Macdonald, and others, and the spiritual and moral dimension of education (see Chapter 2).

The book the reader has in hand is thus timely; it discloses the malaise sparked by such *Freudian* hysterical absence and dominant ill-informed unjust Eurocentric curriculum discourses. Among other issues, Venturini's volume embraces Huebner and Macdonald's proclamation and places 'temporality' at the core of his ruminations. Temporality and consciousness—something that, in his terms, is impossible to comprehend out of spirituality—are intertwined in any 'learning environment.' There is no human existence/non-existence out of spirituality.

The volume also helps to unveil how "the language used by most of us is not helpful" (Huebner, 1999a, p. 257) in grasping our field's challenges and societal needs. The blind denial of an open, frank, and complicated debate on spirituality prevents the epistemic subject—the curriculum reason—from being exposed to new realities, worlds, languages, challenges, and fears. Curriculum reason—victim of an abyssal epistemic subject—thus insists on not losing its pretentious innocence; it is immersed in a fallacy. As I have argued in other contexts (Paraskeva, 2015, 2016, 2018, 2021a, 2023b), the challenge is not that curriculum is a complicated conversation, as identified by William Pinar (2004). As this volume shows, the challenge is that this conversation remains unjust, derivative, abyssal, and eugenic; it is epistemicidal, as Dwayne Huebner (2022) stresses.

The absence of spirituality—or its due centrality—in our field's debates is an unprecedented affront to the historical processes of human societies over the centuries. Such absentee—marginalization or perversion—ostracizes the historical role of spirituality in—classed, casted, raced, and gendered—power struggles within, between, and beyond hegemonic and counter-hegemonic movements, both in the U.S. and worldwide. It distorts human beings' temporality. It disregards crucial spiritual impulses within our field's true people's history. It excludes how it was through spirituality that the oppressed body and mind championed to find strength and craft reason to conquer freedom. It disregards understanding the reason why for billions—in a *Voltairean* way—'if spirituality, faith, God did not exist, it would be necessary to invent.' It ignores that eugenics and racial brutality were so unimaginable and irrational that they could not be understood and challenged on the 'mundane' plane of the—white—reason that created it. Spirituality allowed the enslaved person and 'thinkificated' oppressed to overturn a eugenic reason that undergirded such historical carnage. We will return to this issue later.

Venturini's *Curriculum, Spirituality, and Human Rights towards a Just Public Education* is an essential volume as it brings the spiritual question to the table of our debates in a very crucial moment facing humanity, a moment that I defined elsewhere as an absurd (Paraskeva, 2021b), a significant regression (Geilselberger, 2017). Just over the last three years, the world has faced a pandemic, an increase in environmental disasters, the war in Ukraine, the escalation of massive waves of migration, and the eruption of another economic havoc. While one is speechless by such tragical events, it is also shocked by the policies to address such global malaise. Venturini unpacks spirituality and its importance for curriculum studies and theory in a unique way. Drawing on Santos (2007) and other key anti-colonial and decolonial intellectuals, he confronts spirituality as an egregious sociological absence related to the attack on humanities and liberal arts. Spirituality becomes

> a noisy silence in public curricula and pedagogies. Under neoliberalism, the degree and depth of its absence have escalated to a dangerous stage. Conservative neoliberal attacks on the humanities and liberal arts provide solid ground for the consolidation of treacherous so-called neutral educational forms—deterministic, objectivistic pedagogies, curricula, subjects, and modes of teaching and evaluating students—that are overtly detached from the organic indeterminacy of the personal component and the inner spiritual self. (Chapter 2)

Odd as it might be, a system dominated by economic doctrines as the best way to protect the economy is damaging the economy. Pinar (1992) states

> There is much wrong with the U.S. public school system. For 70 years, curriculum specialists have complained about inaccurate curricula, inadequate teacher preparation, inappropriate evaluation, and dysfunctional administrators. Problems internal to the American public school system do contribute to the nation's economic problems, but the schools are not the major culprit. While schools have not changed much, the economy they were designed to support has. (pp. 228–229)

Such 'absence' has been rubber-stamped 'scientifically' by the monumentality of the coloniality power matrix (Quijano, 1991), legitimizing spirituality—falsely—as non-existent (Santos, 2014). As Venturini (in Chapter 3) advocates, one witnesses 'the absence of an authentic being, the absence of an authentic belonging through the absence of an authentic curriculum.' The absence of spirituality twits and dents individual and social identities. Venturini pushes the envelope into a more 'radical river' in our field, framing spirituality as a—counter-hegemonic—human rights issue. In doing so, he unpeels how the production of spirituality as non-existent is intrinsically related to every reductive and functionalist of modernity reason and its language. Such absence imposed by the 'colonizer' constitutes an explicit denial of human rights—within a society that laudably proclaims the flag of social justice. Moreover, as he argues, the rejection of spirituality constitutes an identity challenge. As he argues in Chapter 4

> there is no genuine identity or citizenship if an individual's culture, which in many cases integrally involves spirituality and language, is forcibly and intentionally disengaged from a mandated, scientized learning process. This mode of education consists of the de facto denial of human rights via the insertion of 'superior' ones, based on the notion that modernity requires rejection of/separation from the past in the interest of the sole 'acceptable' goal of rebuilding a new future. Languages other than that of the colonizer are demonized, 'modern' languages valorized; selected 'rational' knowledge is framed as the only route to success, and 'non-valid' ideas are denigrated and/or rendered invisible. Such attempts are better understood as yet more tentacles of modernity acting in favor of the colonization of minds.

In Venturini's terms, denying the spiritual 'being-in-the-world' is a direct violation of human rights in a society that shamefully advocates social justice yet blindly engages in celebratory human rights practices; unfortunately, dominant and particular counter dominant forces in our field are not innocent in such a facade.

As we excavate his diegeses—which also have a solid overt autobiographical basis and dynamics—we are faced with the possibility of embarking on particular critical, post-critical, decolonial, and anti-colonial rivers within and beyond our field. More than a riverbed of his intellectual duel with the word and the world, and influenced by William Pinar (2004), "he—also—perceives autobiography as a revolutionary act." As he confesses in Chapter 1, Pinar (2004) helps him "to understand how the 'personal' is crucial to unpacking any social engineering so inextricably rooted in curricular content." Echoing Pinar (2004, p. 49), he sees "autobiography as one of the few ways one can genuinely express and legitimize one's experiences acting as the economy of the self, wherein the narration of one's story functions to preserve oneself" (Chapter 1). In Venturini's terms, his narratology 'is an attempt to claim his existence—not only physically, but metaphysically as well, and it involves a methodological approach in which one's lifeblood' allows a "spiritual revolution to happen" (Pinar, 2004, p. 49). This work is his claim to keep alive his non-quantitative self (Chapter 1), a kind of *Whitmanian* yell in which 'I celebrate myself and sing myself, and what I assume you shall assume'—whatever/whoever 'me' one I able to comprehend. Such *Pinarian-Whitmanian* eruption and larva—if I may say—wraps Venturini's journey and consubstantiates what Marian de Souza (2012, p. 291) determines as "relational consciousness, placing relationality as the essence of spirituality," which enables an inner dialogical nexus with these theoretical rivers and their tributaries, thus reinforcing the importance of the debate on spirituality in our field. The *Pinarianian-Whitmanian* larva of relationality wanders throughout Venturini's dialectical metamorphosis.

When we pick up a book to read, we carry a whole past of life, experiences, dreams, imaginations, desires, (non)readings, and anxieties. We never arrive at a text completely naked and deprived of a past/present that makes us 'be' and 'to be.' To draw on Maxine Greene's (1973) existentialist positionality, I argue that 'I am what I am not yet' in any—textual—social interpellation. The phenomenology inherent to each one's hermeneutic processes is an encounter and dis-encounter between the 'text-itself' and all our thesaurus of life experiences. We never engage with a text alone. We are always in a 'populated solitude' (Paraskeva, 2011). Quite naturally, when faced with the exact text, both author/narrator and reader summon different interfaces with all this treasure of life and readings. To engage with a(ny) text is always an exhausting fencing to sift the best 'meaning' from the 'signified-signifier' wrangles that concomitantly inaugurates the sovereignty of the reader—or what Roland Barthes (1977) proclaims as the author's death, which permeates my disputes with Venturini's text. Such wrangles triggered a healthy hermeneutical process calibrating the power of the author's or narrator's intention of any text with the power of the reader's criticism, diluting the absolutist inclination of the author/narrator defined—as well as that of the reader—as 'a subject who collects singularly a set of pre-existing forms of knowledge' (Barthes, 1977). Each text speaks to the reader differently. The unity of the voices of the text is not found in its origin because it is only achieved in its destination/receptor. For example, the writings of Amilcar Cabral speak to the world, projecting different echoes on each reader. Some place Cabral—reductively—just as a freedom fighter, others advocate in Cabral the cult of 'negritude,' others celebrate the political identity antithesis of Pan-Africanism, others outlined the matrix of the anti-colonial and de-colonial intellectual process, and still others—like Paulo Freire—claimed 'Cabralism,' and 'Cabral' within a wrangle 'pedagogue of the revolution' vs. 'revolutionary pedagogy,' and drew clear affinities between Amilcar Cabral and Antonio Gramsci. I remember vividly, though, my first—and radically different—incursion on this particular piece from Paulo Freire, as I footprinted a powerful trilogy—'Antonio Gramsci, Amilcar Cabral, and Kwame Nkrumah—crucial to understanding 'conscientização' and 'consciencism' as a spiritual praxis of the epistemic subject of the Global South.

My engagement with Rogério Venturini's manuscript is just one more example of the authority of the reader—or, if we want to be more lenient, of the calibration between the author's will and the reader's footprint—as Roland Barthes (1977) teaches us—crafted from the idiosyncratic non-derivative itinerant hermeneutical pantheon (Paraskeva, 2022a, 2022b) undermining traditional 'signifier-signified' wrangle, thus triggering the collapse of canonized meanings. As I delved into his diegesis, I built a semiotic matrix—as if I was amid a hermeneutical whirlpool whose intensity kept increasing. I saw myself surrounded by an unraveled violent spiral of themes, sometimes explicit, other times confused—among others, the power of the person, spirituality as individual and social consciousness, spirituality as social capital, as inquiry, as resistance, as critical pragmatic consciousness, the person as a being and temporal being, identity, the neoliberal fervor, the saga of coloniality, spirituality as non-derivative human rights, itinerant curriculum theory—outlining clear secants and tangents with the object of the diegesis. As I carved and soldered affinities and distances with these themes, specific experiences, 'encounters,' 'dis-encounters,' and 'un-encounters,' from the distanced and more recent past took on more preponderance than others. During my hermeneutic disputes with the text, I naturally made some voices—from particular rivers—more audible and visible than others; some of these voices have already been highlighted, such as the cases of Dwayne Huebner James Macdonald and others. However, within such a plethora of diverse epistemic timbres and tones, I would like to highlight some other voices—that gush wildly by mighty rivers within and beyond the Eurocentric riverbed—who repeatedly intruded on my analysis as I flipped through the pages of this book in Glasgow's wet winter, namely Paulo Freire, Paul Robeson, Kwame Nkrumah, Babasaheb Ambedkar, Gloria Anzaldúa, and Joaquim Machado de Assis. While the *Freirean* river may not surprise the reader, I am unsure about the others. These were not the only epistemic tenors that surrounded my hermeneutical metamorphoses, causing successive 'collapses of meaning' (Barthes, 1977). I have underlined just a few of those who most stubbornly decided to walk with me as I obstinately dug and discovered my 'own' textual non-derivative compass. They are part of a plurality of rivers and streamlets on the great scenarios framing the interpretation of 'this text,' which had the matrix outlined by intellectuals such as Dwayne Huebner and James Macdonald as a background. I must open a parenthesis here and confess that as I delved more and more into the text, the background was suffering multiple natural mutations, either revealing *Hueberian* contours, or showing *Nkrumahian* tones, or *Robesonian* nuances, or even Dalit traits, in a permanent non-derivative itinerantology. I chose to embrace Huebner's legacy as a background, as he lends us a rich river flooded with rapids and dams before the contentious estuary of our field.

Each of those voices, though, 'talks' profoundly to my reading of Venturini's journey, and I made each one of them talk to me in different and similar ways on matters related to temporality and human incompleteness, spirituality as a form of social capital, and critical consciousness, as a form of counter-hegemonic human rights and activism, the disgrace of coloniality, the potential of the itinerant curriculum theory as a way to open up the irrational rationalization of the monumentality of Prosperous divisive reason.

## 2   Towards a *Plus Que Parfait Imparfait* Theory

Joaquim Machado de Assis's *The Posthumous Memoirs of Brás Cubas* (2021)—is regarded as the first novel of the Brazilian realist school and dedicated 'as a nostalgic remembrance' to the 'first worm which gnawed the cold flesh of my corpse'—unveils much more 'than the author's delirium.' It echoes Huebner and Macdonald's rationale subscribed in Venturini's "Curriculum Spirituality and Human Rights." It is an oeuvre "which science will thank [him]" (Machado de Assis, 2021, p. 25). Creatively, Machado de Assis (2021) machinates an intrigue hatched in the first person and posthumously. One is before a narrator that is a deceased author—a dead human being—who took the creative task to pencil his memoirs. He crafted a corrosive critique of the nineteen's Brazilian elite's social fabric with mockery and limitless irony, breaking with the parameters of romantic idealism—although the novel is weaved within a particular romance—and traditional realism. His sharp pen—conversely to other realist literary genres—confronts society yet 'from within' through the 'self' of the protagonist and other characters, as well as particular institutions socially constructed as the registry of morality—i.e., marriage, family, and education—a society rammed by the swamps of 'life,' 'death,' 'adultery,' 'greed,' 'mediocrity,' and 'pettiness, ['in]sanity' and the 'defiance of science'; a society whose public institutions are smeared with deformed and arrogant pictorial beings, perfect avatars of social justice and the common good; a society in which the 'personages' are ordinary, routinely maculated, extraordinary incomplete human social beings. Brás Cubas is a vivid example of the epistemic subject struggle from within (Pinar, 1974). The parallels with what is happening currently in Brazil, the U.S., the U.K., and other nations—the loutish level to which the political debate has descended—are frightening.

Machado de Assis (2021)—from an epistemology from the South—crafted a candid reality judiciously that epitomizes the ethos of 'human being's temporality' (Huebner, 1967) and its unending imperfection. Temporality—or historicity—Dwayne Huebner (1967, p. 176) accurately defines, "is not a characteristic of isolated human being, but a characteristic of being-in-the-world." The novel frames the 'being(s)-in-the-world mundanely, flooded with silences, as well as unfinished and incomplete events, giving the protagonist and characters an imperfect, fragmentary, partial, and mundane nature—a truthful example of human finitude in a nineteen-century society turned upside down. The internal unity of the story stems from the mundane and incomplete "being-in-the-world" (Huebner, 1967, p. 177). Such 'being in the world' situates the individual surrounded by multiple dreams, frustrations, conflicts, desires, and joys; it is crafted essentially within a plethora of intersections of a past located on its temporality, the temporality of the present and towards a future whose temporality is only possible to reach within a utopian canvas.

Learning—and consequently curriculum and pedagogy—reflect such temporal intersections—as it doesn't exist out of temporality. That is, Venturini proceeds,

> As consciousness of existence over time emerges, temporality arises. Human temporality (personal history, memory, the whole life) is integrated into education when students are allowed to study and analyze aspects of life through language (spoken and non-spoken) and its meanings. This brings vitality into Freire's conscientização and/or Nkrumah's conciencism and 'spiritual' self-development. In Freire and Nkrumah's proclamation, spirituality unfolds within specific contexts. Bringing the past into the future brings continuity and essential rootedness as students emerge from yesterday into the future. Learning is not just today's forecasting of tomorrow's many possibilities but also threading the historicity of goals, purposes, and objectives as a claim for continuity—and scaffolding for building the changes necessary for tomorrow. (Chapter 2)

Brás Cubas's (2021) life story translates a concrete temporality. His 'story'—related to a specific temporality—is the 'story' of countless 'other Brás Cubas,' stories related to a particular space and time. To situate the human being in its temporality is to perceive the deepest contours of the mundane, the unfinished, the insufficient, the immanent, the non-immanent, the transcendent, and the reality of the real. What makes his 'story' different from so many others is not the absence of temporality. Quite the opposite. What makes each story unique is the endless non-derivative commonalities and uncommonalities within temporality. Perhaps nobody better than Karl Marx defined the impossibility of the human being out of temporality when he claimed that 'human beings make their history, but they do not make it as they please; they do not make it under self-selected circumstances.' It is up to us in 'our' field to seek a curriculum and pedagogical theory that grasps these temporalities. The great challenge we have as curriculum theorists, though, is to build a theory and praxis that is sensitive to the distinctive characteristics of temporality and resolves epistemic challenges that cannot be grasped out of temporality.

Like the social fabric realistically grasped in *The Posthumous Memoirs of Brás Cubas*, our field's solidity and internal coherence are not ahistorical. Our field's temporality, while related to significant accomplishments (Paraskeva, 2011; Pinar, 1995), it is also linked to its non-realizations and vain expectations, deferred promises, lost utopias, incomplete nature of our battles, and reductive nature of our actions—our 'being in the world' (Huebner, 1967), and 'in the field.'

Our field is epistemologically exhausted, though, incapable of breaking with the linguistic web that structures its challenges, a field that somehow has been incapable of taking a just advantage of great revolutionary attempts—the political (Apple, 1979; Giroux, 1981) and autobiographical, yet no less political (Pinar, 1977) turn, for instance—in the recent past and which could have allowed us to be in a different stage today. Instead, like *The Posthumous Memoirs of Brás Cubas*, our field gave in to morbid and putrefied silences and puzzling hiatus. The silence of our field about specific crucial social issues—such as spirituality—is no longer an inconvenient and uncomfortable issue; it pushes us and our theoretical frameworks into a mythomaniac plateau. The statement may seem an exaggeration, and I apologize for that. Our theoretical approaches—both hegemonic and counter-hegemonic—erroneously gave up "to find a just non-derivative meaning in an—*endless and perpetual* [emphasis added]—imperfect world" (Landau, 2017)—an 'imperfect' world with an 'imperfect' human being, an 'incomplete' human being. As I have examined in other contexts (Paraskeva, 2021a, 2022a, 2022b), our field suffers from a theoretical imparity; it is 'de-conexed' with the reality that claims to explain. I would complexify Apple (2018) frustrations and argue that our field,

> has lost its way, [struggles] with historical amnesia [and] has too often forgotten the key questions about what and whose knowledge should be official. It has become lost in 'derivative] postmodern abstractions and deconstructive despair. (p. 689)

Curriculum theory and development are not 'out-of-history,' though. We need to craft the brutality of history and its history—and its socially constructed temporality—acknowledging that "sources of temporality do not reside in the individual, but in the confrontation between the individual and other individuals, other material objects, and other ways of thinking as they are objectified in symbol and operation" (Huebner, 1967, p. 177). The reality challenged by the subject is socially constructed, unfair, unfinished, incomplete, imperfect, and a mirror of people's history—crafted by historically polluted (classed, raced, casted, and gendered) human beings. In *Foucauldian* terms—and rightly so—as reality doesn't have ontological supremacy towards the subject, it is thus crucial to place the individual historically "in a dialectical process in which cause is an effect, and effect is cause" (Huebner, 1967, p. 177). As I argued before—to situate the human being in its temporality is also to de-link from romanticizing the individual being, to deconstruct false and idyllic assumptions of the human being, assumptions that attempt to manipulate the 'authentic'—a metamorphosis of finished, perfect, complete, and unfinished, imperfect, incomplete reified temporality processes, a graded social construction. Inauthentic learning, Yu-Ling Lee (2018, p. 242) argues, is an outcome of an inauthentic understanding of curriculum as human being's temporality. Within such wrangle emerges the tainted nature of the 'self' and society. Marian de Souza (2012) argues that we need,

> to help children realize that none of us are always lovely people. We have our good and bad days, our good and bad times, when we may love the world and when we hate the world and everyone in it. This is being human in all our wholeness, and we remain spiritual in all these experiences. Thus, we need to teach children to be discerning. Until value is placed on the variation and spread of human gifts and children are led to recognize that their individual gifts are as important as others precisely because they complement the gifts of others, human flourishing will continue to be impeded, and the shadow will prevail. (p. 300)

In his germinal piece Critical Theory, Max Horkheimer (1999, p. 188) shrewdly argues that "if experience and theory contradict each other, one of the two must be reexamined." In such a sense, any theory that 'ignores' the spiritual dimension of the very nature of the human being and reality is at odds with both. As Dwayne Huebner (1999e, p. 356) taught us, "theory is not merely an escape into the esoteric. It is part of the necessary work for the redemption of schools." Indeed, "if the theory does not exist to provide practical solutions to everyday problems, why does it exist?" (Pinar, 1992, p. 230). Such a take echoed what Pinar and Grumet (1988) had denounced years before:

> Too often, curriculum theory has been tainted with the self-conscious complexity of academic work, disdaining practical activity to maintain the class privilege that clings to the abstract to aggrandize its status. Although the field situation provides a context where curriculum theory

and practice confront one another, our objective ought not to be to resolve their differences, reducing one to the dimensions of the other.... Rather, let us play theory and practice against each other so as to disclose their limitations and in so doing enlarge the capacity and intensify the focus of each. (pp. 37–38)

Moreover, as Gilles Deleuze and Felix Guattari (1994) argue, "theories and concepts are not waiting for us ready-made, like heavenly bodies. There is no heaven for theories; they must be invented, fabricated, or rather created and would be nothing without their creator's signature." Spirituality—its concepts and theories—constitutes no exception.

Spirituality is experienced by massive waves of communities worldwide. If spirituality is "related to human beings' subjective relationships" (Senreich, 2013, p. 553), and such subjectivity is not ahistorical (Huebner, 1967), then their experiences cannot be theorized out of spirituality. Suppose spirituality is related to the idiosyncratic understanding of the 'self' and the social human being in their relationships with the wor(l)d—"cognitive, emotive and intuitive" (Senreich, 2013, p. 553). Any theory that walks and is guided through a social and cognitive justice matrix cannot ignore these experiences. For millions, the unknown is not impossible to grasp. In Dwayne Huebner's (1999b, p. 403) proclamation, the "spirit is that which transcends the known, the expected, even the ego and the self. It is the source of hope." As I have emphasized before, Venturini highlights temporality as an identity matter. In Chapter 2, he argues that human identity 'unfolds in temporality, forged by social relations, the conditions of the environment in which one lives, and how one accepts and interacts with oneself and other selves.'

Such interaction deals with and in temporality and is related to identity as a perpetually unfinished social and inner transmutation. To be 'mundane,' 'maculate,' unfinished,' and incomplete is related to the 'authentic;' it is to be 'authentic'—however, both social constructions. Inauthenticity, however, crosses our curriculum thinking, theory, and development and forces individuals to stay in modes of 'being' and learning that perpetuate their position as 'abyssal citizens' (Venturini, Chapter 3). Inauthentic reason frames the curriculum logic; it is the compass of the praxis of education toward the infallible—and thus dangerous—assumption of the capacity to fully determined the future (Lee, 2018); its clashes with the praxis of authentic living that should be echoed by an authentic education (Lee, 2018).

Drawing on Greene's (1988) reason, Venturini *Freireanly* 'announces' and 'denounces' how current hegemonic curriculum forms distort any attempt to be transformative and authentic. Denying spirituality as an intrinsic dynamic of human existence, our curriculum theory and development—in its hegemonic and counter-hegemonic Eurocentric forms—frames the individual inauthentically and coarcts its transformative potential. As he argues, "any effort to hinder the transformative nature of the individual and his/her/their authenticity is an attack on his/her/their freedom" (Chapter 1).

We must not give up the dream of a just and perfect world, a world that we all wish to see (Amin, 2008). However, we must understand that one cannot labor towards a 'perfect/just' theory that crafts a 'perfect/just' world without sketching a 'perfect/just' theory that accurately grasps the 'imperfect/unjust' world. As long as we continue to produce and legitimize in our scientific incursions a derivative and abyssal reason—which grants itself the eugenic right to determine what exists and does not exist—our theory will always be just that, derivative and abyssal and therefore inauthentic, an approach incapable to a just dialogue with reality let alone *inherently* predisposed to connect with others (Cazeaux, 2019).

## 3  'Conscientização' and 'Consciencism': A Spiritual Call

While Machado de Assis—from the avenues of the epistemology from the South—opens the door to understanding the temporality of the *maculated* individual, but also within the temporality of a particular society (Huebner, 1967)—so crucial for curriculum workers—Kwame Nkrumah's "Consciencism" offers us an in-depth reading of the existence of such temporality based on a mix between spirit and matter—an implicit wrangle in Venturini's volume. His rationale is a political statement against the laudable silence of spirituality in education and curriculum as a public good. The volume places spirituality as an inherent towering dynamic in constructing social meaning. He persistently argues that it is impossible to understand human beings' existence out of spirituality. If there is no existence out of spirituality—for so many human beings—there is no 'meaning' out of spirituality. As Dwayne Huebner (1967, p. 176) reminds us, meaning is not something out there, but it "is tied to the meaning of time—always a socially constructed matrix—and it can be grasped in its temporality." While such is a controversial statement for so many, it is undeniable that for millions of human beings, 'spirituality' is a structural device in their 'temporality.'

Venturini's rationale unravels a set of channels leading to what Kwame Nkrumah (1964) referred to as 'philosophical consciencism.' Nkrumah's 'consciencism' "suggests simultaneously 'conscience,' 'consciousness' and 'science,' towards a certain anticipated future" (Du Toit, 2015, p. 4).

> If philosophical consciencism initially affirms the absolute and independent existence of matter and holds matter to be endowed with its pristine objective laws, then philosophical consciencism builds itself by becoming a reflection of the objectivity, in conceptual terms, of the unfolding of matter. When a philosophy so restricts itself to the reflection of the objective unfolding of matter, it also establishes a direct connection between knowledge and action. (Nkkrumah, 1964, p. 92)

'Consciencism'—is Nkrumah's 'being-in-the-world' (Huebner, 1967)—or, as William Pinar would term it (1974), a 'struggle from within'—a way of beginning to resolve what he sees as the "crisis of African conscience" (Du Toit, 2015, p. 9)—triggered by colonialism and the persistence of coloniality (Quijano, 1991; Mignolo, 2008). Spirituality is not an abstract dynamic but a significant card within the anti-colonial and decolonial—pan-Africanist river—struggles and thinking. It is a concrete structural feature within a Global south epistemic subject and reason such as Ubuntu.

Ubuntu, Devi Mucina (2019, p. 141) argues, "is a Black philosophical and ethical system of thought, from which definitions of humanness, togetherness, and social politics of difference arise." It is a spiritual scholarship in which "the spirit in the Ubuntu worldview is the energy flux of all things" (Mucina, 2019, p. 141). Spirituality, in Ubuntu terms, Devi Mucina (2019, p. 141) adds, "is the principles and values that allow one to connect to the life force that created all of creation; it is valuing that one is connected to all living forces." Drawing on the Nigerian intellectual Oyeronke Oyewumi (1977), Devi Mucina (2019, p. 142) argues that the Eurocentric notion of worldview is inaccurate in describing indigenous epistemic ways of being and thinking as it is a notion that "privileges only one sense of knowing when indigenous reason centers multiple ways of sensing and knowing the world." Caliban's wisdom—as Paget Henry (2000) would have phrased it—"allows one to understand our common relatedness without undermining our individuality and uniqueness" (D. Mucina, 2019, p. 144). Such wisdom is essential for "spiritual surviving and physical well-being" (D. Mucina, 2019, p. 145). There is no Caliban epistemic existence and legitimacy out of spirituality which "extols the power of such experience as a teaching tool" (D. Mucina, 2019, p. 143), one that understands the intra-play of multifarious senses and knowings—as "the spirit can also be more than just people who can speak to us and advise us." Such endless relatedness implies relatedness forms of 'critical spirituality' as Michael Dantley (2005) advocates, something quite structural in Paulo Freire's *jouissance*—and that crosses Venturini's volume. Nkrumah's 'consciencism' is visible in Freire's 'conscientização.'

Unfortunately, even though Freire's reason has been—and continues to be—much studied in the counter-hegemonic Eurocentric hemisphere, the fact is that such studies persist in 'hiding,' 'ignoring,' 'disparaging' the spiritual impulses that strongly underlie his critical and transformative rationality. Understanding Freire's gateway in the U.S. left academic hemisphere would be crucial. While he is now considered the demiurge of critical pedagogy, it is also true that his gateway in the US academia was not through secular education but through academic groups tenured—and/or directly or indirectly associated with—at divinity studies. Derrell (Drick) Boyd unfolds the academic 'spiritphobia' insightfully. Drawing on Keating (2008) and others, he states:

> A primary reason for the lack of research on Freire's spirituality is mainly because Freire never used the word 'spirituality' in his writings; when he spoke of his spirituality, he referred to it as his 'faith.' Furthermore, he wrote and spoke about his faith infrequently and admitted he was reticent to discuss it publicly. Additionally, in academic circles, what Keating (2008) has called 'spirit phobia' exists. In her study of Mexican feminist popular educator Gloria Anzaldúa, Keating notes that in the rational and empirical world of academia, writing about spirituality can cause a scholar to lose standing and credibility with his or her peers. She quotes Alexander, who writes: 'there is a tacit understanding that no self-respecting postmodernist would align herself (at least in public) with a category such as the spiritual, which appears so fixed, so unchanging, so redolent of tradition' (Keating, 2008, p. 55). Even though Anzaldúa was quite open about the spiritual influences on her life, Keating notes that scholars often dismissed her spiritual language as nostalgic, backward, traditional and naive. (Boyd, 2012, p. 760)

Spirituality feeds Paulo Freire's political reason and action (Boyd, 2012; hooks, 1994; Darder, 2018). While Paulo Freire is generally quiet about his spirituality, Derrell Boyd (2012) adds, "one cannot fully appreciate the depth of his moral vision or his perseverance in the face of rejection, exile, and imprisonment without exploring the spirituality that informed his life and work" (p. 760). Paulo Freire's spiritual dynamic was not esoterical but inherent to his critical consciousness, intimately related to the world's materialities and temporality. He criticality jazzed Marxist and spiritual impulses.

> When I was a young man, I went to the people, to the workers, the peasants, motivated really, by my Christian faith...When I arrived with the people—the misery, the concreteness, you know. The obstacles of this reality

sent me—to Marx. I started reading and studying. It was beautiful because I found in Marx a lot of the things the people had told me—without being literate. Marx was a genius. But when I met Marx, I continued to meet Christ on the corners of the street—by meeting the people. (Elias, 1994, p. 42)

Paulo Freire's critical and transformative reason formed and informed what he calls (feels as) 'conscientização.' As he argues, 'conscientização' is a critical attitude that

is not based on consciousness on the one hand and the world on the other; for another part, does not intend a separation. On the contrary, it is based on the consciousness-world relationship. Taking this relationship as the object of their critical reflection, human beings will clarify the dimensions obscurities that result from their approach to the world. (Freire, 1979, p. 1)

Like Nkrumah (1964), Freire's advocacy of 'conscientização,' frames "the human being in history" (Freire, 1979, p. 1) in its temporality. One's spirituality, "always develops in a specific social and cultural context" (Kirylo & Boyd, 2017, p. 3). Spirituality's historical and temporal reason, according to Freire (1995, p. 104), does not mortgage or dilute forms of agency. Quite the contrary, it "pushes the human being to interpellate dialogically the social sagas of reality, pushing towards the world transformation which allows humanizing humanity" challenging the oppressor.

'Conscientização' was inherently related to Freire's dialogical praxis with the world and the word, a praxis that couldn't happen out of the temporality and spiritual dimension of the human being. He states:

Faith in people is an a priori requirement for dialogue; the 'dialogical man' believes in others even before he meets them face to face. His faith, however, is not naive. The 'dialogical human being' is critical and knows that although it is within the power of humans to create and transform, in a concrete situation of alienation, individuals may be impaired in using that power. Far from destroying his faith in the people, however, this possibility strikes him as a challenge to which he must respond. Without this faith in people, dialogue is a farce that inevitably degenerates into paternalistic manipulation. Founding itself upon love, humility, and faith, dialogue becomes a horizontal relationship in which mutual trust between the dialogues is the logical consequence. Whereas faith in humankind is an a priori requirement for dialogue, trust is established by dialogue. (Freire, 1995, pp. 90–91)

Human being's temporality—in Freirean terms—is intrinsically related to their finitude, incompleteness, and "the completion of such incompleteness is encountered in their relationship with the transcendent creator, a relationship that is always a relationship of liberation" (Kirylo & Boyd, 2017, p. 7).

Kwame Nkrumah and Paulo Freire's notions of 'consciencism' and 'conscientização' are undeniably forms of 'spiritual inquiry' described by Gloria Anzaldúa (2002), 'critical spirituality' defined by Michael Dantley or 'Prophetic pragmatism' as Cornell West would frame it. Such forms are at the core of social transformation Dantley (2005), the latter challenges the western philosophy to take the experiences of the oppressed seriously (West, 1988). They are both quite towering in the struggle against oppression.

Jazzing Marian de Souza's (2012, p. 292) 'relational consciousness' with Kwame Nkrumah's 'philosophical consciencism' and Paulo Freire's 'conscientização' one can argue that "expressions of relationality become expressions of spirituality."

> Living with an awareness of one's relationality is the essence of human spirituality. For many, this includes the connectedness that leads to a search for something 'other' beyond one's physicality, but even without this aspect, the individual still remains a spiritual Being. Important to note is the understanding that the higher the levels of awareness, the higher the consciousness levels that the individual reaches. Movement through these levels of consciousness corresponds to the movement from a focus on the outer self to a focus on the inner self, which, in turn, may lead to the experience of 'letting go' and living in the present moment. These elements may release in individuals a sense of freedom, helping them experience transcendence and, I would argue, spiritual growth. (Souza, 2012, p. 292)

Such 'relatedness relationality'—or non-derivative forms of agency as Boaventura de Sousa Santos (2014) would have put it—also dents the absolutism of the physical, the fallacy of the perfect, the complete, and the immaculate; it alerts us to humans and humanity's temporality—as advocated by Dwayne Huebner (1967) and others (Macdonald, 1975; Phenix, 1964; Greene, 1988). As Dwayne Huebner (1967, p. 176) advocates, "education recognizes, assumes responsibility for, and maximizes the consequences of this awareness of human being's temporality."

Such recognition has been eugenic in our theoretical proclamations, however. That is, 'curriculum as [human being's temporality] has been framed in a derivative way, under an abyssal temporality which obliterates endless ways of experiencing existence. The problem for curriculum theorists thus persists. While it is crucial "to conceptualize human being's temporality and to find means to express his concern for human being's temporality" (Huebner, 1999c, p. 136), such conceptualization needs to be non-abyssal and non-derivative. As Josué Tario (2019, p. 189) stresses, "la Beleza de la vida es que todo es temporal,"[1] a beauty enjoyed by Brás Cubas, and that needs to be at the core of our curriculum labor. Like 'conscientização,' 'consciencism' interpellates—an unfinished—relatedness reality, and 'being-in-the-world;' is a way of thinking and existing of a human being that is "primarily a spiritual being, a being endowed originally with a certain inward dignity, integrity, and value" (Nkrumah 2006, p. 68).

Dwayne Huebner (1999b, p. 410) argues that all human-social constructions "have a spiritual dimension." According to Kwame Nkrumah, then, "the notion of the human being as "primarily a spiritual being" should therefore also not be seen in opposition to, or stark demarcation from, "material being"; rather, "spirituality is an aspect or manifestation of the material being" (Du Toit, 2015, p. 9). He argues that "matter and spirit are on a continuum—even if distinguishable as different types or configurations of matter" (Du Toit, 2015, p. 10), which implies "a radical revaluation of matter as both primary and complex, dynamic and alive with forces" (Du Toit, 2015, p. 11). Kwame Nkrumah's 'consciencism' epitomizes 'Ubuntuism.'

> The supernatural is not seen as the superior or outside (transcendent) origin of the natural world. Instead, the spiritual elements of life are fully incarnated, which means that all life is spiritual while being entirely material. The world is thus fully immanent and material but carries a spiritual dimension within the material itself. While Western metaphysics, therefore, tends, with its sharply hierarchical binaries, to desacralize the sensible, lived reality, to suck out all value, intrinsic worth, and finally, all life of that part of reality that it designates as "nature" (along with specific classes or groups of humans deemed "natural"), reducing it to raw material to be exploited, the African materialism of Nkrumah sees all existence as teeming with "a plenum of [life] forces in tension, capable of self-motion 196), and thus as imbued with spiritual value. (Poe, cited in Du Toit, 2015, p. 9)

The matter-spirit duality—or if I may say endless plurality—at least for millions of human beings, frames inherently the diverse "conceptions of individuals, organizations, and societies" (Noghiu, 2020, p. 45). While some challenge the impossibility of a "higher level of existence" (Tario, 2019, p. 191), it is undeniable that for too many millions, the wrangling matter-spirit pushes them "to a perpetual temporal transcendence" (Tario, 2019, p. 191). Such transcendence temporality is inherently related to various spiritual capital and activism forms (Noghiu, 2020).

As Venturini argues in Chapter 2, Nkrumah's 'consciencism' blends with Freire's 'conscientização' in spiritual terms. While both constitute powerful weapons in the struggle against colonialism, the former overtly assumes an anticolonial decolonial spiritual footprint. He acknowledges the power of Freire and Nkrumah's epistemic consulate, arguing 'consciencism' and 'concientização' as interdependent with spirituality (Chapter 2). Spirituality is the force that awakens and impels the conscience into the modes of 'concientização' and/or 'consciencism' in the fight against the realities of colonialism, imperialism, disunity, and lack of development. It is such spiritual capital and spiritual activism that one sees gushing through the veins of the torn body of the enslaved black communities and other historically oppressed groups—among others, women, indigenous peoples, and the 'untouchables' (Paraskeva, 2022a, 2022b); it combusts and builds up their resilience, struggle, and accomplishments. It constitutes also a structural feature of anti-colonial, decolonial, and indigenous reasons as it structures their powerful intellectuality profoundly and uniquely.

## 4  Critical Prophetic Pragmatism

Spirituality is thus inherently an identity matter. Such spiritual capital is a river also quite palatable within the intellectual veins of Civil Rights leaders—from Martin Luther King Jr. to John Lewis, Rosa Parks, Rosemarie Harding, and Paul Robeson,—a handful of intellectuals who did not let die the masterful legacy of great scholars in the struggle against slavery and oppression such as Frederik Douglass, Sojourner Truth, William DuBois, T. Broker Washington, among others. Paul Robeson's *Here I Stand* is an anthem to the 'self's temporality within the struggle against segregation.' It constitutes a vivid example of 'being-in-a-word'—as a racialized struggle. His commitment to "the struggle of black communities, workers, and immigrants was the foundation for his musical thesaurus, which was built from the unique heritage and gift of enslaved Africans: Negro spirituals" (Redmond, 2016, p. 671). Paul Robeson (1958, p. 33) was vocal about "his spiritual heritage" and the importance of such inheritance in the struggle against slavery.

It was within spirituality that Paul Robeson—a giant in the struggle against racial segregation—found solid pillars to defy the system's original sin, eugenics (Paraskeva, 2022a, 2022b). He provoked a world wave of irreversible indignation related to the dehumanizing conditions of black communities in the U.S. In his trip to Ireland, Robeson was able to "sing in Welsh with a wonderful Welsh choir that made the spiritual sound very near to heavenly music" (Horne, 2016, p. 33). Spirituality through music provided what Robeson and others wanted: transmitting the message of a deplorable apartheid system and its irreversible end. Spirituality allows "[T]he Negro's easy approach to death" (Horne, 2016, p. 33), a commitment adopted creatively given the atrocious conditions faced" (Horne, 2016, p. 33). That is, death was "something which comes even as a comfort, a reward—not something to be afraid of" (Redmond, 2016, p. 671). Spirituals play a crucial role in Robeson's reading of the wor(l)d.

> When I was a young man in Harlem, just round the corner from where I lived was a café. The musicians would go there after the nightclubs closed around 2 A.M. I remember when I was in a show, I'd go along, and we'd have eggs and bacon. People would improvise on their instruments and sing, and many great songs were written that way. For me, it was spirituals on Sunday morning, but on Saturday nights, I rocked. Who rocked with me? Well, there was Fats Waller, Billie Holliday, Chick Webb, Louis Armstrong, Count Basie, Duke Ellington, and many more—and among the youngsters who came along later was Lena Horne, Sammy Davis…I remember a young girl coming in one night. We couldn't see much of her through the tobacco smoke, but when she sings—we stop and listen. She sang "A Tisket, a Tasket," and the Count said, "Where's she from?" Her name was Ella Fitzgerald. She says, "I'm going to Carnegie Hall. (Robeson, cited in Horne, 2016, p. 95)

Paul Robeson epitomizes what Cornell West (1988) calls prophetic pragmatism, "a form of thinking and seeing the world centered on democratic practices. It is an intellectual process built on the premise of existential democracy and requires one to be self-critical and self-corrective" (Dantley, 2005, p. 662). As unpacked by West (1988, p. 17), prophetic pragmatism is an "Afro-American philosophy which takes the Afro-American experience seriously." As a specific expression of contemporary American philosophy, West (1988) felt that Western reason

> has never taken the Afro-American experience seriously. Even during the golden age of Royce, James, Santayana, and Dewey, it remained relatively

unaffected by rampant lynchings and widespread mistreatment of Afro-Americans. Therefore, the West will not be opposed to using Eurocentric thinkers and theories as models, but they must be retrofitted to account for the plight of black people. This plight is often ignored by the very thinkers and theories being employed. (Stone, 2011, p. 93)

Prophetic pragmatism, in West's (1988) terms, is the sublime recognition of the legitimacy of the epistemic oppressed. Since the beginning of his professional performing arts career, the core of his struggle related to songs that he described as "coming from the very depth of the struggle of his people" (Redmond, 2016, p. 617). In his magnum oeuvre, *Here I Stand*, Paul Robeson (1958, p. 32) argues that "consciousness of Africa and its influence in determining values proper to people of African ancestry in America was threatened as never before. A new ideological and spiritual low was reached." As in anti-colonial and decolonial struggles, the battles against apartheid in the U.S. also revealed all the splendor of spirituality as social capital. Drawing on Brad Stone's (2012, p. 93) dieges-es on West's prophetic pragmatism, one would argue that Robeson was able to help "modify the theoretical engines provided by mainstream academia so that they can account of race, class, and gender." Robeson exemplifies "West's ultimate objective, that is Black liberation, followed by the liberation of all the oppressed people of the world." Prophetic pragmatism paves the way to such liberation through a radical co-presence, and non-abyssal epistemic reason—as Santos (2014) would put it. In a dialogue with Eduardo Mendieta (2017), West argues:

> I would want to conceive of philosophy grounded in the very long humanist tradition of the best of the West that is open to the East and North and South, but what I mean by that is that I began with "human," which means burial. I begin with the humanity and the humility, which is very different than the biological species like homo sapiens. Humanity versus homo sapiens. They are very different things. We are biological creatures, we are animals, no doubt, but when you talk about human, you're talking about that particular kind of animal who are aware of its impending extinction and have the capacity to be sensitive to catastrophe and disaster and calamity and profound crisis. The question for me is, how do we love wisdom—philosophia—in the face of impending catastrophe given the kind of thinking, loving, caring, laughing, dancing animals that we are? So that it's a very, very historicist, contextualist, fallibilist, concrete, fleshified conception of philosophy. (Mendieta, 2017, p. 140)

Prophetic pragmatism is related to human beings' temporality and finitude. Leading contemporary battles for the recognition of alternative theoretical new engines—to smash oppressive historical dynamics—is Michael Dantley, who blends non-derivatively critical and prophetic pragmatist impulses and, in doing so, "transcending his head-heart tension" (Boyd, 2012, p. 765). Dantley (2005, p. 656) champions the notion of 'critical spirituality,' which allows "one or a community to invoke a hope that critically interrogates current situations vis-à-vis a backdrop of a brighter future." As he argues, "schools for African American children grounded in spirituality become places where the discourse is replete with notions of hope, struggle, purpose, victory, and accountability" (Dantley, 2005, p. 656). Critical spirituality is the epicenter of African American struggle and "has served as the catalyst to continue African Americans" quest for equity and equality in a less-than-welcoming culture; African American spirituality is the internal grounding of many Black people's ontology or sense of being. It crafts a sense of self and provides the impetus to resist forms and practices of dehumanization and oppression sometimes promoted by the dominant culture" (Dantley, 2005, p. 657). Critical spirituality is at the core of what Davis (2016) frames as "systemic change." Drawing on David Purpel (1999, p. 161), Dantley (2005) reinforces that spirituality authorizes for each of us our engagement in the process of what he calls counter-imagination, that is, "an imagination that is not at all congenial to dominant intellectual or political modes." Critical spiritual activism was a significant liberation force in tearing down segregated social structures (Dantley, 2005; Noghiu, 2020). To ignore the role that spirituality plays in the civil rights struggle is tantamount to ignoring the relationship between the blues and the civil rights movement and the fight to end segregation—a perfect intellectual delirium.

Venturini (in Chapters 2 and 3) places such intellectual delirium at the center of our school structures that function as segregation machines. Drawing on Maxine Green's rationale, he argues that most teachers do not know what education must mean (Chapter 2). They produce instead fear or a lukewarm sense of social responsibility based on a long-ago engineered, indefinitely perpetuated democratic absence of the exercise of freedom and citizenship grounded in an ideology that claims only one knowledge is possible and guided by striving for material possessions. The civil rights struggle was undeniably an identity struggle against racialized cleansing. For the African American oppressed, spirituality, Michael Dantley (2005, p. 657) argues, "is a tool of connection and identity."

As Venturini argues in Chapter 5, spirituality—a powerful dynamic within the Civil Rights struggles—is intrinsically a counter-hegemonic human rights issue and a path to freedom. His rationale distances mainstream forms of human rights. The civil rights battles were not detached from spiritual calls—triggered by social constructions such as 'conscientização' and 'consciencism' crossing individual, institutional and social identities; moreover, one cannot disengage such calls from the intricate path towards liberation and emancipation of one's identity. Civil rights struggle against the deracialize society was a spiritual battle for the legitimacy of equal existence; a struggle for double recognition, that is, the recognition of the brutality of white supremacist power and the recognition of the brutality suffered by the black community; the civil rights struggle—superiorly epitomized by intellectuals such as Paul Robeson— was an individual and collective 'here I stand' which frame a concrete temporality—that unfortunately, it seems that it is not completed eradicated, as one can see from eugenic impulses of the police brutality on black communities and individuals, the attacks on critical race theory, etc. The civil rights struggle was/is a struggle for the recognition of the identity of the black epistemic subject as equal. Such epistemic thesaurus has no historical existence out of spirituality.

## 5    Confronting the 'Chamber of Horrors'

Spirituality—as a form of social capital and activism (Noghiu, 2020)—was/is also a powerful 'tool' within the epistemic of the indigenous subject, a subject that faced ethnic cleansing. In this context, spirituality was/is inherently a revolutionary ethos "situated in a space and place called home" (M. K. Mucina, 2019, p. 36). Spirituality was/is an "indigenous way of place" (M. K. Mucina, 2019, p. 40). Coming to terms with injustice, Mandeep Kaur Mucina (2019, p. 40) argues, "is an act of liberation." Within the context of the native American struggle, spirituality was/is also viewed as an identity matter. Nurturing spirituality "is an important factor in promoting identity and belonging in the individual, leading to individual and community well-being" (Souza, 2012, p. 293).

Kalyani Unkule (2011, p. 346) stresses that wellness is "a spiritual endeavor helping to comprehend and transcend the binary between colonized and colonizer." Erroneously some of our field's theoretical incursions 'cherry picks' what is 'comfortable' to theorize on the—indigenous—epistemic 'Other.' Unfortunately, the indigenous question has often been treated epistemically, either out or at the margins of spirituality. In doing so, spirituality—and other dynamics—is either persistently produced as non-existent or 'folkloreized' or addressed in a very marginalized way. As Mandeep Kaur Mucina (2019), George Dei (2011), and others documented, 'the indigenous epistemic subject is the everyday experiences that have been ignored, forgotten, misunderstood, and invisible'—as Boaventura de Sousa Santos (2014) frames, the 'non-existences.' Through spirituality, the indigenous subject frames its *Gurudwara*—a social justice praxis, a safe place, a gateway to a revolutionary space where individuals and community to gather worship and be free" (M. K. Mucina, 2019, p. 32). Spirituality is also perceived as a form of social capital and activism idiosyncratically constructed by the indigenous epistemic subject. Spirituality is structurally indigeneity's onto-epistemic reason. As Gloria Anzaldúa alerts us, "body, mind and spirit constitute an indissoluble that places the indigenous epistemic subject—its thinking and existence—in a perpetual articulation, de-articulation and re-articulation of 'nepantla' or 'in between' reality" (Tirres, 2019, p. 119). Such 'in between' paves the way for a *nepantlaistic* way of existence and of reason, a non-binary, non-dichotomic feeling and existence in the word and of the world since it is an 'itinerant' (Paraskeva, 2016, 2021a, 2021b, 2022a, 2022b) 'in-between-existence' that propels alternative ways to read and feel the world and the word alternatively—as Santos (2014) would put it. Anzaldúa terms such non-divisive non-binary reason as 'conocimiento' that not only challenges dominant forms of 'reason and rationality' (Anzaldúa, 2015) by questioning but also concomitantly unfolds the splendorous endless epistemological latitude and longitude of "spiritual inquiry, and activism" (Tirres, 2019, p. 125) 'Conocimiento' is, Anzaldúa (2002, 2015) argues, a sublime form of spiritual inquiry.

> Those who carry conocimiento refuse to accept spirituality as a devalued form of knowledge and instead elevate it to the same level occupied by science and rationality. A form of spiritual inquiry, conocimiento is reached via creative acts—writing, art-making, dancing, healing, teaching, meditation, and spiritual activism—both mental and somatic (the body, too, is a form as well as site of creativity). Through creative engagements, you embed your experiences in a larger frame of reference, connecting your personal struggles with those of other beings on the planet with the struggles of the Earth itself. To understand the greater reality that lies behind your personal perceptions, you view these struggles as spiritual undertakings.

Such spiritual inquiry amplifies what Angela Valenzuela (2017, p. 907) defines as "spiritual oneness," unpacking alternative forms of co-existing and co-learning that recognize the legitimacy of indigenous ways of knowing and being in the world, alternative ways which are not esoteric, but right "at the heart of indigenous communities" (Valenzuela, 2017, p. 906). The emergence of Nuestro Grupo and Academia Cuauhtli—triggered by an unfortunate health issue—as examined through Valenzuela's (2017) approach, constitute clear examples of the role of spirituality in the struggle for social justice, bringing children "into the fullness of their own stories, languages, culture, community, ancestry, and a deep sense of identity that precedes modern, oppressive constructions like 'nation states,' 'borders,' and 'citizenship' which is in direct contrast to so much of the toxic rhetoric that refers to them as 'illegal' or 'alien' and that regularly positions them as 'foreigners' and 'outsiders' even when they officially hold permanent resident or citizenship status (Valenzuela, 2017, p. 909).

Anzaldúa's 'conocimiento,' Christopher Tirres (2019, p. 125) insightfully decants, "in its highest expression is spirituality; it is a 'form of spiritual inquiry' that offers a 'larger frame of reference' that gives us insight into 'the greater reality that lies behind' our individual epistemologies." As a form "politics of embodied spirituality" (Anzaldúa, 2015), 'conocimiento,' Christopher Tirres (2019, p. 125) stresses is not limited to "the subject-centered hemisphere of reason, but rather more capacious and universal." 'Conocimiento,' Martina Koegeler-Abdi (2013, p. 80) argues, "refers to an alternative form of relational, spiritual knowing and acting that is based upon intuition, the body, its "intellect of the heart and gut, and spirituality." Through spirituality as a form of social capital, indigenous subjects dissect and challenge the inner contradictions of the struggle against many oppressive forms. By not giving up an authoctone epistemic reason—i.e., 'conocimiento,'—indigenous individuals and communities have been able to short-circuit great regressions. While "twenty years ago we struggled with the recognition of difference within the context of commonality and today we grapple with the recognition of commonality within the context of difference" (Anzaldúa, 2002, p. 2), indegenity cannot abdicate of its most powerful weapon to challenge oppressive dynamics; 'conocimiento' Anzaldúa (2002) proclaims is the 'inner works and public acts' sentient of the need "to dissolve the categories of abyssal reason" (Koegeler-Abdi, 2013; Santos, 2014). While the indigenous epistemic subject was tortured to live in denial—that is, "we're supposed to ignore, forget, kill those fleeting images of the soul's presence and the spirit's presence; we've been taught that tile spirit is outside our bodies or above our heads somewhere up in the sky with God; we're supposed to forget that every cell in our bodies, every bone and bird and worm has spirit in it" (Anzaldúa, 1987, p. 37)—they refuse to compromise their identity saturated through spiritual impulses and "roamed in indigenous attributes, images, symbols, magic, and myth" (Anzaldúa, 1987, p. 38).

Also, spiritual capital and activism (Noghiu, 2020) are not absent from the Dalit anti-caste struggle against the yoke of Hindutva reason. As I have been able to examine in great detail elsewhere (Paraskeva, 2023a), while caste is a social system that precedes colonial occupation, it persists within the contemporary yoke of coloniality. It has been around for over two thousand years, rooted in the Hindu religion and spirituality and its traditions, and it emerges from the bloody wrangles between Buddhism and Brahmanism (see also Ambedkar, 2016; Teltumbde, 2010; Paraskeva, 2023a). The caste system and caste-based discrimination is a eugenic grading system that operates historically not only in the culture of several countries of South Asia, especially Nepal, Siri Lanka, India, and Pakistan but also in the world's diaspora, so visible, for example, in Europe, Japan, and Africa. It has also been framed as a crucial category in the sanguinary historical path of the United States. It pervades the Roman (aka gypsy) community across "vagrant tribes in Northern India, true nomads, living in temporary huts and wretched tents," as well as Western and Eastern European nations (Blunt, 1969, p. 148; Čvorović, 2007). Coincidently the 'Roman Question' is out of the curriculum debates.

Babasaheb Ambedkar (2016) digs even more deeply into historical terms and places caste and, consequently, untouchability and Dalitism, emerging into an Indian society due to a bloody wrangle between Buddhism and Hinduism. While there are some clear commonalities between them—metempsychosis, karma, and devotion towards salvation—they are strikingly different. While the latter constitutes the maternity of the caste system, the former vehemently rejects the caste system and the inherent divinities undergirding such a graded system. As I have examined elsewhere (Paraskeva, 2023a), Hinduism frames society within the Purusha Hymn of the Rig-Veda, 'thy' hymn that describes the creation of Castes,[2] a hymn that places the Brahmans within the perpetual bubble of purity. Indeed, in Book X, Hymn 90, verses 11–12, "an account is given to the creation of the four castes from the body of the great god Purusha" (Cox, 1959, p. 85). Conjeevaram Hayavadana Rao (1931) describes such a hymn:

> When they divide the Purusha into how many parts do they divide him? What was his mouth? What were his arms? What were his thighs and feet called? The Brahman was his mouth, of his arms, the Rajanya was made; the Vaisyas were his thighs; the Sudra sprang from his feet. (p. 53)

The casted Brahman blessed protectorate graded society crafted the world between the four graded varnas and a non-monolithic 'whatever would be the rest.' Such non-monolithic 'rest,' the fifth varna (Pachamas), aka Untouchables—(Asprushya and Achhuts), low born (Antyja), also referred to as Dalits, scheduled castes, and backward classes—socially tagged as dirty, polluted, smelly, cursed, hopeless savage primates—constitutes a pluriverse plethora of maculate human beings, whose existence and visibility wasn't blessed and only doable out of the four varnas (Paraskeva, 2023a). Outside the graded bouquet of caste are the *Ati Shudras*, also known as 'Untouchables,' who are forced to perform the most 'polluted' and menial work (Ambedkar, 1989). More to the point, the caste system created an outcasted society. Leading Dalit intellectual Anand Teltumbde defines untouchability as

> a diverse but distinctive community in India, who are treated unequally in daily life because of the lowest status, according to them, the Hindu social order. At its worst victims, they characterized India's hierarchical caste society at its most essential. They were historically excluded from most social, cultural, religious, and economic situations for over two millennia. Although castes have undergone significant changes in their configuration as well as in their operation, for the majority of the Dalits at the bottom, they continued to be as oppressive as ever. (Teltumbde, 2018, p. 24)

Demiurges of the anti-caste struggle, such as Jyotiba Phule, Babasaheb Ambedkar, and others, turned to the spiritual vein of Buddhism not just to face the brutality of Hindutva, but to be able "to unify untouchables with the altered socio-cultural and religious identity Buddhism offered, which they hoped would see social transformation along the ideals of liberty, equality, and fraternity" (Teltumbde, 2010, p. 26). In supplementing this transformational project with political struggle, "they sought the inclusion of the downtrodden of both caste and class" (Teltumbde, 2010, p. 26).

Caste is the face of the barbary of Hinduism, which frames casteized human beings' temporality—and so well defined by Babasaheb Ambedkar (2009, p. 296) as "a veritable chamber of horrors." Caste looks like a refined social chameleon not just with the capacity to adapt to different historical phases in the history of humanity but also to be responsive to the diverse cultural and political graded needs and structures of the various historical stages, placing resiliently "Dalit's aspirations as a breach of peace" (Roy, 2016, p. 22). The Hindutva eugenic ideological impulses and the economic logic underpinning segregated materialistic global forms are "reconcilable but complementary" (Ahmad, 2008, p. 15). Caste and other segregational categories and dynamics—such as class, race, ethnicity, and sexual orientation—are deplorable categories of cleansing and related to different forms of indigeneity (Harney, 2015). Any curriculum theory that obliterates such eugenic metamorphosis is the lab of such a chamber of horrors.

As I have examined in great length in other volumes (Paraskeva, 2011, 2014, 2022a, 2022b), the struggle for the U.S. curriculum was not just confined to the intellectual republic of academia. Important revolutionary social events triggered significant irreversible changes in our field's history, theory, and development. I have examined and argued that one cannot accurately grasp the struggle for the U.S. curriculum out of the battles fought by the so-called Romantic Critics, the Students' Revolt, and the Civil Rights struggle to eradicate racial apartheid (Paraskeva, 2011, 2014, 2022a, 2022b). We are what and where we are, thanks to the intellectual honesty of such a revolutionary social wave of individuals and movements that stormed the nation and our educational and curriculum fields. It is a mistake, in my view, to debate our field—its history, theory, and development—ignoring the defeats, the accomplishments, and the slaughter suffered by millions in the struggle for a just society and education (Paraskeva, 2011, 2014, 2022a, 2022b). We will never be able to preserve these achievements if we do not respect who and how they have been accomplished.

I stressed elsewhere (2016, 2021a, 2022a, 2022b) that it would be a mistake to examine historical battles against oppression and ethnic cleansing—i.e., the Civil Rights movement, anticolonial decolonial, feminist, and LGBTQ+, Native American, and Dalit anti-caste struggles—ignoring particular spiritual, moral and ethical impulses at the heart of such struggles. I have framed such obliteration as one of the symptoms of our field's theoretical atrophy. Spirituality is not a minor device in the battle against oppression. The oppression and annihilation of the most historically disadvantaged communities have been so atrocious that it tramples the most elementary criteria of any rationality. There is no rational understanding of the brutality of eugenics—much less when bestowed as 'scientifically justified.' The struggle against oppression epitomizes the endless potential of the Caliban reason capable of confronting the Prosperous eugenic praxis, a wrangle in which the oppressed saw spirituality as a powerful way to comprehend and smash segregation and ethnic cleansing. The rationalization of the irrational also took place through the path of spirituality. In so many ways—some argue—such a path couldn't be avoided. This is quite visible, for instance, in the struggle against indigenous cleansing in the U.S. and elsewhere and in the Dalit anti-caste struggles. Notwithstanding, spirituality persists as the 'visible absence' in our counter-hegemonic curriculum discourses, which constitutes a glaring error. It makes our theoretical incursions inaccurate.

The civil rights, the anti-colonial and decolonial, the Native Americans, and the anti-caste Dalit struggles against segregation, oppression, exploitation, and genocide overtly show an endless rich spiritual capital and activism in a non-negotiable commitment for recognition of oppressive and eugenic structures and the legitimacy of the oppressed epistemic subject.

Alain Adrian Noghiu (2020, p. 47) defines such a form of agency as framed within a language of spiritual capital, exhibiting "accumulated and enduring collection of beliefs, knowledge, values, and dispositions that drove societal, organizational, and interpersonal behavior" (Noghiu, 2020, p. 47). He places Adam Smith, Adam Muller, and Max Weber as the pioneers of the notion of spiritual capital, which paves the way for the spiritual capital theory, aiming to "address a missing moral link at the core of modern economics" (2020, p. 48). Social change for such oppressed groups is a political battle. A victory cannot be achieved by ignoring spiritual activism, that is, "spirituality for social change, spirituality that recognizes the many differences among us yet insists on our commonalities as a catalyst for transformation" (Anzaldúa, quoted in Noghiu, 2020, pp. 188–189). Spiritual activism challenges the socially constructed eugenic inability to think of the Global South and its subjects from-and-in their epistemological framework. Dalitism and untouchability, indigenous knowledge and methodologies, and anti-colonial, decolonial, and Civil Rights struggles were/are historical stages of spiritual capital and activism that need to be situated within an epistemic matrix out of the Prosperous reason (Henry, 2000).

Venturini's *Curriculum, Spirituality, and Human Rights towards a Just Public Education* stands on the shoulders of scholars concerned with the human being's immanent and transcendent temporality reason. In Venturini's terms, the real issue is not "how can one talk about the education, specifically, curriculum and also talk about the spiritual" (Huebner, 1999b, p. 401), but precisely the onto-epistemological impossibility of talking about education and curriculum out of spirituality. Or, as we articulate and re-articulate his reason, such impossibility is made possible by truncating and misrepresenting the very essence of humanity and its human and non-human temporality (Huebner, 1967) its very nature; in so doing, spirituality—the spiritual being—and other dynamics have been produced, sometimes as non-existent, sometimes as a wound on-and-of the 'Other,' eugenically constructing their inferior condition, crafting the 'Other' not as an epistemic subject, but as a subject destitute from any epistemic matrix, and in desperate need of the only and legitimate epistemology available to humanity—Modern Western Eurocentric epistemology. The idea that there is no humanity out of Modern Western Eurocentric—physical reason—hides the fact that such humanity and its reason is only possible through its sub-humanity (Santos, 2018).

As this volume unveils, the noisy silence around spirituality not only obliterates from our theoretical debates in our field a 'reality' that structures the lives of billions of human beings but also constitutes a symptom of the eugenic construction of the 'Other.' It speaks volumes about the Eurocentric arrogant construction of the 'Other' establishing the violence of the identical (Han, 2019). We cannot construct a just knowledge by permanently nullifying or mutilating the 'Other' as a powerful epistemic subject in its temporality. If we agree with Dwayne Huebner (1999b, p. 408)—and others—that "knowing is a process of being in relationship with that 'Other' and knowledge is an abstraction from that process," we must admit that by perverting the 'Other's' identity and epistemic matrix, we are fatally perverting the act of knowing. Such unjust construction is not inoffensive; the 'lack of knowledge about realities beyond the West, about the 'Other' is not innocent; that is, "there is no knowledge in general, as there is no ignorance in general. What we ignore is always the ignorance of a certain form of knowledge, and vice versa; what we know is always knowledge about a certain form of ignorance" (Santos, 1999, p. 205). Ignorance is a form of knowing. Slavoj Žižek (2013) asserts that we feel free 'because we lack the language to articulate our unfreedom.' The inability to think, imagine, and envision that 'myself' could well be the 'Other-self,' that there is an 'epistemic self' in the eugenically constructed 'Other,' is appalling. Dwayne Huebner (2022) states:

> One of the insights I had many years ago was that if I grew up in a different culture, I would think differently. Why do I think the way I do, and why do they think the way other cultures do? This is a curriculum issue. If you deny the validity of what and how different cultures think and impose ours, it is very unjust and unfair, to say the least. It assumes a power relation that is inappropriate and unacceptable. We must be able to get out of our shoes and see and live in somebody else's shoes. We must ask what we have been able to learn and accomplish and share our perspectives with others. If other cultures reject, we need to accept that. It is a totalitarian thought and way of acting that is unacceptable. (p. 235)

Our field lacks a non-derivative linguistic competence to grasp the world's endless epistemological differences. As Huebner (1999a, p. 267) would argue, our "curriculum utter meaning and utterance meanings are meaningless." Both curriculum subjective (utter) and objective (utterance) meanings are lost regarding a socially just education. Such loss and lack of meaning pushed Huebner (1976)—and others—to claim the moribund state of the field, insisting that there is no curriculum theory.

As I have argued before, the search for a theory for a 'perfect' and 'just' world is doomed to failure if we do not realize and grasp the endless diversity of epistemological colors framing our 'imperfect' and 'unfair' world. The lack of a non-derivative curriculum theoretical approach is intrinsically related to what Boaventura de Sousa Santos (2018) defines as the monumentality of modern Western Eurocentric non-derivative thinking, a sharp feature within the coloniality power matrix (Quijano, 1991; Mignolo, 2008) as this volume documents.

## 6 The Monumentality of a Prosperous Divisive Curriculum Reason

The absence of spirituality in 'our—mythomaniac—conversations' speaks volumes about the epistemicidal nature of our field. Such conversations have been weaved through a graded language that produces and mirrors a segregated Eurocentric reason. The modern Western reason, Boaventura de Sousa Santos (2009) argues, is an abyssal reason." That is

> a system of visible and invisible distinctions, and the invisible sustain the visible. The invisible distinctions are established through radical lines that divide social reality into two distinct realms: the universe from this side of the line and the universe from the other side of the line. The division is such that the other side of the line vanishes as reality, becomes nonexistent, and is simultaneously produced as nonexistent. Everything that is made nonexistent is radically excluded, for it lies beyond the realm of the accepted conception of inclusion. (p. 28)

Our curriculum discourses highlight particular visibilities and existences through the invisibilities and non-existences they promote (Santos, 2014). Atrociously, spirituality is just one of such invisibilities and non-existences produced through our field's theoretical journeys. Such an abyssal matrix frames "how can one plan educational futures" in a field highjacked by behavior objectives (Huebner, 1975a, p. 215). The very curriculum just meaning is tainted. Curriculum person's dependency on scientific thought patterns, Dwayne Huebner (1975a, p. 215) argues, "has broken its linkages with other great and important intellectual traditions of East and West which have a profound bearing on the talking about the practice of education." The curriculum constitutes a "set of meanings, but only those that preserve the status quo, perpetuating realities of the social order as perceived, structured, and defended by the dominant group" (Zaret, 1975, p. 38). According to Macdonald and Zaret (1975, p. 4), "most of the curriculum talk is confused about modes of valuing and motives for talking." The curriculum should be seen as a liberating force (Macdonald & Zaret, 1975) and teaching as a commitment to helping others to develop their possibilities, which could only be achieved if the children were not deprived of specific meanings, and their memories, life experiences, and desires (Huebner, 1975a, 1975b). Venturini places the absence of spirituality in our curriculum framework as a consequence of the modernity and coloniality matrix. He stresses:

> Coloniality is *per se*—for itself—intrinsic and omnipresent in texts (whether written or streamed), altering knowledge production and the

validation of knowledge, acting directly on academic performance, playing in cultural spheres, influencing how the self is defined by society and how the self in turn defines common sense and reason, redefining the truth and the aspirations one may aspire to, thereby radically and totally shaping the future. (Chapter 4)

Coloniality is different from colonialism; it supersedes colonialism and deepens the abyssal line affecting millions who immigrate to the U.S. (Chapter 4). Coloniality is about power and control emanating from both coloniality-modernity and 'abyssalism,' leading to the destruction of the individual's realm and 'being.'

As I have examined elsewhere (Paraskeva, 2022a, 2022b), there is no white reason out of the Modern Western and Eurocentric which frames what anti-colonial and decolonial intellectuals termed a coloniality power matrix (Quijano, 1991; Mignolo, 2008). As I argued previously, such reason reflects a selective way of thinking, an abyssal logic, and divisive thinking (Santos, 2007, p. 45). Modern Western Eurocentric white reason and its divisive nature coarct its capacity to address the world's epistemological differences and diversity. Its eugenically divisive nature, though, doesn't recognize the epistemological legitimacy of any other reason beyond the Eurocentric framework; it annihilates the possibility of Eurocentric and non-Eurocentric epistemologies as *primus inter pares*; it is a monumental reason Santos (2018) that feeds its eugenic exceptionalism. Unfortunately, specific sectors of the counter-hegemonic hemisphere cannot get out of this straitjacket that is the monumentalism of Eurocentric thought, which prevents thinking the 'other' of and about the 'other' in terms of the 'other'; that is to commit to what Santos (2014) calls epistemologies from the south—going to the south, living in the South and learning from and with the South.

Patently, critical and post-critical counter-hegemonic approaches laudably edified by leading intellectuals and movements within what I have coined 'the generation of utopia' (Paraskeva, 2021a)—a generation that sails and swims with a very crucial curriculum river (Paraskeva, 2011)—echoes such eugenic abyssal divide. By fundamentally operating within a Eurocentric epistemological matrix, critical and post-critical counter-hegemonic approaches ended up aggravating such abyssal lines and inadvertently legitimizing their reductive visibility and the false legitimacy of this side of the line through the invisibility and non-existence of the other side of the line. It is actually in this context that anti-colonial and decolonial intellectuals have strongly and forcefully denounced Western Eurocentric modernity in its dominant and specific counter-dominant forms as tout court inconsequential to address global and local needs (Dussel, 1995, 2000, 2013; Grosfoguel, 2010, 2011; Maldonado-Torres, 2003, 2008; Paraskeva, 2014, 2016; Santos, 1999, 2014; Walsh, 2012; Darder, Mayo, & Paraskeva, 2016).

Moreover, critical and post-critical counter-hegemonic approaches by refusing to get out of the Modern Western Eurocentric epistemological straitjacket bluntly ignore that the 'masters tools cannot dismantle the master's houses (Lorde, 2007), and in doing so, they labored in one of their crucial deficiencies, that is refusal "to admit that in a world that is epistemologically diverse it is impossible to understand and transform it from one and only one fixed epistemological position" (Paraskeva, 2021a, p. 259). To this end, critical and post-critical counter-hegemonic approaches become the sublime advocates of the monumentality of a divisive reason (Santos, 2018)—reprehensibly eugenic—a monumentality that paves the way for one-dimensional thinking—which is fundamentally Eurocentric. In doing so, like the dominant traditions, critical and post-critical counter-hegemonic intellectuals—inadvertently, I concede—become the sublime ambassadors of the world's unparalleled monumentality of Modern Western Eurocentric science and knowledge forms and overtly incapable of 'demonumentalize' it. In a way, critical and post-critical counter-hegemonic approaches lost their innocence—as Terry Eagleton (2003) would put it—and they are pretty oblivious that the reason that criticizes can never be the reason that emancipates (Santos, 2018); they were incapable of understanding how their epistemological hemisphere was irreversibly exhausted; they exhibit painful incapability to run away from mechanistic frameworks and move toward an overhaul theoretical reconstruction to address the problems of the present (Lukács, 2009). In Eagleton's (2003) terms,

> Structuralism, Marxism, Post-structuralism, and the like are no longer the sexy topics as they were. What is sexy instead is sex. On the broader shores of academia an interest in French philosophy has given way to a fascination with French kissing. In some cultural circles, the politics of masturbation exert far more fascination than the politics of the Middle East. Socialism is not out of sadomasochism. Among students of culture, the body is an immensely fashionable topic, but it is usually the erotic body, not the famished body. There is a keen interest in coupling bodies but not in laboring bodies. (p. 2)

A similar take is exhibited by Frederic Jameson (2016), who argues that the great utopias of modernity, promised and pursued by powerful political movements and intellectuals over the past centuries, namely communism, socialism, and social democracy, for so many people, are today a heap of concepts and obsolete practices in the suburbs of the scrapyard theory, a specimen of ideological scrap that for most even functions as a nightmare that offers nothing to the rail of utopia. The intention to believe in a utopia just painted with certain tones—'from this side of the line'—was one of the most significant pitfalls of modernity and an undeniable symptom of the epistemicide. Even the form of combating the epistemicide appeared to be proposed and defended in the form of another epistemicide—the reversive epistemicide (Paraskeva, 2016, 2018, 2021a, 2021b, 2022a, 2022b). The critical post-critical republic fell short of the utopian path. Painstakingly counter-hegemonic critical and post-critical republic is no less epistemicidal than the hegemonic territories. They have been incapable of a non-derivative critique of the White reason (Mbembe, 2014).

Venturini's volume helps us understand this gap that transpires from the contradictions of the Eurocentric platform—whether hegemonic or counter-hegemonic. By selflessly defending spirituality as a counter-hegemonic human right, Venturini unmasks how human rights are woven and found kidnapped by the reductive and segregated logic of coloniality. Drawing on crucial decolonial and anti-colonial intellectuals (Mignolo, 2018; Quijano, 2008; Dussel, 2000), Venturini argues "spirituality as the stark absence within the hegemonic human rights framed by the colonial power matrix" (Chapter 5). Deeply influenced by Santos (2015, p. 63), he stresses the celebratory tone undergirding the hegemonic logic of human rights

> The current human rights hegemony is fragile, lacking as it does any genuine regard for what most humans need most. The (related) insensitivity of the current modern Western Eurocentric matrix towards spirituality is not innocent; to be more precise, it is both evolving and intelligent. It is, as I have demonstrated, eugenic. Suppose spirituality is a human rights issue; it becomes crucial to understand, along with Santos, how we can edify counter-hegemonic forms of human rights in which spirituality stands as an uplifting and powerful principle.

Venturini is not sidelining the historical gains of the struggle for human rights—i.e. "great accomplishments of oppressed groups throughout history are related to human rights battles, as with, for example, the civil rights movement, women's rights, children's rights" (Chapter 5) However, he argues that

> despite such indisputable historical accomplishments, it is undeniable that extant hegemonic forms of human rights have been historically silencing not just religion, but spirituality as an integral component of

human rights struggles. Granted, large swathes of the civil rights movement had a religious base.

Drawing on Santos (2014, 2015) and Mignolo (2018), Venturini maintains "that it is crucial to develop a counter-hegemonic platform of human rights that explicitly positions spirituality at its very core" (Chapter 5). In doing so,

> we will be able to question the real epistemological colors of the current hegemony of human rights that, in so many ways, produce specific visibilities at the expense of the invisibilities it creates. The resulting paradoxes are entirely and overtly irrefutable. (Chapter 5)

Fatally, the struggle for the U.S. was developed within fundamentally Eurocentric terms. Both dominant and counter-dominant pundits clashed in tough epistemological battles, however strictly within the framework of a Eurocentric epistemological matrix and within limits allowed by such a matrix. Neither dominant nor counter-dominant movements dare challenge themselves, going beyond the Eurocentric epistemological platform—explicitly eugenic. To this end, and as the historical and theoretical multifarious trajectories of the field vividly show, hegemonic and counter-hegemonic traditions were never producers and carriers of 'a theory' that could adequately capture a particular curriculum metamorphosis responsive to the world's epistemological difference and diversity. In fact, out of the wrangle between hegemonic and counter-hegemonic impulses, one witness a theoretical impasse (Paraskeva, 2016, 2018, 2021a, 2021b, 2022a, 2022b).

Allow me a little pause here—albeit briefly—to safeguard a critical issue that cannot be developed within the scope of this introduction but which deserves future attention in our field. Spirituality is not only related to the epistemic subject of the Global South.

Although it is a fracturing topic between the hegemonic and counter-hegemonic blocs, the truth is that it is also a divisive topic within each of these blocs. Spirituality—visibility/invisibility—saturates the epistemic existence of the Global North and South subjects. History teaches us how through spirituality, the epistemic subjects of the Global North—in their successive temporalities—committed themselves to the development of 'a' humanity at the cost of inexhaustible brutality and carnage. Venturini's volume is sentient of such a challenge. To obliterate this bloodbath—within and between each bloc from our theoretical expeditions—pathetically justified and learned in classrooms around the world as the unavoidable scientific reason to spread the Christian faith—also taints how one's attempts to understand and transform the epistemic subject of the Global North. Furthermore, strange as it may seem, it is still a deeply fracturing issue between the two Eurocentric blocs—hegemonic and counter-hegemonic—and the endlessly diverse and dispersed non-Eurocentric bloc. The abyssal lines drawn by Santos run 'rhizomatically'—as Deleuze would say—the multitude of territories related to spirituality and its real essence—or not.

Paradoxically, we perceive a parallelism between the epistemic subject of the Global North and the Global South. This parallelism is expressed in both hemispheres' individual and collective subjects, who understand that their nature and human existence also cross the spiritual dimension. These epistemic subjects enjoy an affinity overshadowed by the logic of modernity. This logic manages to raise and maintain the yoke of an abyssal reason over the centuries: ' the other side of the line' does not exist. The visibility of the invisibility on the other side of the line has been diluted, canceling any possible parallelism with 'this side of the line.' This is not a minor issue as it is probably one of the rivers to engage in what Boaventura de Sousa Santos (2014) frames as 'radical co-presence.' I will return to Santos (2014) radical co-presence later.

Two questions—among many others—arise from here. If, on the one hand, it is understandable why within the scope of the hegemonic Eurocentric blocs, the hegemonic and counter-hegemonic homilist perspectives are silenced, on the other hand, it is difficult to understand how certain circles within the counter-hegemonic Eurocentric hemisphere persists in a manifest insensitivity, marginalizing the homilist Eurocentric and non-Eurocentric perspectives. As I have flagged, this is not the place to go deep on such a puzzle; however, it is crucial to signal. When we unstrap the epistemic subject—whether from the Global North or South—from one of its essential 'features'—spirituality—we are constructing, deconstructing, and reconstructing them in a fallacious way, we are describing them in a way in which they don't exist. The way to address such a dynamic—both for those who agree and those who disagree with its existence and legitimacy—is not to 'invisibilize' it and capriciously edify it as 'non-existent.' The persistence in such epistemicidal curriculum praxis is a commitment to craft our theoretical treks within a mythomaniac plateau. In other words, we pervert a crucial aspect linked to the identity of the oppressor and oppressed. Such perversion speaks volumes to "the difficulties we have with the language we have, which is a consequence of the limitations of our communicative competence" (Huebner, 1999a, p. 267). Our field refuses to open to a different *langue* and *parole*, to explore it, to articulate our theoretical journey in neophyte non-Eurocentric discourses, helping to grasp our fears better, sweep our doubts, solve our doubts, perceive the torment, the dream, and the utopia as experienced by the other.

I mentioned earlier that my argument might seem excessive and unfair. I don't see it that way if one examines the text in its context. In all my work, I have respected the legacy of the intellectuals who preceded us. I have defended as best I can how our work would not be possible without what past generations have achieved. But the truth is that we cannot ignore that we have not been able to manage and capitalize on the outstanding achievements of the past, and—somehow—it is not good for us to persist in certain mistakes. One of these mistakes is that we fight for a theory entirely out of line with reality. A theory that is not even close to the reality of millions of human beings. We have been engaged and committed to an erroneous process wrapped up in a metamorphosis of fallacies. Any theoretical 'model' for a more just and equal society passes through the curriculum. Although curriculum theory is not the master key to explaining how we can have a fair and equal society, the truth is that we will never be able to even dream of a fair and equal society without a fair and equal curriculum theory. We will never be able to enter a more just and equal society with the historically dominant theoretical models. We need to look for new theoretical paths that will help us—in each local—to design, and develop a new reality that is fairer and more equal.

As I write this piece, there are human beings—elderly, mothers, pregnant women, children, and babies crossing the ocean that separates France from the United Kingdom in rubber boats with a capacity of 50 people and carrying more than 250. Life confirms itself for these human beings as a game in the destiny of an ocean, a life they didn't ask for. There countless migrants jumping onto lorries underway at the Calais border to try to enter the UK. Yet our schools—not only in the United Kingdom—continue to cling to everything but pedagogies that help resolve—or at least comprehend—this social saga. Some kids who cross the channel—the lucky ones—will sit on our school benches and hear everything but the reasons that 'brought them to where they are,' their 'reality,' their 'challenges,' and their dreams.' The world is going to bed with veiled threats of a nuclear meltdown in Ukraine, and the users of the classrooms—students of teachers—remain kneeling before the sanctuary of learning theories and tests. Nothing but nothing breaks the spirit of the tests. It has been a truism to hear that there has always been and will continue to be inequality, poverty and misery throughout the world. What we must never forget is that the reason behind this saga is theoretically debunkable.

The world's end is more easily discussed than the end of tests and learning theories. It is worth saying that curriculum as 'currere' is 'nostrum mendacium est.' Our theory is out of joint (Paraskeva, 2021a, 2021b, 2022a, 2022b). Part of the imparity 'curriculum theory and development' and reality—in which spirituality constitute an intrinsic dynamic for millions of individuals—is due to the monumentality of Eurocentric reason that produces sociological absences, thus legitimizing particular 'social absences.' Such 'social absences' find in our curriculum the perfect place to evolve and perpetuate their unjust existence within educational apparatuses and society that consistently deny the tears, struggles, and suffering of the people they serve (Chapter 5).

It is our task to open up the cannon of the monumentality of dominant and counter-dominant curriculum reason and place the metaphysical dimension at the core of our 'conversations' as well. Venturini's exegesis challenges the dominant and counter-dominant power matrices that relegate to the cloud of the anodyne, peripheral, and marginal humanistic-holistic (physical–metaphysical) approaches sculpted by intellectuals working from and within an epistemological platform from the Global North—and subjected to one of the most repugnant strategies of the academic tribes—silence. The examples of Paul Tillich, Dwayne Huebner, James Macdonald, and so many others leave no room for doubt as to how our field has not been and is still not receptive to incursions that attempt to understand the curriculum beyond what is thought to be seen. While Tillich (2014, p. 7) advocates transcendence and spirituality "as an ethical reality, but it is rooted in the whole breadth of human existence and ultimately in the structure of being itself," Macdonald (1986) placed transcendentalism as a crucial stage in human development, a critical asset to explain how can we live together. As Alexander (2003, p. 236) shrewdly argues, "spirituality involves engagement with the transcendent, and this is what education [and curriculum] is all about." In Macdonald's (1975, p. 12) terms, curriculum as a "study of how to have a world" involved an act of faith, or, as Tillich (2014) would put it, 'a courage to be.' Macdonald's (1995) vision of a humane existence is an "epistemology that would come to grips with the so-called hard knowledge of our culture" (p. 85). Again, Huebner (1966) continues to be very present—a quite *Avant la Lettre* intellectual, as I keep reminding in my work—when he voiced the need for a new language over the way we think and debate education. The counter hegemonic Eurocentric plataforms are as epistemicidal as the hegemonic plataforms. I have called such a paradox a reversive epistemicide (Paraskeva, 2018, 2021a, 2021b, 2022a, 2022b).

The inability to perceive the limitations of the Western Eurocentric epistemological modern matrix is one of the wires plugged in the clock bomb thrown at radical critical progressive curriculum theory. We need a radical epistemological overall in the way we think and do curriculum theory and development. Counter-hegemonic Eurocentric perspectives—critical post critical—need to de-link from the absolutism imposed by the matrix of coloniality; they need to decolonize, to deterritorialize curriculum theory; they need to commit to a curriculum turn from ossified inflexible Eurocentric territories and towards an itinerant path that responds to the worlds epistemological diversity and difference. An approach that will help transform our way of thinking and co-exist. As Kwame Nkrumah (1964) eloquently argues, "one cannot change society if it is incapable of changing mentalities." The itinerant curriculum theory is a just path for such transformation.

## 7  Itinerant Curriculum Theory: Towards a Non-Derivative Curriculum *'Langue'* and *'Parole'*

As myself and others have advocated (Paraskeva, 2011, 2014, 2016, 2018, 2021a, 2021b, 2022a, 2022b, 2023a, 2023b; Jupp, 2017, 2022; Shubert, 2017), it is vital for the diverse tributaries within the radical critical curriculum river drastically de-link from its own oppressive epistemological Western Eurocentric matrix—without renegade it—and engage in what I coined (Paraskeva, 2011, 2014, 2016, 2017, 2021a, 2021b) as itinerant curriculum theory (hereafter ICT), one that pushes for a "non-abyssal non-derivative" momentum (Paraskeva, 2021a, 2021b, 2022a, 2022b; Santos, 2019). As Weili Zhao (2019) states,

> ICT is a form of decolonial thinking that recognizes an ecological co-existence of varying epistemological forms of knowledge around the world paying attention to knowledge and epistemologies largely marginalized and discredited in the current world order. (p. 27)

ICT, as Eagleton (1990, p. 86) would have put it "attempts to take theory back to the routne of curriculum affairs"; it unleashes a new conceptual grammar (Jupp, 2017) that moves itinerantly within and beyond "(a) the coloniality of power, knowledge, and being; (b) epistemicides, linguicide, abyssality, and the ecology of knowledge; and (c) poststructuralist hermeneutic itinerancy" producing a new non-abyssal alphabet of knowledge (Paraskeva, 2021a, 2021b, 2022a, 2022b). It challenges the predominance of global north white architects (Watkins, 2001). ICT is thus a way to challenge curriculum epistemicides (Paraskeva, 2016; Santos, 2014)[3]; the *ICTheorist*, knows full well that the struggle against the epistemicides cannot be won with old weapons (Latour, 2005). It implies "to deterritorialize both curriculum and teacher education fields which cannot be done without counteracting linguisticides or epistemological euthanasia" (Moreira, 2017, p. 3; Paraskeva, 2011, 2014) carried out by the colonial powers in the past (but still going on in the present). In so doing, it floods the terrain with a language beyond Western Eurocentric linguistic formations, hoping for alternative philosophy of praxis.

ICT aims toward "a general epistemology of the impossibility of a general epistemology" (Santos, 2007b, p. 67). As Santos (2009) would undoubtedly frame it, it is a counter-hegemonic human rights theory. ICT is human beings' temporality. It is about the diverse and different ways of 'being in the world.' ICT responds to the "death of our field and its ghosts," as Nathan Snaza (2014) proclaims; it addresses the field's desideratum "of figuring out how we can learn to think and act together in ways that might disrupt the neoimperialist and biopolitical control that has emerged with globalized capitalism" (p. 20). ICT "[re]theorizes about theory," as Eagleton (1990, p. 24) would have framed it.

Sentient that subaltern and marginalized individuals and communities have been oppressed by theory (Smith, 1999, p. 39), ICT implies a theorist that is an epistemological radical, an epistemological pariah, who is challenging and challenged by a theoretical path that is inexact yet rigorous; the *ICTheorist* "runs away" from any unfortunate "canonology." Such itinerant theory(ist) provokes (and exists in the midst of) a set of crises and produces laudable silences. It starts abstinence of theoretical uniformity and stabilization. The theory(ist) is a volcanic chain that shows a constant lack of equilibrium; the theory(ist) is always a stranger in their language. It is not a solo act, however; it is a populated solitude. ICT challenges the sociology of absences and how specific non-Western epistemologies have been rendered as non-existent; it challenges any form of *indeginestoude*; that is, it challenges any form of romanticization of indigenous cultures and knowledge, and it is not framed in any dichotic skeleton of West-rest (Paraskeva, 2011, 2014).

ICT, Venturini argues, "empowers us to see beyond the abyssal line, and thus to challenge the Western epistemological framework's position as the only legitimate one" (Chapter 5). It confronts the monumentalistic fallacy of the Eurocentric reason. ICT opens the veins of the oppressive Modern Western Eurocentric epistemological canon. It is against any canon (Paraskeva, 2011, 2016, 2017). It is, as Darder (2016) argues,

> an epistemology of liberation that can persistently challenge structures of authority, hierarchy, and domination in every aspect of life must be cultivated, nurtured and embodied within the blessed messiness and unwieldy chaos of every-day life within schools and communities. (p. 12)

ICT confronts and throws the subject to a permanently unstable question of "what is there to think?" (Paraskeva, 2011). ICT pushes one to think in the light of the future as well as to question how 'we' can claim to know the things that 'we' claim to know if 'we' are not ready specifically to think the unthinkable, to go beyond the unthinkable and master its infinitude (Paraskeva, 2011, 2014,

2016). ICT "is a real social practice" as Eagleton (1990, p. 24), would put it, "it destabilizes social life" (Eagleton, 1990, p. 27) In this sense, ICT is "a theory of change" (Spivak, 1988, p. 3) that goes beyond confrontation as the matrix for change and assumes a commitment to "radical co-presence" (Santos, 2014), or, better said, a subaltern radical co-presence toward a non-abyssal path. IC*theoristis,* though complexify Santos's notion of 'radical co-presence'. ICT goes beyond 'such presence' and argues that any 'non-derivative co-presence' implies more than a 'co-presence,' a 'co-habitance,' an itinerant 'co-habitus' (Paraskeva, 2023a); while doing so, it provides a 'theory of translation' that walks away from conventional notions of 'translation' as

> translingual and/or transcultural practice crossing and equivalizing two languages, epistemes, cultures, or practices entangled within the issue of power and resistance [and advocates translation as] mediating between cross-cultural differences on the principle of transparency, precisely produces 'the partly opaque relationship called difference.' Cultural episteme are entangled practices, with one not reducible to the other. Thus entangled-ness allows for seeing different epistemes as existing side by side in the sense that each has its own integrity and historical sensibility in forming a relational rather than the hierarchical notion of difference. (Zhao, Popkewitz, & Autio, 2022, p. 9)

ICT "travels extensively through the 'other side of the epistemic abyss" (Moreira, 2017, p. 2). ICT challenges book worship (Tse Tung, 2007, p. 45) and the yoke of writing as a *prima facie* condition to the legitimacy of what is knowledge (Smith, 1999). In that sense, ICT is an ethical take; it is the subaltern momentum within subalternity. ICT is a clear call against the precariousness of any fixed theoretical position. ICT is "not merely invocation or evocation; it exemplifies how ideas can be added powerfully to the sources of curriculum studies by substantially including Works" (Schubert, 2017, p. 10) above and beyond the Modern Western Eurocentric epistemological dominant and counter-dominant traditions. Venturini (Chapter 4) embraces the 'non-derivativity' of ICT; Drawing on Santos (2009), he endorses ICT as a non-derivative counter-hegemonic human rights issue to respond to the endless diverse and different spiritual immanent and transcendent readings of the world's epistemological matrix. In Venturini's proclamation (Chapter 4), ICT is a just approach.

> In all relevant aspects of education, from the discipline of curriculum studies and the various academic and institutional levels of administration to teacher education and the classroom. This inclusive theory presents a

powerful force against the epistemicides, silences, absences, abyssalism, and sub-humanization of modernity-coloniality-neoliberalism. It seeks to add diversity, delve into many ways of 'being' and knowing, ask questions, share freely, and liberate education from its longtime hegemonic dependency and the intellectual pandemic of oppression it imposes. In so doing, ICT still grants spaces for differences to be settled, humanity to be cultivated, pain to be acknowledged, tears to be understood and addressed, spirituality to be acknowledged, cultivated, and supported, and metaphysics to be respected as unmeasurable but valid, knowledge to be free of frontiers while allowing the local to hold its cultural value, freedom to be dreamed of as a constant aim, diversity to exist as genuinely diverse, not forced to be unified, and, finally, for 'beings' to cease to exist, and instead fully live. In sum, ICT will allow the educational system to serve our students in such a way that their individual sovereignty will be restored, and they will regain the right to be.

ICT, as inherently an exfoliation metamorphosis, a "sill of infinite mourning" (Couto, 2008, p. 105), champions an anti and post "mechanotic" (Al-L-Ahmad, 1987, p. 31) momentum that seeks to create "a powder, gentle, maneuverable, and capable of blowing up the human beings without killing them, a powder that, in vicious service, will generate a life, and from the exploded "beings" will be born the infinite humans that are inside such beings" (Couto, 2008, p. 68). ICT is a "new form of political affirmation grounded global *epistemological* visions and interests to be favored and courses of action to be followed that are sustained in people's history" (Popkewitz, 1978, p. 28). ICT interpellates science and what constitutes science differently (Autio, 2006). In this regard, an itinerant theoretical path is without floodgates because the best sentinels always have no floodgates (Couto, 2008). In so doing, the itinerant curriculum theory honors a legacy of accomplishments and frustrations, understanding that de-linking will always be to make theory a just theory. To de-link and decolonize—while keeping the legacy of the critical path and taking it to a different level—is also a decolonial attempt to do critical theory (Kellner, 1989, p. 2). In so doing, an itinerant curriculum theory re-thinks utopianism. I am not claiming ICT is a perfect theory; neither does Venturini. There is no such thing as a perfect, ideal theory (Quantz, 2011). ICT reflects that another scientific *langue* and *parole* is natural and confronts dominant Eurocentric forms of science that legitimize 'the modern epistemicidium' and are thus natural obstacles to social and cognitive justice.

In this context, ICT provides an endless different and diverse curriculum *langue* and *parole*, an endless non-abyssal semiotic latitude and longitude on the subject and objective meanings, championing a "de facto protest against the constraints of the *Eurocentric* ideology of meaning" (Barthes, 1973, p. 1016). ICT is thus "a meaning that denies the meaning" (Barthes, 1990, p. 127). If Susan Sontag (2001, p. 96) is accurate—in her masterpiece *Against Interpretation*—when she claims that "all Western consciousness of and reflection upon art have remained within the confines staked out by Greek theory of art as mimesis of representation," it is also prudent to admit—and accurate to claim—that our dominant forms of curriculum reason have 'remained within the confines of an epistemic matrix that is heir to the Greek theory and reason.' ICTheorists echoed Sontag's (2001) alerts that "to interpret is to impoverish, to deplete the world—to set up a shadow world of meanings. It is to turn the world into this world" (p. 99). ICT aims such a 'world of meanings'; it tirelessly aims to a mimesis 'of the world into this world.' Knowing full well that "there is no meaning without interpretation and to understand is to interpret" (Sontag, 2001, p. 98), ICT is, however, a commitment to "interpretation as a liberating act" (Sontag, 2001, p. 98) since it is non-aligned, non-derivative, and non-abyssal (Santos, 2014) way of 'turn the world into this world'; ICT has no-existence out of the 'radical co-habitance' (Paraskeva, 2023) of endless different and diverse epistemologies.

It is thus an itinerant posture that is profoundly committed to a 'radical co-habitus' (Paraskeva, 2023). It is non-abyssal since it challenges the modern Western cult of abyssal reason and attempts to dilute such fictional vacuums between the lines. ICT is an act of resistance also at the metaphysical level. The struggle against modern Western abyssal thinking is not merely a policy matter. It is also above and beyond that: It is an existential and spiritual question. The struggle against the Western Cartesian model cannot signify substituting one Cartesian model for another. Also, the task is to refrain from dominating such a model or to wrap it in a more humanistic impulse. The task is to pronounce its last words to prepare its remains for a respectful funeral. The task is to keep the language and concepts the same, although these are crucial elements. The task is to terminate a particular hegemonic geography of knowledge that promotes epistemological euthanasia.

As educational scholars, our task is to de-link and decolonize it, a crucial commitment toward a ruthless critique of every existent epistemology as a *sine qua non-condition* for a just curriculum theory. This is undeniably the best battle we can engage to open up the Western Eurocentric canon of democracy (Santos, 2007a) and, in doing so, pave the way for a non-abyssal and just society through a non-derivative curriculum theory. ICT "theorizes about curriculum theory," as Terry Eagleton (1990, p. 24) would put it; ICT is an onto-epistemological declaration of independence. It is the people's theory.

Since its first incursions, ICT has worked to break with traditional methods and the more Cartesian views of critical and post-critical theories. The dialectical method—under a non-derivative perspective as the itinerant theory adds—allows for a construction that is always unfinished, which always starts from a reality that is never finished, never ossified, a reality, not being mechanical, cannot be apprehended in any mechanical way. As Marx and Engels (1955) taught us, in today's modern world, things happen at such a speed that "everything solid melts into the air" (p. 13). Marx and Engels are in many domains, and in some ways, post-spiritualists *avant la lettre*. They demonstrate, among other things, the impossibility of the crystallization of 'Eurocentric or non-Eurocentric' perspective. Where and how does ICT go, one may ask? Itinerantly and precisely where/how it moves, where/how it collides, where/how it 'encounters and dis-encounters' with other theoretical approaches, creating constellations, promoting 'co-habitus' of 'radical itinerant co-habitations,' not only with different and diverse epistemological multitudes—within and beyond the Eurocentric platform—but also with policies, curricula, teachers, students, classrooms, social and grassroots movements, with the reality that makes it possible to tear paths that are itinerant that are not fixed and cannot be.[4]

*Curriculum, Spirituality, and Human Rights towards a Just Public Education* examines the integration of spirituality—not religion—into U.S. public education and curriculum debates. The volume challenges celebratory 'curricularized' forms of human rights and frames spirituality as a counter-hegemonic human right. Drawing on autobiography as inquiry, Rogério Venturini unpacks his spiritual struggles—'from within'—and experiences as a progressive spiritual person and educator. The volume examines the subjectivity and objectivity of spirituality, exploring the lethal social impact triggered by the absence of spirituality at the table of the so-called curriculum conversations. The volume places the struggle for spirituality in our field as a political struggle that recognizes and respects the authenticity of the complexity of human beings in their socially constructed graded temporality. In doing so, the text challenges the epistimicidal nature of such conversations, arguing the need to recognize the importance of spirituality as an unavoidable human being's inner dynamic.

Venturini draws on critical, anti-colonial, and decolonial frameworks and argues for an epistemological move towards an itinerant curriculum theory that responds to the world's endless epistemological diversity and difference by assuming a non-derivative non-abyssal approach. His reason echoes the 'spirit' of the series *On (De)Coloniality: Curriculum Within and Beyond the West*, which is a beacon in the struggle against epistemicide and the colonialities of being, power, and knowledge. It attempts to bring to the fore an analysis that focuses on non-Western/non-Eurocentric epistemological frameworks. In a world that still struggles to see 'its own' overt epistemological diversity, *On (De)Coloniality*

*Curriculum Within and Beyond the West* is an open just, non-derivative space to challenge epistemological fascism. It encourages curriculum scholars to engage in dialogues about non-Western/-Eurocentric epistemologies within and beyond the Western Eurocentric platform. The 'series invites 'just conversations' that dig into new avenues such as those of Itinerant Curriculum Theory (ICT), and, in so doing, introduce a new language that will take us to alternative levels of articulation and re-articulation of meanings, through endless and spaceless processes of coding, decoding, re-coding, and 'encoding.'

The *(De)Coloniality: Curriculum Within and Beyond the West* series is about 'curriculum from the South in the Global South and curriculum from the South in the Global North,' as connected with the different metamorphoses of coloniality. It is about 'nuestros locales'—our locals—introducing in the field alternative ways to think and to do educational and curriculum theory; it intends to help establish various corpus of scholarship that will open the curriculum canon to foster social and cognitive justice through an itinerant theory a commitment toward a non-abyssal approach; Venturini's volume advocates new itinerant theoretical non-derivative rivers in our collective struggle against the curriculum epistemicide, advocating for a post-abyssal turn challenging the absolutism of Modern Western Eurocentric epistemic forms.

## Notes

1   The beauty of life is that everything is temporal.
2   The Rig Veda is an ancient Indian collection of Vedic Sanskrit hymns. It is one of the four sacred canonical Hindu texts called the Vedas. The Rigveda is the oldest known Vedic Sanskrit text. Its early layers are one of the oldest texts in any Indo-European language.
3   Although some have argued that ICT proposes itself as *the* only alternative theory, this has never been said. ICT has been crafted as *an* alternative theory.
4   I would like to thank Alvaro Hypolito for some of the arguments unfoled related to ICT in this paragraph.

## References

Addams, J. (2023). Trade unions, and public duty. In J. M. Paraskeva (Ed.), *The curriculum: A new comprehensive reader* (pp. 417–426). Peter Lang.

Ahmad, A. (2008). *In theory: Classes, nations, literature*. Verso.

Alexander, H. (2003). Education as spiritual critique: Dwayne Huebner's lure of the transcendent. *Journal of Curriculum Studies*, 35(2), 231–245.

Al-l-Ahmad, J. (1987). *Occidentosis: A plague from the West*. Mizan Press.

Ambedkar, B. R. (1989). Untouchables or the children of India's ghetto and other essays. In *Dr. Babasaheb Ambedkar. Writings and speeches* (Vol. 5). Education Department, Government of Maharashtra.

Ambedkar, B. R. (2009). *What Congress and Gandhi have done to the untouchables*. Gautam Boom Centre.

Ambedkar, B. R. (2016). *The annihilation of caste*. MJ Publishers/Moven Books.

Anzaldúa, G. (1988). *Borderlands. The new mestiza*. Aunt Lue Book Company.

Anzaldúa, G. (2002). *This bridge we call home*. Routledge.

Anzaldúa, G. (2015). *Light in the dark/Luz en lo oscuro: Rewriting identity, spirituality, reality* (A. Keating, Ed.). Duke University Press.

Apple, M. (1975). Autobiographical statement. In W. Pinar (Ed.), *Curriculum theorizing: The reconceptualists* (pp. 89–93). McCutchan.

Apple, M. (1979). *Ideology and curriculum*. RKP.

Apple, M. (2018). Critical curriculum studies and the concrete problems of curriculum policy and practice. *Journal of Curriculum Studies, 50*(6), 685–690.

Assis, J. M. (2021). *The posthumous memoirs of Brás Cubas*. Liveright.

Autio, T. (2006). *Subjectivity, curriculum, and society. Beyond and between German Didatkik and Anglo-American Curriculum*. Routledge.

Barros, P. M. (2020). Rethinking women's suffering and holiness: Gloria Anzaldúa's "Holy Relics." *Journal of Feminist Studies in Religion, 36*(2), 7–24.

Barthes, R. (1973). Texte. *Encyclopaedia Universalis, 15*, 1016.

Barthes, R. (1977). *The death of an author*. Fontana.

Barthes, R. (1990). *S/Z*. Blackwell.

Blunt, E., & Aa, H. (1969). *The caste system of Northern India*. S. Chand & Co.

Boyd, D. (2012). The critical spirituality of Paulo Freire. *International Journal of Lifelong Education, 31*(6), 759–778.

Cazeaux, C. (2019). Art, philosophy and the connectivity of concepts: Ricoeur and Deleuze and Guattari. *Journal of Aesthetics and Phenomenology, 6*(1), 21–40.

Chu, E. L. (2019). *Exploring curriculum as an experience of consciousness transformation*. Palgrave.

Čvorović, J. (2007). Caste behaviors among Gypsies in Serbia. Културу у трансформацију/*Culture in Transformation*, 151–168.

Couto, M. (2008). *Terra Sonambula*. Leya.

Cox, O. (1959). *Caste, class, and race*. Monthly Review.

Dantley, M. (2005). African American spirituality and Cornell west notions of prophetic pragmatism. *Education Administration Quarterly, 41*(4), 651–674.

Darder, A. (2016). Ruthlessness and the forging of liberatory epistemologies: An arduous journey. In J. Paraskeva (Ed.), *Curriculum epistemicide* (pp. IX–XVI). Routledge.

Darder, A. (2018). *Students' guide to Freire's pedagogy of the oppressed*. Bloomsbury.

Darder, A., Mayo, P., & Paraskeva, J. (2016). *International critical pedagogy reader*. Routledge.

Davis, A. (2016). *Freedom is a constant struggle*. Penguin Books.
Dei, G. (2011). *Indigenous philosophies and critical education*. Peter Lang.
DeLeuze, G., & Guattari, F. (1994). *What is philosophy*. Verso.
Du Toit, L. (2015). When everything starts to flow: Nkrumah and Irigaray in search of emancipatory ontologies. *Phronimon*, 16(2), 1–20.
Dussel, E. (1995). *Philosophy of liberation*. Wipf & Stock.
Dussel, E. (2000). Europe, modernity, and Eurocentrism. *Nepantla: Views from South*, 1(3), 465–478.
Dussel, E. (2013). *Ethics of liberation: In the age of globalization and exclusion* (A. Vallega, Ed.; E. Mendieta, N. Maldonado-Torres, Y. Angulo, & C. Pérez Bustillo, Trans.). Duke University Press.
Eagleton, T. (1990). *The significance of theory*. Basil Blackwell.
Eagleton, T. (2003). *After theory*. Basic Books.
Fenwick, T. (2001). Religion and science. In A. Einstein (Ed.), *Ideas and opinions* (pp. 36–54). Crown.
Freire, P. (1974). *Education for critical consciousness*. Continuum.
Freire, P. (1979). *Conscientização. Teoria e Prática da Libertação*. Cortez e Moraes.
Freire, P. (1995). *Pedagogy of the oppressed*. Continuum.
Geilselberger, G. (2017). *O Grande Retrocesso. Um Debate International sobre as Grandes Questoes do Nosso Tempo*. Objectiva.
Giroux, H. (1981). *Ideology, culture & the process of schooling*. Temple University Press.
Greene, M. (1973). The passionate life of Maxine Greene. In W. Pinar (Ed.), *The passionate life of Maxine Greene*. Routledge.
Greene, M. (1988). *Dialectic of freedom*. Teachers College Press.
Han, B. C. (2019). *Topologia da Violência*. Relogio D'Agua.
Harris, W. (2023) Report of the fifteen. Correlation of studies in elementary schools. In J. M. Paraskeva (Ed.), *The curriculum: A new comprehensive reader* (pp. 179–210). Peter Lang.
Henry, P. (2000). *The Caliban reason*. Routledge.
Hogan, M. (2009). On spirituality and education. *Thinking Skills and Creativity*, 4, 138–143.
hooks, b. (1994). *Etching to transgress*. Routledge.
hooks, b. (2009). *Teaching critical thinking*. Routledge.
Horkheimer, M. (1999). *Critical theory*. Continuum.
Horne, G. (2016). *Paul Robeson the artist as revolutionary*. Pluto Press.
Huebner, D. (1959). *From classroom action to educational outcomes: An exploration in educational theory*. University of Wisconsin-Madison.
Huebner, D. (1966). Curricular language and classroom meanings. In J. Macdonald & R. Leeper (Eds.), *Language and meaning*. ASCD.
Huebner, D. (1967). Curriculum as concern of man's temporality. *Theory into Practice*, 6(4), 172–179.

Huebner, D. (1974). *Curriculum...with liberty and justice for all* [Unpublished paper].

Huebner, D. (1975a). The recreative and the established. In J. Macdonald & E. Zaret (Eds.), *Schools in search of meaning* (pp. 27–37). ASCD.

Huebner, D. (1975b). Poetry and power: The politics of curricular development. In W. Pinar (Ed.), *Curriculum theorizing, the reconceptualists* (pp. 271–80). McCutchan Publishing Company.

Huebner, D. (1976). The Moribund curriculum field: It's wake and our work. *Curriculum Inquiry*, 6(2), 153–167.

Huebner, D. (1985). Babel: A relection on confounded speech, In V. Hillis (Ed.), *The lure of the transcendent: Collected essays of Dwayne Huebner* (pp. 312–320). Routledge.

Huebner, D. (1999a). An educator's perspective on language about god. In V. Hillis (Ed.), *The lure of the transcendent: Collected essays of Dwayne Huebner* (pp. 257–284). Routledge.

Huebner, D. (1999b). Education and spirituality. In V. Hillis (Ed.), *The lure of the transcendent: Collected essays of Dwayne Huebner* (pp. 401–415). Routledge.

Huebner, D. (1999c). The tasks of the curricular theorist. In V. Hillis (Ed.), *The lure of the transcendent: Collected essays of Dwayne Huebner* (pp. 213–230). Routledge.

Huebner, D. (1999e). The redemption of schooling. The work of James Macdonald. In V. Hillis (Ed.), *The lure of the transcendent: Collected essays of Dwayne Huebner* (pp. 353–357). Routledge.

Huebner, D. (1999f). Spirituality and knowing. In V. Hillis (Ed.), *The lure of the transcendent: Collected essays of Dwayne Huebner* (pp. 340–352). Routledge.

Huebner, D., & Paraskeva, J. (2022a). A curriculum afterword: The dialogue Dwayne Huebner and João M. Paraskeva. In J. M. Paraskeva (Ed.), *Conflicts in curriculum theory* (2nd ed.). Palgrave.

Huebner, D., & Paraskeva, J. (2022b). A curriculum afterword: The dialogue Dwayne Huebner and João M. Paraskeva. In J. M. Paraskeva (Ed.), *Curriculum: A new comprehensive reader* (pp. 529–558). Peter Lang.

Jacobs, A. (2012). South African teacher's views on the inclusion of spirituality education in the subject life orientation. *International Journal of Children's Spirituality*, 17(3), 235–253.

Jal, M. (2023). Epistemological untouchability. The deafening silence of Indian Academics. In J. M. Paraskeva (Ed.), *Critical perspectives on the denial of caste in educational debate: Towards a nonderivative curriculum reason*. Routledge (forthcoming).

Jameson, F. (2016). *American Utopia: Dual power and the universal army* (S. Žižek, Ed.). Verso.

Kay, W. (2003). Spirituality and education: Two millennia of thought and practice. *International Journal of Children's Spirituality*, 8(3), 291–295.

Keating, A. (2008). I am a citizen of the universe: Gloria Anzaldúa's spiritual activism as a catalyst for social change. *Feminist Studies*, 34(1–2), 53–70.

Kellner, D. (1989). *Critical theory, Marxism and modernity*. The John Hopkins University Press.

Kirylo, J. D., & Boyd, D. (2017). *Paulo Freire: His faith, spirituality, and theology*. Sense Publishers.

Kliebard, H. (1995). *The struggle for the American curriculum*. Routledge.

Koegeler-Abdi, M. (2013). Shifting subjectivities: Mestizas, Nepantleras, and Gloria Anzaldúa's legacy. *MELUS: The Society for the Study of the Multi-Ethnic Literature of the United States, 38*(2), 71–88.

Landau, I. (2017). *Finding meaning in an imperfect world*. Oxford University Press.

Lee, Y.-L. (2018). Discerning temporal philosophy of education: Understanding the gap between past and future through Augustine, Heidegger, and Huebner. *Philosophy of Education Society*, 242–248.

Lukács, G. (2009) *Lenin: A study in the unity of his thought*. Verso.

Lorde, A. (2007). *Sister outsider*. Crossing Press.

Macdonald, J. (1975). Curriculum theory. In W. Pinar (Ed.), *Curriculum theorizing: The reconceptualists* (pp. 5–13). McCutchan.

Macdonald, J. (1986). The domain of curriculum. *Journal of Curriculum and Supervision, 1*(3), 205–214.

Macdonald, J. (1995). A transcendental developmental ideology. In B. Macdonald (Ed.), *Theory and a prayerful act: The collected essays of James B. Macdonald* (pp. 69–98). Peter Lang.

Macdonald, J., & Zaret, E. (1975). *Schools in search for meaning*. ASCD.

Marx, K., & Engels, F. (1955). *The communist manifesto*. Appleton-Century Crofts, Inc.

Mbembe, A. (2014). *Crítica da Razão Negra*. Antigona.

McMurry, F. (2023). Discussion on the report on Dr. Harris. In J. M. Paraskeva (Ed.), *Curriculum: A new comprehensive reader* (pp. 385–387). Peter Lang.

Mendieta, E. (2017). "What it means to be human!": A conversation with Cornel West [Special issue]. *Critical Philosophy of Race, 5*(2), 137–170.

Mignolo, W. (2008). The geopolitcs of knowledge and colonial difference. In M. Morana, E. Dussel, & C. Jauregui (Eds.), *Coloniality at large: Latin America and the postcolonial debate* (pp. 225–258). Duke University Press.

Moon, S. (2015). Tasanhak, Korean neo-Confucianism, and curriculum studies. Complicated conversations in human nature, knowledge, and justice. In J. M. Paraskeva (Ed.), *Curriculum: Whose internationalization?* (pp. 129–136). Peter Lang.

Moreira, M. A. (2017). 'And the linguistic minorities suffer what they must?' A review of conflicts in curriculum theory through the lenses of language teacher education? *Journal for the American Association for the Advancement of Curriculum Studies, 12*(1), 1–17.

Mucina, D. (2019). A journal of Ubuntu spirituality. In N. N. Wane, M. S. Todorova, & K. L. Todd (Eds.), *Decolonizing the spirit in education and beyond: Resistance and solidarity* (pp. 137–151). Palgrave.

Mucina, M. K. (2019). Spirituality and a search for home. The complexities of practising Sikhism on Indigenous land. In N. N. Wane, M. S. Todorova, & K. L. Todd (Eds.), *Decolonizing the spirit in education and beyond: Resistance and solidarity* (pp. 23–43). Palgrave.

Nkrumah, K. (1964). *Consciencism*. Monthly Review Press.

Nkrumah, K. (2006). *Class struggle in Africa*. PANAF.

Noghiu, A. A. (2020). Spiritual capital: A framework for spiritual-infused leadership education and organizational spirituality. *New Directions for Students Leadership*, *166*, 45–59.

Oyewumi, O. (1977). *The invention of women: Making an African sense of Western gender discourses*. University of Minnesota Press.

Paraskeva, J. M. (2011). *Conflicts in curriculum theory: Challenging hegemonic epistemologies* (1st ed.). Palgrave.

Paraskeva, J. M. (2014). *Conflicts curriculum theory: Challenging hegemonic epistemologies* (upgraded paperback edition). Palgrave.

Paraskeva, J. M. (2016). *Curriculum epistemicides*. Routledge.

Paraskeva, J. M. (2018). *Towards a just curriculum theory. The epistemicide*. Routledge.

Paraskeva, J. M. (2021a). *Generation of utopia*. Routledge.

Paraskeva, J. M. (2021b). Did Covid-19 existed before the scientists? Towards curriculum theory now. *Educational Philosophy and Theory*, *54*(2), 2–13.

Paraskeva, J. M. (2022a). *Conflicts in curriculum theory: Challenging hegemonic epistemologies* (2nd ed.). Palgrave.

Paraskeva, J. (2022b). The generation of the utopia: Itinerant curriculum theory towards a 'futurable future.' *Discourse: Studies in the Cultural Politics of Education*, *43*(3), 347–366.

Paraskeva, J. M. (2023a). *Critical perspectives on the denial of caste in the educational debate*. Routledge (forthcoming).

Paraskeva, J. M. (2023b). *The curriculum: A new comprehensive reader*. Peter Lang.

Parker, F. (2022). The Quincy method. In J. M. Paraskeva (Ed.), *Curriculum: A new comprehensive reader* (pp. 393–398). Peter Lang.

Phenix, P. (1964). *The realms of meaning*. McGraw Hill.

Pinar, W. (1974). *Autobiography*. Peter Lang.

Pinar, W. (1975). *Curriculum theorizing: The reconceptualists*. McCutahan.

Pinar, W. (1992). Dreamt into existence by others: Curriculum theory and school reform. *Theory into Practice*, *31*(3), 228–235.

Pinar, W. (2004). *What is curriculum theory?* Lawrence Erlbaum Associates Publishers.

Pinar, W., & Grumet, M. (1988). Socratic caesura and the theory-practice relationship. In W. Pinar (Ed.), *Contemporary curriculum discourses* (pp. 92–100). Gorsuch Scarrusbrick.

Pinar, W., Reynolds, W., Slattery, P., & Taubman, P. (Eds.). (1995). *Understanding curriculum*. Peter Lang.

Poe, D. Z. (2005). Consciencism. In M. K. Asante & M. K. Asama (Eds.), *Encyclopedia of Black studies*. Sage.

Popkewitz, T. (1978). Educational research: Values and visions of a social order. *Theory and Research in Social Education*, 4(4), 28.

Purpel, D. (1999). *Moral outrage*. Peter Lang.

Quijano, A. (1991). Colonialidad y Modernidad/Racionalidad. *Perú Indígena*, 29(1), 11–21.

Radford, M. (2006). Spirituality and education: Inner and outer realities. *International Journal of Children's Spirituality*, 11(3), 385–396.

Rao, C. H. (1931). *Indian caste system: A study*. Asian Educational Services.

Redmond, S. (2016). And you know who I am: Paul Robeson Sings America [Special issue]. *The Massachusetts Review*, 57(4), 615–619.

Robeson, P. (1958). *Here I stand*. Dennis Dobson.

Roy, A. (2016). The doctor and the saint. In B. R. Ambedkar (Ed.), *Annihilation of caste* (pp. 17–179). Verso.

Santos, B. (1999). Porque é tão difícil construir uma teoria crítica? *Revista Crítica de Ciencias Sociais*, 54, 197–215.

Santos, B. (2005). *Democratizing democracy: Beyond the liberal democratic cannon*. Verso.

Santos, B. (2007). *Another knowledge is possible*. Verso.

Santos, B. (2014). *Epistemologies of the South: Justice against epistemicide*. Paradigm.

Santos, B. (2018). *The end of the cognitive empire*. Duke University Press.

Schilbrack, K. (2012). The social construction of "religion" and its limits: A critical reading of Timothy Fitzgerald. *Method and Theory in the Study of Religion*, 24, 97–117.

Schubert, W. (2017). Growing curriculum studies: Contributions of João M. Paraskeva. *Journal for the American Association for the Advancement of Curriculum Studies*, 12(1), 1–20.

Senreich, E. (2013). An inclusive definition of spirituality for social work education and practice. *Journal of Social Work Education*, 49(4), 548–563.

Smith, L. (1999). *Decolonizing methodologies: Research and Indigenous peoples*. Zed Books.

Snaza, N. (2014). The death of curriculum studies and its ghosts. *Journal of Curriculum and Pedagogy*, 11, 154–173.

Sontag, S. (2001). *Against interpretation*. FSG.

Souza, M. (2012). Connectedness and 'connectedness': The dark side of spirituality. Implications for education. *International Journal of Children's Spirituality*, 17(4), 291–303.

Stone, B. E. (2011). Prophetic pragmatism and the practices of freedom: On Cornel West's Foucauldian methodology. *Foucault Studies*, 11, 92–105.

Tario, J. (2019). Critical spirituality: Decolonizing the self. In N. N. Wane, M. S. Todorova, & K. L. Todd (Eds.), *Decolonizing the spirit in education and beyond: Resistance and solidarity* (pp. 179–193). Palgrave.

Teltumbde, A. (2010). *The persistence of caste: The Khairlanji murders & India's hidden apartheid.* Navayana.

Teltumbde, A. (2018). *The republic of caste.* Navayana.

Tillich, P. (2014). *The courage to be.* Yale University Press.

Tirres, C. (2019). Spiritual activism and praxis: Gloria Anzaldúa's mature spirituality. *The Pluralist, 14*(1), 119–140.

Todorova, M. (2019). Conclusion: The politics of spiritaulity. In N. N. Wane, M. S. Todorova, & K. L. Todd (Eds.), *Decolonizing the spirit in education and beyond: Resistance and solidarity* (pp. 221–233). Palgrave.

Tse Tung, M. (2007). Oppose book worship. In S. Žižek (Ed.), *Slavoj Žižek presents Mao on practice and contradiction* (pp. 43–51). Verso.

Ukule, K. (2011). Decolonizing the spirit in education and beyond: Resistance and solidarity. *Journal of College Character, 22*(4), 346–348.

Valenzuela, A. (1999). *Subtractive schooling: U.S.-Mexican youth and the politics of caring.* State University of New York Press.

Valenzuela, A. (2017). Academia Cuauhtli; (Re)locating the spiritual, if crooked, the path to social justice. *International Journal of Qualitative Studies in Education, 30*(10), 906–911.

Walach, H. (2011). *Secular spirituality. The next steps towards enlightenment.* Springer.

Walsh, C., & Mignolo, W. (2018). *On decoloniality: Concepts, analytics, praxis.* Duke University Press.

Wane, N. N. (2019). Is decolonizing the spirit possible? In N. N. Wane, M. S. Todorova, & K. L. Todd (Eds.), *Decolonizing the spirit in education and beyond: Resistance and solidarity* (pp. 9–21). Palgrave.

Watkins, W. (2001). *The White architects of Black education.* Teachers College.

West, C. (1988). *Keeping faith: Philosophy and race in America.* Routledge.

West, C. (1988). *Prophetic fragments: Illuminations of the crisis in American religion and culture.* Eerdmans.

Zhao, W. (2019). *China's education, curriculum knowledge, and cultural inscriptions: Dancing with the wind.* Routledge.

Zhao, W., Popkewitz, T., & Autio, T. (2022). Historicizing curricuoum knowledge transition and onto-epistemic coloniality. In W. Zhao, T. Popkewitz, & T. Autio (Eds.), *Epistemic colonialism and transfer of curriculum knowledge across borders* (pp. 3–18). Routledge.

Žižek, S. (2013). *Welcome to the desert of the real.* Verso.

Žižek, S. (2019). Why there are no viable political alternatives to unbridled capitalism [Video]. *Big Think.* https://bigthink.com/videos/slavoj-zizek-on-the-failures-of-the-leftist-movement/

CHAPTER 1

# The Truth about My Schooling

*"A Struggle to Fly Inside a Bottle"*

I was side-by-side with my father and mother as they drove me on the bumpy road to my first day of school. My heart was pounding, anxious, joyful, apprehensive, and a little lost. I had so many hopes at the beginning of this long journey, a journey I could never have imagined would take so long to really make sense, and bring me from that day in Brazil to my current existence in the United States. That I was leaving a safe home environment and going into a fun, fair, and integrative setting was my parents' expectation. Unbeknownst to them, something bigger was fighting against this very reasonable expectation. Back then, I could not imagine that 35 years later I would be in a different world, admitted into a doctoral program in which I would learn to better theorize my life, especially my school experience, in such a way as to offer a path towards human liberation via our educational systems.

In this chapter, I intend to critically examine my past realities and lived experiences, my life story (Goodson, 2006), how I struggle from within (Pinar, 1974) in light of what some scholars (Santos, 2014; Mignolo, 2005; Escobar & Dussel, 2008; Paraskeva, 2011, 2014, 2016, 2018) call a Eurocentric way that perpetuates a set of damages on the individual and society, a context in which "Eurocentrism [is] framing social norms," as Cronk and Wasielewski (2008, pp. 285–289) wisely point out. More specifically, I unravel how education and curricula as a whole work towards the emasculation of freedom, as well as incentivize the dominance of thinking shaped by social constructivism.

In the first section of this chapter, I examine my early life. As, "in the beginning, there was the word," I will chronicle my first steps into education. What I expected from education was not so simple, especially in light of how academic life daily presents itself as the bureaucratization of learning and the preparation of minds to meet "socially constructed" expectations. I will unpack moments beginning with my "un-schooled" happiness prior to kindergarten and proceeding to my increasingly contested cognizance of the deceptions pervading my education. I will discuss the lack of relevance and meaning in public schooling and its curriculum (Macdonald, 1995; Huebner, 1996; Apple, 1979; Paraskeva, 2011), relating those absences to my struggle to survive an education in life's desert[1] and revealing the suffering of my mind/self, which needed to learn in different ways and time frames that varied from dominant reductive pedagogical expectations. I attempt to make sense of the specific contexts imposed on me. I struggle to read through my "existence" through the world and word (Freire & Macedo, 1987)—or through the wor(l)d as Paraskeva (2011, 2016) would frame it. Furthermore, I use my experiences to reflect on the official knowledge (Apple, 2000) and the cult of positivism (Giroux, 1981) produced by schools, as well as the curriculum and teaching materials they employ (Giroux, 2009; Apple, 1979). I grapple with defining how schools label students, and how students are especially identified by racialized definitions (Leonardo, 2019). Consequently, I unravel how this culture is passed on to society as a whole, with the educational environment as the shoulders upon which this destructive way of thinking is carried forth (Apple, 2000).

As I think back in time, I fish through events that are still fresh in my memory, many of which in fact became markers of my inner struggles, questions, and decisions as I was pursuing my education and life. With this in mind, I want to ask readers to not just read and come to their own conceptual conclusions about this work, but to reflect deeply on the very real ways in which children can be tremendously impacted and traumatized by the way they are addressed/acknowledged/approached in the classroom, as well as on the influence society exercises on human "beings" aspirations and expectations of and from the world. In this particular chapter, my intention is to invite the reader to see a little piece of "myself" within a specific context and to introduce the real epistemological colors (Santos, 2014) of the bottle I was in and how I was functioning within it. Like so many others—some similar to me, others quite different—I survived. Along with Borges, "I confess that I survived." I intentionally want to open myself to local realities, so I can be better understood and avoid the wrong conceptualizations. In addition, this approach will aid the reader to better understand where I am coming from epistemologically, more specifically, emotionally, socially, and spiritually, and, thus, how I theorize my personal journey.

Needless to say, this is not an easy task; however, one's life story (Goodson, 2006) is only transformative at this level if one has the capacity to situate one's theorization—in a particular temporality (Huebner, 1975)—so as to connect it to the reader's experience or their desire to explore other's experiences, regardless of how painful the process is. This manuscript explicitly endeavors to avoid ventriloquial self-expression (Gay & Hall, 2013). I claim the journey, the self, a story, my story, spirituality, and the cultural web in which I exist and resist, as well as all the other animate and inanimate things that co-existed as part of the unique and solely maternity of who I am. With the terms spirituality, spiritual "being," and (spiritual) self, I refer to a way of existing, being, and thinking, of rationalizing and irrationalizing reality, a dynamic inner sense and sensibility, "an infinite source of faith and will power, as well as an ultimate end, nonsectarian, that goes beyond the creeds and are universal, and non-dimensional and timeless" (Solgi & Safara, 2018, p. 86). Furthermore, this notion frames my own rationality, my reasoning, which goes

> beyond all sciences, philosophies and religions. Reality is both transcendental and beyond time and space, and physical domain and is higher than any conceptualization of the mind, but at the same time it dominates all of these realms; it cannot be understood, meaning that, it cannot be encompassed because no one can understand any infinite fact. At the same time, the infinite fact can be recognized with reason, as one of the divine epistemic powers in the center of existence; this fact is absolute, ultimate, and infinite. (Solgi & Safara, 2018, p. 88)

In this sense, spirituality cannot be submerged in any religious creed, as it doesn't necessarily imply a philosophical stance or refer to religious rituals or institutions per se, but rather is an embodied praxis.

My dissatisfaction with the way education and curriculum were addressing my "potential development" stemmed from not being educated for the world I was aiming to be part of,[2] but rather for a world in which I had to maneuver around the thorns in order to dream about the flowers. My frustration lay in being not only the instrument but also the outcome of the pedagogy of the oppressed (Freire, 1995). As I began my initial reading and examination of critical pieces during my doctoral studies, I was increasingly exposed to revelatory ideas, such as Freire's banking concept of education. Interestingly and oddly, while I am from Brazil and did my studies in Brazil, I never "encountered" Paulo Freire's reason the way I did in my educational journey in the U.S. His *Pedagogy of the Oppressed* was a "revelation" for me in one of Professor Paraskeva's doctoral courses.

The fragmented pieces and unconnected dots of my educational journey started making even more painful sense. Freire (1991) claims that

> Education thus becomes an act of depositing, in which the students are the depositories and the teacher is the depositor. Instead of communicating, the teacher issues communiques and makes deposits which the students patiently receive, memorize, and repeat. This is the "banking" concept of education, in which the scope of action allowed to the students extends only as far as receiving, filing, and storing the deposits. They do, it is true, have the opportunity to become collectors or cataloguers of the things they store. But in the last analysis, it is the people themselves who

> are filed away through the lack of creativity, transformation, and knowledge in this (at best) misguided system. For apart from inquiry, apart from the praxis, individuals cannot be truly human. Knowledge emerges only through invention and re-invention, through the restless, impatient, continuing, hopeful inquiry human beings pursue in the world, with the world, and with each other. (p. 72)

Freire (1991), Nkrumah (1964) and many others gave me the language—the semiotics, the discourse—I had so desperately needed to make sense of my oppressed experiences. I had not dared to even dream about such a realization of my inner needs. To dream is not a rebellious force, but rather a living, revitalizing force. Daily, I had felt my inner aims and needs slowly being reshaped, redefined, reorganized—but also oppressed, as my own dreams were not a priority. Education deferred my dreams (Ladson-Billings, 1994). I felt betrayed by seeing education changing the course of my life while I, in my role as a student, had my hands tied, and that is one reason why I claim that my body, the exteriority of my human "being," was in the classroom but not my mind, not my soul. Unfortunately, my untouchable and invisible "self"—who I really was—was not there because I was empty of identity, much like, in Giroux's (2015) words, a social zombie.

Regardless of how my educational experience made me feel, I followed the requirements of a ubiquitous and oppressive model of education (Freire, 1990) that attempts to produce one-dimensional individuals for a supposedly one-dimensional society (Marcuse, 1974); nonetheless, nothing in my education ever responded to my inner requests or acknowledged my existence as an individual, in the true sense of the word. When I could no longer give in to the fictitious educational requirements being imposed upon me, I had a higher price to pay. Instead of education fulfilling its responsibility to empower me (Freire, 1995), it did the opposite, becoming an agent of oppression until the day I realized something else was guiding the whole process—not towards the amelioration of the "being" (in this case, me), but instead to satisfy a macro-societal agenda. This education, which fulfills Giroux's (2001) critical pedagogical deviation ideal, served me, in retrospect, as a way to reset my "conscientization" (Freire, 1990) or "consciencism" (Nkrumah, 1964) processes, uncovering a profoundly unconscionable lack of "proper balance between public values and commercial power, between identity founded on democratic principles and identities steeped in forms of competitive, self-interested individualism that celebrates selfishness, profit-making and greed" (Giroux, 2001). Education never engulfed my complete "self" in the process of "educating" me; I was only intermittently motivated, and never entirely invested in the schooling process, which I will define more extensively in the following chapters. It is necessary to first understand my beginnings in order to unravel my analysis of how spirituality is perceived, explained, and dialoged within the context of my maturation.

1      Let Me Begin from the Beginning, as "in the Beginning Was the Word"

At the age of six, I entered school for the first time in the city of Altamira, Brazil. I was following my sister's path and wanted to avoid staying home without her companionship and friendship, but I was, undoubtedly, also moved by curiosity arising from the positive impression my friends and my parents' friends had created about school. They each insinuated that "kids" loved school, especially the children in my neighborhood, which was populated by farmers, immigrants, and unemployed miners. At this young age, the attention, care, companionship, and one-on-one dedication offered by my teachers—and my classmates, as well—proved to me that schools were places where, regardless of ethnicity, skin color, or social class, we had the same expectations. Furthermore, I felt that our expectations (such as they were at 6 to 10 years old) were being met.

Given that this was such an early stage of my life, I was unable to discern oppression, but as requirements, homework, little projects, and quizzes began to be assigned, and I observed teachers' attitudes changing towards me, I for the first time perceived the educational environment (Dewey, 1916) as a space in which bias was operating. For instance, class, race, caste—a problematic concept in itself—and gender divisions manifested through the selection of group work.

Along the road to fourth grade, the society I was part of prompted me to look around and question myself about specific points, such as why the gap between school and real life was so wide as to constitute a form of injustice. The injustice I am talking about is the self-denying requirements of school vs. the requirements of life. Why did the school and curriculum get to define part of who I was/we were, but never bring my/our social struggles (real life) into consideration? I perceived education as a necessity of life. Yet my social challenges and the needs of my community had no meaning at all in the education I was enduring (see Macdonald & Zaret, 1975). There was no correspondence between my completion of school requirements and life. I began to understand the disparity between the school curriculum and students' ages and realities. Educators really committed to social justice, Macdonald and Zaret (1975) claim, need to articulate curricular knowledge within the praxis of everyday life in each unique community and through emancipatory pedagogical forms.

Thus, by fourth grade, my admiration and liking for education began to diminish to the point where even the idea of going to school was distasteful. Later on, I started experiencing painful contradictions, beyond what I could articulate at the time, as I attempted to internally wrestle with, even rationalize, the disparities between my school and society in general. Almost 30 years later, as a father of three, I've listened as my children express an even greater dissatisfaction with the way they are perceived, treated, and taught. It is painful.

As I am seated here today writing this piece, I am reflecting on my daughters' perceptions of the schooling process. I'm reminded of how the critical approach of certain scholars, including Freire, Giroux, Apple, McLaren, Pinar, Wexler, Huebner, Macdonald, hooks, Darder, Paraskeva, Tillich, and many others, helped me to dissect how schools function as segregation machines. The ongoing perpetuation of this discriminatory and community- and self-denying schooling process, with its regimented, segregated, and divided activities, has not abated. Every day, I sit with my children to oversee their homework and what they are being taught in class. In this close family context, moments of discomfort certainly arise. I know that my school and curriculum did not meet my expectations or needs as a child, and, as I help them, I realize that it is very possible that my children will someday look back and have even greater frustrations with their education. In my mind, the whole situation keeps evolving into a monster—and I cannot help but ponder that monster's ultimate academic and social mutation.

I remember how hard it was as a child to go back and try to remember a large quantity of detailed information in order to regurgitate it on a piece of paper called a test or exam in which my journey of two or three months of schooling could be judged by a letter grade. Even though I was passionate about geography, social studies, and philosophy, my love for a subject was not measured on any test. Moreover, I was passionate about thinking, thinking over abstract matters. Yet, it wasn't until later on, through my encounters with the critical/progressive works of scholars such as Antonio Gramsci, Raymond Williams, Terry Eagleton, Angela Davis, bell hooks, Dwayne Huebner, Samuel Bowles and Herbert Gintis, Paulo Freire, Cornel West, Henry Giroux, Michael Apple, Stanley Aronowitz, Peter MacLaren, Thomas Popkewitz, Antonia Darder, Jean Anyon, William Pinar, Angela Valenzuela, Franz Fanon, Kwame Nkrumah, Aimé Césaire, Amílcar Cabral, Walter Mignolo, Boaventura de Sousa Santos, João M. Paraskeva and so many others, that I ended up understanding that the very act of thinking is dismissed in our educational systems, since not only is critical and abstract thinking un-measurable and un-testable, but the standardized curriculum strenuously blocks any potential forms of emancipatory rationale (Giroux, 1981; Darder, 2017).

There was no sense of virtue and humanity in my educational process. Clearly, as Huebner (1962) would frame it curriculum conceptions were inadequate, in that they tie the educative process only to the world of man's technique and exclude ties to the world of his spirit (p. 95). My classroom context represented a sphere that I later learned to classify as an environment of survival, an example of the outcome of a cultural politics of cruelty (Giroux, 2011), an oppressive community (Freire, 1991) instead of a learning environment. Ideas and knowledge were imposed, without dialogue or collaboration. Freire (1995), questioning the teaching and development of virtues[3] in *Reading the Word and the World*, wisely claims the following: "Dialog is not an empty instructional tactic, but a natural process of knowing" (p. 15). From this, I conclude that non-dialogic curricula and pedagogy are products of the oppressors' agenda, currently wearing a neoliberal face and directed towards the industrialization of minds. It is also clear that teachers themselves are also oppressed, "colonized" by a deplorable system that de-skills and de-intellectualizes them. As Césaire (1977) insightfully contends, the best weapon of the colonizer is the mind of the colonized.

Thus, we teachers and students were—and are—all, in effect, inside of a bottle. So we must interrogate what is inside of the bottle and why it is there, why I and so many others were inside that bottle. And, to extend the metaphor, we must also ask who pours from, and, above all, who benefits from, such a bottle. We were in some ways deliriously happy thinking that we were touching reality, yet we were just touching the bottle from within. This is not a minor issue, and it contributed deeply to who I am once I was exposed to critical possibilities presented by the scholars mentioned above, along with many others. Pinar's autobiographical matrix was crucial to my understanding of "my curriculum." My educational curriculum-currere (a living, or infinitive form of curriculum [Pinar, 1975/1994])—or the currere of "my"self—was an act of violence against my own "being." More than a method, Pinar's "currere" is for me a way of existing, of "being," as it involves a complex matrix of relations between academic experiences, life histories, identity, and social (re)construction (Pinar, 1975/1994). Pinar aptly frames the futility of addressing these acts of violence within the system that perpetuates them:

> Education and curriculum have been very reluctant to abandon social engineering. If only we can find the right technique, the right modification of classroom organization (small groups, collaborative learning,

dialogue), if only we teach according to "best practices," if only we have students self-reflect or if only we develop "standards" or conduct "scientific" research, then students will learn what we teach them. If only we test regularly, "no child [will be] left behind." (p. 1)

However, such "current" cannot only talk to me if it is non-derivative, that is a-abyssal as Paraskeva (2011, 2016, 2021a) advocates. As the focus on social engineering escalates, there is cognizance of the need to pay attention to the full person, to the individual in all their inner complexities. Before an oppressive pedagogical matrix (Freire, 1991), Pinar (2004) rightly advances autobiography as a revolutionary act. Needless to say, of all the personal moments that I will be sharing and analyzing in this work, most, if not all, are embedded in an attempt at social engineering that can be understood deeply only via an autobiographical approach. Pinar (2004) helps us understand how the "personal" is crucial to unpacking any social engineering so inextricably rooted in curricular content. He states:

> Autobiography is a first-person and singular version of culture and history as these are embodied in the concretely existing individual in society in historical time. In European and European—American culture, scholarly studies of culture and history have expressed disinterested and spectator-like structures of epistemology and knowledge. In contrast to these fictive universalisms are fiction and poetry. What would be the curriculum look like if we centered the school subjects in the autobiographical histories and reflections of those who undergo them? The "subjects" in school subjects would refer to human subjects as well as academic ones. Indeed, the academic disciplines are highly systematized, formalized, bureaucratized conversations among human subjects, circulating in a specific regime of reason, sometimes estranged from bodies of knowledge. (2004, p. 38)

When one is inserted in just such a social context, autobiography is one of the few ways one can "genuinely express and legitimize one's experiences acting as economy of the self, wherein the narration of one's story functions to preserve oneself" (Pinar, 2004, p. 49). To draw on Paraskeva (2011, 2016, 2021a, 2022) my "currere"—spiritually—was a profound itinerantology. In this sense, I would argue that this text is an attempt to claim my existence—not only physically, but metaphysically as well. It involves a methodological approach in which one's lifeblood allows a "spiritual revolution to happen" (Pinar, 2004, p. 49), contradicting the technicalities of modern curriculum, which has been shaped over the decades and centuries by a global social engineering mentality. Therefore, this work is a claim to keep alive the non-quantitative me.

This social engineering is the basis of our education-for-jobs doctrine—and clearly a façade for the humanity-crusher that is the curriculum. The justifications for ameliorating education by making it into preparation for the workforce were challenged more than a century ago by Dewey's (1897) claim for the superior social mission of education. In his Creed, Article Two, he argues that education should prioritize the simplification of life, instead of complexifying education and society in the learning setting, first and foremost to avoid bias and "[m]ake education more palpable than just theoretically" (p. 7). Also writing many decades ago, Pear (1944) intelligently articulates the collateral damage wrought by the excessive theorization of subjects that don't match the varying mental maturities of each pupil and vehemently states that this approach might adversely affect the outcome of the learning process. This is yet another barrier preventing dialogic spaces, wherein knowledge could be constructively exchanged, and where classrooms could be aligned with—and generative of—Freire's (1990) notion of knowledge as virtuous, noble, accessible to anyone. As research documents (Krug, 1969; Kliebard, 1995; Schubert, 1986; Baker, 2009), and as we will see later, the more "technicfied" curriculum becomes less attention is paid to students and teachers as spiritual beings.

In retrospect, I highlight two key things that struck me by the time I reached fourth grade. First, I noticed that the importance of the appearance of my projects could override the actual quality of my work. Second, I realized that if I had money to invest in my class project, it would be much more attractive-seeming, blinding my teacher from looking deeper into the genuine knowledge and efforts I had invested. These realizations constituted an awakening to "modernity's shine," as Andreotti (2011) so wisely framed such phenomena. As I see it, such attitudes on the part of teachers reflect the negligent act of contemplating academic efforts driven by the incentive of modernity; this modernity shines from the very early formation of the students and onward over the entire course of their educations. In this case, hooks (2000) helps me better understand the message delivered to the students, one which competes with the positive elements of community, financial power, and solidarity, nullifies mental maturity and readiness to learn, and, from my perspective, exchanges the fast results of modernity for the glory of genuine momentum. By the same token, maturity, not in the sense of mental readiness but in the sense of practicing the deeds of modernity—externalized in a shiny way—is combined with current educational expectations, manifesting ultimately in what I would call the educational new right.

An absence of values or moral common ground generating mutual respect precisely because of differences is obviously related to individual temperament and character, but such attitudes are also reflected in schools and curricula, making students susceptible to practicing the only options offered. The works of hooks (2000) as well as Andreotti (2016), and Geo-Jaja and Majhanovich (2016), offer vivid explanations of the downhill paths that become common routes when students receive hidden incentives to position themselves in a more fast-food academic way without knowing that they are also being trained to take shortcuts in life. In these contexts, there is no space for reflection, no appreciation for heartfelt efforts and intellectual growth, only a superficial grading process that crushes the human "being," spirituality, and meaningful interconnection. Moreover, curriculum theory and development don't aim an abstract existence. In fact, education and curriculum will always bear, Huebner (1975) highly claims, a concern for human temporality. Such temporality cannot be reductively defined just in technical terms aimed towards a pragmatic outcome framed by future "jobs."

As mentioned previously, I believe that efforts to mechanize and box in the humanization of the "being" begin with attempts to benchmark learning that grant students the so-called privilege of continuing to learn while reducing them to mere word learners or memorizers. On this, Huebner (1966) teaches us a great deal:

> For centuries the poet has sung of his near infinitudes; the theologian has preached of his depravity and hinted of his participation in the divine; the philosopher has struggled to encompass him in his systems, only to have him repeatedly escape; the novelist and dramatist have captured his fleeting moments of pain and purity in never-to-be-forgotten aesthetic forms; and the [man] engaged in the curriculum has the temerity to reduce this being to a single term—learner. (p. 10)

As the emphasis on the scientific management of the curriculum increases and dominates curriculum and pedagogical theory and practices, we see a gradual increase in an anti-intellectual stance on the part of educators. The curriculum assumes an anti-intellectual matrix and today a very strong concern with management devices controlling pedagogical practices has become normal. School administrators—superintendents and principals—are much more concerned with hiring teachers who are experts in classroom management than experts in their subject areas.

Drawing from Giroux (2011), who adamantly challenges our curriculum's anti-intellectualism, and Paraskeva's (2017) notion of anti-intellectual intellectualism, I argue that the attack on intellectualism corresponds with the total nullification of the human "being" and its spirituality. But this is not the only problem we face. We must acknowledge that there is more than one point to which we should pay attention. In tandem with the political and intellectual realms, there are other aspects through which ideas about visible and invisible "beings" are to be engaged. Santos (2014) unquestionably advocates on behalf of the latter, in the sense that a multitude of things cooperates in the process of deep realm negation. The holistic perception of a world-system is imperative to understand that "abyssalism" and the denial of the "being" are departmentalized.

Up to here, I have purposely externalized my world in order to allow the reader to understand how and why I approach the denial of spirituality in public education as a human rights issue. But it is necessary to pay attention to a correlation between what gives structure to the expression of the interior and exterior of the "being."

The labyrinth where abyssal-neoliberal epistemologies work—to rely on Santos' (2014) approach—oppresses and muddles culture, individuality, and spirituality. My experiences led me to believe I was just one "guinea pig" among others, part of a captive audience (Apple, 2000) in an educational system designed to solidify regulation over emancipation. Are we "beings," the structured "products" of a programmed machine ever supposed to awaken? In the following section, I highlight the claims/excuses of modern education as it places human "beings" face-to-face with the subtractive "learning process," and I examine the tensions between the "beings" enduring this racist/classist/sexist structural violence and the system itself.

## 2  A Subtractive Culture of Learning

There are subtle, intrinsic curriculum nuances in which unseen social phenomena rub up against each other all the time, intrinsically framed by what Benedict (2005) calls a culture-pattern. This helps structure how culture and ethnicity play a significant role in students' mental readiness to learn. Therefore, teachers must be aware of what to expect from them. It is not that they are cognitively incapable of marching in the same row, but each will vary temporally in achieving his or her own maturity vis-à-vis different aspects of life. Human "beings" have differing cognitive skills—and these skills are in no way detached from cultural, economic, ideological, and spiritual dynamics. In this context, as Santos (2016) argues, there is no equality or social justice without cognitive justice.

Here, I situate one of my claims: Teachers, instead of just teaching the curriculum and acting as mere executors of a prescribed classized, racialized, and genderized epistemological matrix, should perform as real intellectuals

(Giroux, 2011, 2019). In so doing, they must openly engage in spontaneous strategies not just to teach (and challenge) the (required) curriculum content, but to create knowledge without undermining the need to know students as individuals, understanding their culture in order to adapt to their cognitive maturity and needs (hooks, 1994; Darder, 1991, 2017; Valenzuela, 1999; Sleeter, 2011). Most children are not ready to learn, to listen to, and reflect on a colossal amount of information, when confronted by a one-dimensional, non-reflective interpretation of curriculum materials.

Valenzuela (1999) calls this a subtractive culture of learning, which is "organized formally and informally in ways that fracture students' cultural and ethnic identities, creating social, linguistic, and cultural divisions. As a consequence of such divisions, teachers also fail to forge meaningful connections with their students" (p. 5). As we will see later, the absolutism of learning theories, behavioral sciences and the language of psychology—helped consolidate a functionalist curriculum praxis manipulating and shrinking the language we "use" to debate our curriculum affairs and—made spirituality a non-existent factor in the life of the human being. Learning, Huebner (1985a, p. 404) argues, "too quickly explains and simplifies life." In fact, the language that we use to debate education and curriculum, Huebner (1985b, p. 257) is "not helpful in the search for understanding life." Some of the reasons for such lack of understanding is related to "the prevailing taken-for-granted language of education, and hence unrecognized positivism and scientism" (Huebner, 1985b, p. 257). Following Huebner's (1985b) reason, Pinar (2015) argues for an education in which these terrible pitfalls may be avoided, involving a type of study that

> in contrast to learning, is self-paced and its end unknown; it supports subjective and social reconstruction threaded through academic knowledge and everyday life, between "popular" and erudite knowledge. Self-formation specifies no "standards" or "best practices," as the paths of study are numerous. (p. 11)

Moreover, the correlation between emotions and maturity is significant in this context. Arya (1984) claims that not only are "intelligence and emotional maturity...highly related to each other" (p. 121), but "superior emotional maturity among children varies due to gender differences and different residence—urban and rural" (p. 212). This underlines the need for teachers to focus more on the emotional maturity level of each child, instead of simply dumping the same selective traditional/official knowledge (Apple, 2000) alike on all, with the assumption that all students learn at the same time and can reproduce that learning at the expected level of institutional expectations.

In short, the level of maturity necessary for "genuine just learning"—one that responds to the endless different epistemological river—is generally underestimated. Further, while students are in this vulnerable state, our educational systems use students' spirituality as part of a colonial mechanism of control and preparation for workforce (Mignolo, 2018). How? Spirituality, for the majority of individuals, is not something stratospheric and abstract; it is instead a very concrete mundane reality that is deeply ingrained in their values and daily lives. Our educational and curriculum systems treat this reality with both neglect and disdain, rejecting or denying our values, limiting our freedom, denying our personal rights and social necessities, and denying our emotional and affective needs. The ultimate crushing happens when we mistakenly think that abuse manifests only as overt physical or verbal expression. With others, I contend that treating students in this way constitutes abuse.

We are all so different. We each learn and grow in our own ways. Each student produces, and he or she has been produced through, a specific narrative, a life story (Goodson, 2006), which is classed, raced, and gendered (Bowles & Gintis, 2011; McCarthy, 1991; Grumet, 1988; hooks, 2014; Anyon, 1997). Grumet and McCoy (1997), scholars of feminist studies in education, recognize that

> the masculine codes and commitments of curriculum are often portrayed as neutral, and feminists have challenged the arrogation of feminine experience and viewpoints to generalizations of male experience, for too often public life and letters are seen as inscribing only male experience, thus excluding the private domain and the specificity of women's experiences. The caution that defends the subjectivity and specificity of women from being subsumed in male interests has been extended to feminist practice as well, as ideologies related to feminism or the needs and experience of women and girls are examined for their effacement of the idiosyncratic experiences of individual women as well as the specificities of race, class, religion, ethnicity and sexuality. (p. 5)

Similar marginalizations occur for other intersectionalities, including disability, gender identity, sexual preference, ethnicity, poverty, and so on. These connect back to the false measurement of students via the one-size-fits-all metrics of standardized assessment. Pinar and colleagues (1995) stressed curriculum as a classed, raced, and gendered text. The commonsense assumption that standardization and high-stakes testing policies are neutral is a vivid example of how deeply class-, race-, and gender-segregated these policies are (McCarthy, 1991; Weis, 1989; Hursh, 2012).[4] Here is where the tension between the presumably assimilating individual and the demands of the mechanical environmental begins to emerge. Every student responds differently. Thus, the battle for social justice cannot be effectively undertaken if the concomitant need for cognitive justice is minimized (Santos, 2014; Paraskeva, 2016). Such a battle cannot be fought and won when teacher educators have not been prepared and supported to fight for social and cognitive justice—and to respect and respond to the student's "inner" spiritual struggles—and instead remain mere workers promoting standardization. Pinar (2015) claims that:

> perhaps persuaded by our own educational experience, egged on by politicians and parents and, perhaps, by our own megalomania, we imagined we could produce literate and docile workers, or self-reflective and politically engaged citizens, well, name your outcome. We have known for a long time that, in fact, if human conduct could be regulated and rendered predictable, then the costly and ongoing "scientific" research mounted in the social sciences would have by now succeeded. (p. 19)

Teachers must be cognizant of the diverse minds and bodies within their classrooms. They must reflect on, for instance, how a question asked of one student might constitute entertainment when to another it could be offensive. Given my life struggles, I often felt unable to learn what I wanted to learn. Moreover, in many occasions, I felt that to "learn what I need wanted to learn" I had to "unlearned" what I had learned. I had to learn to unlearn (Tlostanova & Mignolo, 2012). This was due both to my mental state and the multiple outside expectations weighing on me at any given time. Like so many others, I was brutalized by my education. I was brutalized through education. In sixth grade, for example, I had a lot of responsibilities, including early hours helping my father, not to mention a great deal of homework. As a kid, I also felt I needed more time to process and ingest what was introduced to me as "knowledge," and there were many subjects that I only fully understood by the end of the school year. Thus, during most of the school year, I was tested and then condemned for my lack of "knowledge," to the point where, by eighth grade, I seriously considered taking a break from school. Like many others that "smell like me," I was racially labeled. Labeling is a very crucial activity in the system as it helps to resolve a racialized problem bureaucratically. Needless to say, such pervasive attacks on cognitive justice—of which my story here reflects just one of millions of instances—are not neutral, either; rather, they reveal racialized and centralized policies and pedagogies that help perpetuate schools and education as segregational places (Giroux, 1981; Apple, 2000; McLaren, 2015) producing and legitimizing the fallacy on a unique mythical scientific pedagogy (Popkewitz, 1976).

Paradoxically, even conservative voices seem to take issue with such a segregational curriculum. Bennett (2012), for example, boldly points out that the curriculum packages that students receive over the years include within them the ultimate drivers of our current educational system, that is "educational consumers, target markets, corporate management perspectives, competitiveness, values, efficiency, productivity, regulatory burden, stakeholder demands, return on investment" (p. 148). As well, Hirsh (2016) claims that such forces are the main justification for deploying an overwhelming amount of learning assessments that contradict themselves by measuring outcomes rather than what students have actually learned. What conservatives conveniently ignore is that their blind creed in the absolutism of leaning theories and behavioral objectives and objectivism taints the holistic dimension of the subject.

Furthermore, schools have utilized certain principles of selection to discriminate against minority classes and people of color (Giroux, 1981). The notion that this system is more proactive in legitimating the disadvantaged rather than working to ameliorate their realities (Giroux, 1981, p. 145) is undeniable. Note that there are no spaces for self or inner development in our educational package. What in fact drives these forces is instead "mounting anxiety about the state of the economy and widespread joblessness" (p. 148). Personal expectations and aims of liberation now are replaced by attempts to achieve predetermined learning outcomes in order to secure "a better place under the sun." These misdirected interpretations of learning push the need for drilling more and more knowledge into students in order to have scores that match academic expectations; these educational aims are in turn directly linked with market expectations. Students who can't "keep up" with these institutional expectations are deemed—at best—inferior learners.

This process of subculturalizing or subculturalization, Santos' (2014) claims, perpetuates sub-humanity, a necessary factor in the well-being of modern Western Eurocentric humanity. Modern humanity is not conceivable without modern sub-humanity (Santos, 2007). Such sub-humanity in turn pollutes the well-being of the individual students subsumed in this system, and yet it is sustained through our curriculum forms in all its aspects.

Not surprisingly, given these sub-humanizing forces, my perception is that the inversion of values away from individuals' socio-culturally situated intellects is more than latent within the academic context. This oppressive approach is not the only option. Vygotsky (1931, 1997, pp. 105–106) claims that through a broad range of joint activities students are able to grasp and hold the inner effects of working in a participatory environment, wherein students may acquire new ways, approaches, and strategies, and develop a much broader knowledge not only of the world, but of other cultures—both highly local and wider—as well. Although Vygotsky was looking into the consequences of such development as an internal process, he notes that if the environment promotes such actions and interactions within its reflected and exchanged culture, personal growth and maturity will naturally ensue. Instead of prioritizing mental, emotional, and social development in education, however, the constitutively human processes of reflection and building relationships are deviated to and through a mechanized system of intellectual growth that standardizes minds to accept specific inputs and outputs.

Every student walks into school with an intact, whole culture, a phenomenon which is even more heightened for "bussed," immigrant and/or bilingual students, who are cradled in the intimacy[5] of a more specific social group (Darder, 1996). The school then rips apart these crucial bonds and forces the student to shift from shared affection to a level of discomfort, especially in the case of bilingual (and other "bi-cultural" students), who are common in U.S. classrooms. Such discomfort caused by the school environment provokes an instability in the "sense of self" (Hall, 2011, p. 597), leading to a dislocation or de-centering of the subject. Hall (2011) also claims that this instability or set of double displacements—de-centering individuals both from their place in the social and cultural world, and from themselves—constitutes a "crisis of identity" for the individual, leading to another problem, affecting the "interaction" between self and society. In my school days, they were moments when I did not know who I actually was. Such not knowing became my identity, and the seeds for my spiritual inquiry (Anzaldua, 2002a).

The mother tongue spoken at home is endowed with many positive affective variables, such as intimacy and solidarity (Darder, 2014). This sense of intimacy is what Guy (1999) defines as culture. Adding onto this, across the ages and throughout life, is the fact that while everybody has a different level of mental maturity and readiness, we all have some sense of unity and connectivity, not just with family and friends but with our selves, as in "myself," or "oneself." For our "selves," learning actually can occur in different ages and stages of the exchange process. The key determinant is whether, even in a culturally diverse environment (classroom), our shared and similar needs are met. Gaps between age and mental readiness to learn and/or emotional strength can be compensated for by the safe environment provided by the school. A safe environment encompasses all cultures as "normal/legit" and of equal value. Therefore, if culture is ordinary (Williams, 1989), and spirituality is part of culture, then spirituality is ordinary as well. We cannot then desensitize or dismiss spirituality, because it is an integral part of the individual. Eradicating it is a biological and social impossibility. Culture is ordinary and is intimately related to the context in which one matures and the metamorphoses that one faces (Williams, 1989).

As an intrinsic element of a state or process of human "being," we must allow spirituality to become part of the transformative educational process.

In our current system, the transitions between one stage and another are in no way ideologically transformative, they simply increasingly reveal what's at stake. "Cooperativism" (teamwork and collaboration) and appreciation for intellectual progress are emasculated as students gradually come to understand that toeing the educational line is a matter of survival. From one year to another, their teachers create activities of isolation instead of activities for building community and individualized student success. Such activities are used to fill temporal gaps between "valid" pursuits and thereby avoid "non-valid" pursuits.

Students naturally begin to internalize the intended lessons. After taking tests, for example, my friends and I went home understanding that the most important thing to do was to memorize as much information as we could to pass our tests and final examinations. Hursh (2008) denounces this sort of high-stakes testing as an ideological artifact that certifies that the educational system is efficient as a sorting machine. I and others were the guinea pigs of what I learned later on in my doctoral studies as "mind as a muscle" (Kliebard, 1995; Schubert, 1986; Paraskeva, 2011, 2016, 2023).

To succeed in this system, my friends and I composed extensive questionnaires about the accumulated subjects. We each spent many hours formulating question-answer sheets to memorize, to the point of distorting the learning process. There was no more room for true cooperativism. Slowly, I noticed that we were becoming more and more self-centered as we focused on learning the required materials in the required way. As Deutsch (1979) claims, these types of grading systems render us more anthropocentric, increasingly liable to view humankind—and then ourselves—as the center of everything. Indeed, our study habits began to reveal anthropocentric traits, such as selfishness, egoism, and competitiveness. Is this the process by which humans understand that, in order to succeed, they have to "only" worry about themselves? Is this how we are taught the postmodern-anthropocentric way of success through overcoming others at any cost?

Undeniably, the nature of schooling and its curriculum frameworks, along with the eugenic engineering of education (Selden, 1999), drove us all to this anthropocentric behavior, and, as I stated before, put us in survival mode. Deutsch (1979) vehemently claims that this method of merit distribution—which is in fact only an attempt to locate those individuals to whom merit shall or shall not be distributed—forcibly inculcates in students and teachers the *Mad Max*[6] notion (see explanation below) of *meritocracy* as a way of determining whether one is worthy or not, via educational symbols (grades). The persistence of "uneducated" elements who aren't achieving the "right" grades or viewpoints forces competitive education to enter into a wrestling match against cooperative education "creating a competitive-hierarchical atmosphere," as Deutsch (1979, p. 391) affirms. This is so negatively biased on both sides of the duality that, whichever side pushes, it will flutter and redefine distributive justice in the classroom and in society.

This is the act of colonizing education by recolonizing and reinstituting knowledge by how it "must" be counted, understood, and replicated on a piece of paper. Such act frames the latitude and longitude of coloniality. My frustration with this cycle goes far beyond the famous question of "why Johnny can't read" and ossifies instead into the matter of why "Johnnies" can't be happy, to wit, why they cannot experience an organic happiness triggered naturally from being exposed to the process of learning.

Of course, my own experience (and probably yours as well) gives us the answer. The school I was attending in Brazil during the testing period described above, had—and still has—the following as part of their mission statement: "We prepare students for success in life." What does this phrase actually mean? And how may we define what success means for the various stakeholders in this process? "Whose success?" Are we talking about "financial success" or "*pura vida*?" Like so many communities in Latin America and Africa, success is "*pura vida*." Coloniality reduces success to material assets, though. In a world where humanity "exists" at the expense of its sub-humanity, it is impossible to frame success for all in such way. Different parents, for example, may define success very differently. Furthermore, while many professionals work in education to enhance human life, they do not realize that preparing a student for success in life may come at the cost of denying the empiric knowledge that each brings to the classroom. Such limited and graded notions of success do not acknowledge that students bring their cultural and daily experiences to the classroom as knowledge. Moreover, they explicitly devalue that knowledge, via the subtractive nature of the school curriculum, which is not detached from the subtractive nature of modern Western Eurocentric hegemonic epistemologies. This subtractive nature (Valenzuela, 1999) so intrinsic to the curricular framework is in truth a fundamental pillar of the sub-humanity that sustains modern Western Eurocentric humanity (Santos, 2014).

Critical decolonial and anti-colonial scholars add great insights to the problem of subtractive curricula (Valenzuela, 1999)—that is racialized selective pedagogical process of assimilation that oppressed minorities and peoples of color. Santos (2014) brings to the fore the claim that modern Western Eurocentric reason is an abyssal reasoning. As we will examine later on, such eugenic approaches establish a clear abyssal line, defining what exists and is legitimated, thus "granting to modern science the monopoly of the universal distinction between true and false" (Santos, 2007, p. 119). Spirituality is right at the very core of what has been rendered nonexistent by such Eurocentric abyssal reasoning. Although I intend to explore coloniality further, allow me to sketch here a small trait related to the true epistemological colors of coloniality that structured the subtractive curricular matrix.

Quijano (1991) also helps us to place the subtractive nature of school curricula within the context of the colonial power matrix, as it builds the fundamental cognitive pillars of coloniality of power and of knowledge, "which do not permit one to see or to invent any other path" (Mignolo & Escobar, 2013, pp. 152–153). In this sense, the curriculum is indeed an ideological artifact of coloniality—the eugenic framework that both preceded and endured after colonialism (Mignolo & Escobar, 2013). Spirituality is just one of the casualties of this repressive system, but it is a significant one.

The way history has been taught also exemplifies these casualties—and speaks volumes about such decolonial and anti-colonial claims. History is taught as neutral, a simple repetition and memorization of particular "facts"—"facts" that just happen to demonize the "other" and highlight modern Western Eurocentric exceptionalism (Zinn, 1999; Goody, 2008, 2011). The way Columbus has been curricularized (Paraskeva, 2011, 2022) shows what this sort of history actually represents: an engineering process (Chomsky, 2002), a process of obliteration (Zinn, 1999), an intentional fallacy that has been justified by the process of civilization (Paraskeva, 2011, pp. 64–65). Columbus was a mass murderer (hooks, 1994) transformed into a hero. Basically, students are educated under a secular curriculum that reproduces these atrocities as tales of heroes (Loewen, 1995). I contend that such attacks on the historicity of history, or as Goody (2011) would say, such pilferings of history, are also an attack on students' spirituality. The very nature of these "heroic" so-called "discoveries" also involved a spiritual clash, a eugenic one, in which the Europeans forced their religion upon native populations. The manipulation and prevention of history were part of my curriculum processes, as a student as well.

When teachers present Brazil's 1896 Canudos Rebellion, for example, they rely upon literature that romanticizes the wilderness of locals and localities, introducing this information to students as a tool meant only for academic growth. Yet the Canudos Rebellion was a direct consequence of a long process of marginalization, violence, and social exclusion in the community of Canudos, which had grown rapidly following the arrival of Antônio Conselheiro in 1893. The press, clergy, and landowners in the region were bothered by the new independent city and the constant migration of people to the area. The messianic movement, rooted in the misery of the rural population (the majority) in the face of the deep religiosity of, and oppression by, colonial landowners (the minority), was a strong force against the interests of the elite of the time. With the colonial landowners fearing a loss of labor, the Church observing the growth of a religious movement it considered heretical, the government losing control, and the press stirring up anger and discord, the messianic movement soon became a target. This resulted in two failed expeditions by the state of Bahia, and two missions carried out by the national army, culminating in the massacre of the Canudos camp. Martins (1991) states that the conflict ended in 1897 with approximately 25,000 casualties.

So, what about the abyssalism and meritocracies suggested in Euclides da Cunha's[7] 1902 work on the subject, Os Sertões? Student readers are not exposed to the full background of the subject of the book, instead they are taught to praise the author for writing an elegant piece. In schools, da Cunha is framed more as a melancholic writer than as someone who denounces European-driven inequality and opportunism, or who, as Sarmiento (1961) claims, decries Western ideas about monarchic civilization and barbarism. Da Cunha describes the terrible battles that occurred during the four expeditions to Canudos, creating the only real portrait available via reports from eyewitnesses to the hunger, plague, misery, violence, and insanity of war. In the end, it was just a violent massacre where they were all "wrong" (barbarism), and the weaker side endured to the end with their last defenders—an old man, two adults, and a child. Isn't hunger, plague, misery, violence and insanity of war, exactly what we are facing right now?

I grew up and attended school near the state where the Canudos Rebellion happened. In all the time that elapsed between my first encounters with da Cunha's book as a student and 2021, when I read Mignolo and Escobar (2013), I hadn't fully realized that I had never been given the "privilege" of a critical reading of "my own realities." I was "educated" and "tested" through a curriculum system that fostered and legitimized epistemological blindness (Santos, 2014; Paraskeva, 2016, p. 211, 2022). Many academics and influencers had access to da Cunha's writings, but most, including me, could not actually hear his voice. I, too, approached da Cunha from the perspective that the modernization of the content could lead to positive positivist lessons, thereby avoiding his deeper aim of advancing conscience. One such incident occurred when I took the Vestibular, a mandatory eight-hour test covering the entire curricular content taught in high school that must be taken before entering college in Brazil. Depending on their grade, students may gain access to a better, accredited university/college or choose to enter a different school and/or field, where a "lower" grade is acceptable. In the test's literature section, students perform text interpretations and, of course, must select the "correct" answers to a series of questions.

When it came to questions on da Cunha and the Rebellion, the "correct" answers glorified the bravery of the locals while fighting until the end, instead of questioning why they had no choice but to do so. There was in reality no sense of heroism or bravery, but rather indignation and rage over people's land—their families' only means of survival—being taken away. Many fought because they wanted to be free to grow, but such fighting is not a way out. In this context, if you do not fight, you will become homeless and a slave once again, or you will be killed, since you have knowledge of a dangerously liberating ideology. Here again, modern history is far from a believable truth. As a teacher, I often used mathematics to motivate my students to override an abyssal living, and thinking condition (Santos, 2014), when I could use the same to deconstruct abyssal ways of existing. For how long was I unaware of my compatriots' true story of their history? My frustrations were triggered by an education and curriculum that every day ran away from the superior praxis of my spiritual utopia and towards a society pilfered of the common good. For a long time, I had no other choice but to believe in what I had been taught.

As a walking victim of the "pedagogy of the oppressed," I realized that such pedagogy also oppresses because it alienates any possibility of even the foggiest attempt to design and pursue a utopia, a better world saturated with social justice. I am not arguing that there is no resistance to such dominant pedagogical forms, actually, resistance typically comes from the marginalized and/or dominated groups that refuse to give up a dominant utopia.

There is a specific group of participants in this process that we need to address: educational "professionals." When we remember past school experiences, good or bad, we especially remember our teachers. There is plenty to blame on teachers' performances, but teachers do not govern all the phenomena in the world, nor are they always responsible for all the pain and educational oppression students go through. When I read and thought about hooks' *Teaching to Transgress*, in my doctoral studies here in the U.S., it struck me that I was never exposed to the kind of teaching that would trigger a different "me." I never saw a teacher who dared to defy the required curriculum. Perhaps those teachers, too, had never encountered such inspiring teaching and/or writing. Curricular knowledge consists always of pale and crude information (hooks, 1994), aimed towards a culture of obedience. In hooks' (1994) terms,

> Despite the contemporary focus on multiculturalism in our society, particularly in education, there is not nearly enough practical discussion of ways classroom settings can be trans-formed so that the learning experience is inclusive. If the effort to respect and honor the social reality and experiences of groups in this society who are nonwhite is to be reflected

in a pedagogical process, then as teachers-on all levels, from elementary to university settings-we must acknowledge that our styles of teaching may need to change. Let's face it: most of us were taught in classrooms where styles of teachings reflected the notion of a single norm of thought and experience, which we were encouraged to believe was universal. This has been just as true for nonwhite teachers as for white teachers. Most of us learned to teach emulating this model. (p. 35)

The deskilling of teachers (Apple, 1982) means they are not considered intellectuals (Giroux, 1988). Teachers' practices now have the potential and inclination to be a sick and degenerative reflection, repetition, and perpetuation of an imperial colonialism that, over the years, has twisted teachers' mindsets, castrating the definition of education for citizenship and child development, exchanging sides from liberator to oppressor, transforming teachers from someone who guides students to help give form to their ideas and intellectuality to someone who boxes in their way of thinking and denies the existence of their individuality—all with the justification of "teaching," and all while imposing a third party's knowledge as a savior of the educational endeavor.

These *Matrix*[8]-style teachers only repeat what they have been programmed for according to their artificial intelligence, itself an engineered product. Like the robots in the movie, each teacher receives their materials—viewpoint, ideology, cultural understanding and awareness, political standing, biased perceptions of knowledge/non-knowledge and ideal behavior, spiritual denial, perception focused on appearance, testing addiction, and behavior control—as a download consisting of justifications for the "superior" educational services to be provided. By the time someone becomes a teacher, that individual is already a reflection of the maximized mode of postmodern identity, ready to serve the purposes of those forces and "humans" behind the ideology.

It can sometimes be frustrating and painful to return to the past and reflect on the memories that we carried so placidly along through our lives and realize, ultimately, that the school setting was not in fact on board with our needs. Going back to the past is also a "struggle from within" (Pinar, 1974). This doesn't happen to us because educators, in general, are/were not sincere, but because education/educators are/were already hooked and dominated by colonial endeavors; they are/were thus aiming to change society and indoctrinate students with a new ideology, the ideology of cyclic servant dependence.

The expectations I personally have around education are heavily impacted by the writings of Harmon (1952); furthermore, her work has shaped my view of teachers when it comes to the call for teaching. The reason why I decided to use the phrase "the call for teaching" is personal. I do still strongly believe that education, being part of the educative process of someone's life, is the most important endeavor one can undertake. To me, the call for teaching—which was spiritually flavored—means understanding what education is about, first and foremost. Teaching is not a stagnant job, wherein you learn the "right" way to teach and then repeat what you've learned until retirement—it's a calling. As such, the position of teacher should only be occupied by someone who understands that growth must be a constant. Being an educator is inherently a commitment that one makes to social and cognitive justice (Santos, 2014; Paraskeva, 2016). It is thus a political act (Freire, 1970) and a labor of love (Marti, 2009).

In this context, I continually ask, "for what and to whom?" and vice versa, and I do so from, in Harmon's (1952) words, *beginning-end*,[9] meaning from birth until death (see footnote for more clarification). This process best represents my personal way of understanding education and fulfills me as human "being" as well. My eschatological perspective encompasses the reality that I cannot deny or change what happened in my past, what is happening in this very moment, and—stemming from my past and present experiences—where my hopes and forecast for public education might point my senses as I make my way towards my "end." I am using a "going back to the source" (Cabral, 1973, p. 12) approach, but in a historical and humanistic way, to make sense of my life and the expectations it has engendered.

I take this stance in direct defiance of the dominant socially engineered curricula that constitute an overt block on any attempt to be transformative and authentic. Any effort to hinder the transformative nature of the individual and his/her/their authenticity is an attack on his/her/their freedom. Greene (1988) teaches us great deal:

> Freedom shows itself or comes into being when individuals come together in a particular way, when they are authentically present to one another, when they have a project they can mutually pursue. When people lack attachments, when there is no possibility of coming together in a plurality or a community, when they have not tapped their imaginations, they may be thinking of breaking free, but they will be unlikely to think of breaking through the structures of their world and creating something new. It does not matter whether those structures are as everyday as constraining family rituals, as banal as bureaucratic supervisory systems, as shabby as segregation practices. (p. 17)

Very often we (teachers), claiming to be educators but without any notion of what education genuinely must mean, produce instead fear or a lukewarm sense of social responsibility based on a long-ago engineered, indefinitely perpetuated democratic absence of the exercise of freedom and citizenship grounded in an ideology that claims only one knowledge is possible and guided by striving for material possessions. We disseminate the belief that "only" the glorification of certain hard skills can promote success—and that the only way of achieving said success is through denying other ways of knowing by means of a standardized, massive, one-dimensional educational curriculum model. I call this the de-intellectualization of the intellect, a process which pays zero attention to the fulfillment of the essence of our existence, numbs our ideas, creativity, and needs for human interconnection, and detaches our culture and spiritual values from our social being. In addition, the vampiric lifeblood of this phenomenon is the ability of we humans—our children, ourselves—to "be" broken and restructured from our unique individual selves, in the process removing our cherished hopes and substituting fulfilment by business endeavors to replace all that has been overridden by social engineering, to the point that many of us no longer know who we are or what we truly want to do. Greene (1998) adds,

> Stunned by hollow formulas, media fabricated sentiments, and cost-benefit terminologies, young and old alike find it hard to shape authentic expression of hope and ideas. Lacking embeddedness in memories and histories they have made their own people feel as if they are rootless subjectivities-dandelion pods tossed by the wind. What does it mean to be a citizen of the free world? What does it mean to think forward into a future? To dream? To reach beyond? (p. 3)

Many factors can contribute to the exploration of these crucial questions. I see myself as a Brazilian progressive spiritual educator, father, and husband, and so it would be unjust on my part to deny any worthy analysis of the various micro and macro timelines of local and/or worldwide historical momentum—or any personal perspective on such local and global matters. I personally have tremendous awareness that there is much I do not know, and I still have many questions about education and life in general. But I do nonetheless believe that there is a purpose in and for life, and I will address that claim in the following chapters. I realize that many students and parents may feel that the struggles of education and educators are just a reaction to the ongoing changes in the world caused by globalization, especially because many do not have access to relevant historical, speculative, argumentative, critical, and/or doctrinal literature. Further impediments are presented by the fact that the intellectual skills necessary for reading such texts are rarely part of the educational curriculum for obvious reasons.

The school's "mind as a muscle pedagogy" (Paraskeva, 2011, 2014, 2023; Kliebard, 1995; Schubert, 1986) drove many of my classmates to delinquency and me. The oppression of any knowledge outside of (or other than) that promulgated by the school environment pushed me to the outer limits of the school space. Clearly, dropouts—or, as the latest research documents, forced-outs— represent oppressive social constructions that particularly impact minorities, in most cases irreversibly (Fine, 2003; Valenzuela, 1999; Darder, 1991; Pinar, 1874). To read Santos (2007) and other critical and decolonial thinkers and to not think about our past life in school and society is also almost impossible. An increasing awareness of the hegemonic power of coloniality—a historical process that interrelates the practices and legacies of European colonialism in social orders and forms of knowledge beyond colonialism itself (Quijano, 1991)—has stirred my thoughts in a very counter-hegemonic way, opening my eyes to the many aspects of coloniality that impinged upon my life as a student and young human "being." Going back to these memories and many others turned my curiosity into indignation.

Nonetheless, I do recognize the almost perpetual evolution of colonialities into new decades and centuries, and more specifically the current decade, wherein colonialism has evolved from its colonial cocoon into different postmodern colonialities and their various permutations. Thus, coloniality has changed in regards to how it operates along its global-capitalist-hegemonic path. I will discuss this more extensively in Chapter 4.

Like so many others, I've experienced a mixture of justice and injustice in my personal life. Theology and Christianity provided an "agora" that allowed me not just to resist but to "re-exist" (Mignolo & Walsh, 2018), even as modernity and coloniality were speaking the same language in different territories of my everyday life. As Mignolo (2012) states, "history has contributed to creating the conditions and to perpetuating the results of global epistemic un-justice" (p. 2). Injustice is not something abstract waiting to be researched by dominant and counter-dominant groups. What actually is becoming an abstract concept for the vast majority of the world is justice itself. There are generations of individuals who don't know any existence outside of oppression (Walsh & Mignolo, 2018). This is not injustice merely because it is unjust, but because millions of educators and others genuinely think they are acting humanely and honestly towards promoting social-educational amelioration, when they are in fact trapped in a destructive ideology in which there is only one way of seeing things.

In this case, knowledge, along with the expression and acknowledgement of that knowledge, as Žižek (2012) states, might constitute an honest trap or well-meaning in which we situate ourselves as ideologically or politically correct. This is worrying, especially when it comes to the judgmental moments students face after their teachers classify the student as incapable, despite the fact that what students are receiving as "knowledge" does not acknowledge their most basic needs, even the need just to be who they really are. In the following pages, I will present some of the core attitudes that contradict the sense of education as a liberating process in itself, much like a superhero who shoots their own foot, shifting the potential for transformation into a dehumanizing tool that guarantees power and oppression in perpetuity.

## 3     Contradictory Education

After attending the final trimester of seventh grade, I was forced to undergo a high-stakes test to measure what "we had learned" in the last few months. The test was based on the aforementioned *Os Sertões* (1902), da Cunha's denouncement of the woeful and unjust lack of state and federal management of lands and roads, the local and federal states' complete abandonment of, and apathy about, the struggles of the people enduring the northeast region of Brazil's challenging environment. Da Cunha was a sociologist and engineer who clearly wrote as an eyewitness to injustice, yet we students had serious concerns about whether we were really understanding the message he was trying to deliver. The problem was not in da Cunha's message itself, but in the interpretations thereof that were passed on to the students. Instead of using the text to create awareness of the need for liberation from oppression, and to awaken resistance to conformity and conscientization, his writings were deployed to oppress students. Students—generally, those from already marginalized populations—who received poor grades on these tests would thereby be further marginalized by being denied key future opportunities.

As I have mentioned before, this all occurred in the south of Brazil, where I was born and raised, an area well beyond the abyssal line (Santos, 2007). This status was embedded in my daily life. Santos (2017) claims that this line divides social reality into two realms, the realm of "this side of the line" and the realm of "the other side of the line" (p. 118). It is important to recognize that abyssalism (Paraskeva, 2017) is a reality that cuts into every single aspect of the lives of those who live in the Global South; nonetheless, when I state that the abyssal line was embedded in my daily life, I feel that I have to justify why and how.

For the oppressed, abyssalism is reality as it is. Every mindset structured by society, the education received in schools, and the very way I perceived myself all took place in the position of submission to other cultures. Here and there I encountered dissatisfaction with that forced submission, not to mention the lack of alternatives. The Brazilian people call the latter "sentimento de cachorro vira lata" (street dog feeling), which is caused, perpetuated, and justified by the lack of alternatives that might enhance the personal vision and mission one has in society and life. This feeling is originated by and through an abyssal condition of existing that is not equal or equivalent to fully living.

Starting in kindergarten, I was taught to uncritically admire "important" Eurocentric books; but those books did not inspire me to read the world through other lenses, such as those of the great European poet, Luís Vaz de Camões. From what I did read, I was able to reflect on a dream of a future in a "great" place. But when, as an adult, I arrived in this allegedly great, prosperous, free place (the United States), I came to understand that the consequences of abyssalism had brought me to the land of conformity where I eventually realized that the great land I had come from could actually be seen through a different lens to have a different past and—more importantly—a different future, if only people were free to "Be":

> By the rivers that flow,
> past Babylon I found myself
> sitting and weeping
> for the memory of Zion
> and the days I lived there.
> The river of my own eyes
> poured into the waters,
> and I compared everything:
> Babylon to present evils, Zion to a different past. (Camões et al., 1843, p. 8)

The severity of the abyssalism is such that it penetrates the deepest strongholds of one's soul, making even the truth, the most inconceivable fact, nonexistent, before it even gets the "chance" to become a lie. Abyssalism hunts the epistemic oppressed. Abyssalism is, thus, more than just a line, it is a way of living (with a pervasive Eurocentric viewpoint), existing (in the reality of the Global South), and resisting being relegated to a constant position of non-living/in complete denial. Abyssalism is also the brutality praxis through which the oppressed is forced to exist and to think. Santos (2007, 2008) describes this abyssal reality as structurally ubiquitous in modern Western thinking and vibrantly powerful in the sense that the knowledge and social realities of the realm on the other side of the abyssal line are made invisible. In other words, they are rendered nonexistent.

Why am I saying this? I was not able to fully grasp the poetic and stimulating way da Cunha described the aridness of the land. My literature teacher, Mary (pseudonym), gave me a sub-mediocre grade on the high-stake test—which was inextricably linked with the fact that, along with several of my friends in the class, I was living with the pervasive physical/emotional/intellectual/spiritual implications of being from the South and being treated as sub-South non-"being." Interestingly, as an oppressed in perpetual pain, I was always being psychologized, and labeled as emotionally unbalanced. To psychologize the oppressed is the "clinicalize" a social constructed racialized saga. The oppressed is soon a statistic to be addressed either with a pill or jail.

My teacher herself was of African descent, and she stated many times that her great grandfather was the son of a slave, and therefore a "quilombola."[10]

Here is the contradictory education perpetuated by some educators: A teacher from the South, herself a descendent of slaves, using powerful, liberating content to exercise power and control and segregate students despite the fact that her own family had been segregated and auctioned off as non-"beings." Years later the reading of Césaire and others in my doctoral program echoed this experience so vividly. I could have schooled all of my friends in regard to what da Cunha was trying to express and inspire—if only my teacher had acknowledged my knowledge. We heard her (and other teachers) say, again and again, "Well, s/he was honestly participating, even though s/he did not meet the requirements." Such sincere efforts were/are never enough! Why not? Are the standards too high? Or is it that the standards themselves are warped? If so, why choose and retain these specific benchmarks? Such contradiction is so visible in the curriculum inadequacies that "stems from an overdependency upon a conception of values as goals or objectives, and a consequent overdependency upon learning as the major characteristic of man's temporality" (Huebner, 1962, p. 94). My school curriculum "didn't relate at all with a just environment" (Huebner, 1962, p. 94). Paraskeva (2021a, 2021b, 2022) refers to such malaise as "curriculum imparities," that there is no nexus between curriculum content and pedagogies and the world's endless diverse and different epistemological realities.

The link between effective performance measures and effective management has been articulated most in the business sphere and has long migrated from there to the world of education. In 1995, Peter Drucker—then considered a top management guru—had a novel and prescient vision regarding business performance. He had the idea of comparing a specific company's performance to that of another concurrent company in the same line of business in order to identify opportunities for improvement in such a way as to maximize performance across every department of the corporation. Likewise, in education, different jargon is used to perpetuate what is essentially the same process. The performance or underperformance of teachers and students vis-à-vis a broader (district, state, and/or nationwide) metric is addressed to "improve" both types of participants" "outputs," and, in turn, their "value." The ensuing results are then used to penalize, label, and classify the human "beings" subject to this system, while also pinpointing where they are in need of further improvement. We become accustomed to such benchmarks being inherently, unquestionably valid and important as we proceed through the schooling process. Thus, schools and curricula are quite powerful vehicles of the cultural politics of labeling, producing dangerous, damaging commonsense categories (Apple, 1995, 1979).

As we grow up, we carry this dysfunctional tendency to classify, label, and measure others by these "implanted" standards. We also use self-penalizing measures to judge ourselves according to the same social expectations. This is a reciprocal behavior that occurs across all ages, teachers and students, children and parents, as we grow into adulthood and beyond. It is almost impossible to escape this cycle. I am sad to say I've inflicted this type of judgment on my students and coworkers, even family members.

Many times, my parents left parent-teacher conferences embarrassed and sad, ashamed of the student I was. School simply was not making sense to me. I was failing, as I was labeled as a failure. Disposability was how I was institutionally "identified." I did not know whether my parents felt embarrassed about my behavior or if they gradually lost hope in the possibility that I might change. I did know that I was fed up with my teachers' lack of concern for me as a unique "being." In my heart, I still don't understand why it is that when you are taught concepts in school, and you diligently practice these concepts in your daily life but just do not know how to practice or regurgitate (on quizzes, and so on) the theoretical aspects of what you've learned, you get left behind and blamed—and, especially as a child, you don't even understand why.[11] Shaw (1966) enthusiastically underscores the importance of validating who the person is in order to validate the existence and worth of each individual self. Needless to say, the attempt to produce one particular yet universal outcome, through a single supposedly "best system" (Tyack, 1974), makes schools and curricula one of the drivers of what Paraskeva (2011, 2014, 2016), drawing on Santos (2014), calls the "curriculum epistemicide." Paraskeva (2011, 2014, 2016) claims that we should challenge such epistemicides by engaging in a battle against "the monoculture of scientific knowledge and [instead] fight for an ecology of knowledge" (Paraskeva, 2016, p. 153).

We should strive to have schools that understand cultural pluridiversity, and that, within a context of multiple diversities, accept that diverse students learn and understand subjects differently from one another on a variety of levels. In my case, what I did know, and had already experienced in different forms, was unilaterally denied. It's interesting to note that even Drucker (2002) urges businesses not to forget that those who compose their companies are "people" and thus need to be approached as "people." So, basically, as humankind reaches the maximum level of production and robotization, as we achieve the pinnacle of correspondence between schooling and the labor force, this claim comes back! It is a biased, incongruent situation, to be sure, but at least someone is making a claim. The same applies to the educational environment and all those who compose this environment, but especially those for whom the education system allegedly exists—the students. I was not given the opportunity to do things differently than the Eurocentric way that was codified in our curriculum. My thinking, my being, my existence needed to be validated by "authorities" that could not comprehend my "inner" self. They actually deny such "inner" existence. My education consisted of book worship, in which every (Western, European) text was inevitably framed by modern Western Eurocentric reasoning and views of the world (Escobar, 2004).

My experiences with their enforcement of rigid benchmarks and curriculum made it clear that teachers had been blinded to others' realities and interpretations. They did not even seem able to see through a different lens, but rather perceived the world through the "one" orthodox, ordinary way of doing so. Now, I finally have a "better" language to understand that the curriculum I had as student was not ideologically free. Why I had to wait until my doctoral studies to be exposed to such language? Why I had to enroll in doctoral studies to engage in crucial readings that helped me to understand not just my pain, but also I could fight such historical sagas? Žižek (2016) wisely talks about the trap our ideology can become when we think we have achieved "freedom" from different ideological forms of oppression. He claims that ideology makes us think we are free from other ideologies, when in fact such ideologies of "freedom" can make us more embedded and deluded. They also render us more critical of others' ideologies, causing us to act as if there is only one way of seeing the world. I respect Žižek, but I also contend that there is no way to dissect ideology and thereby prove that someone else is ideologically wrong without being ideologically grounded. Even though ideology cannot be separated from certain power dynamics, again—as I have stated and will continue to argue—our lifeblood (meaning the essence of who we are, our emotional, spiritual, cultural and intellectual foundation aggregated along the life), plays a significant role in how one thinks and acts in life. Eagleton (1991) perceptively acknowledges that it is quite hard to concretize the definition of ideology, since it has so much to do with individual perceptions of the word. He ultimately offers 15 attempted definitions, but, for our purposes, "the process of production of meanings, signs and value in social life" (p. 6) will suffice.

The teacher needs to "educate,"[12] and the students are to exchange their experiences for that education, externally professing their acquaintance with that culture and its claims and essentially abandoning their own experiences and inner needs. Santos (2008) vehemently points out the non-recognition of pretty much anything that transposes the scientifization imposed from the North. Santos (2016) also notes that the lenses of coloniality denigrate "identity vs. scientific knowledge as the only valid claim of truth" (p. 22); aside from this "science," there is no knowledge, no truth. The worst aspect of this manufactured terrain is that students are more than able to feel this oppressive reality within their not-so-satisfactory educational process, regardless of their age and whether they are able to articulate it—and they react to it, behaviorally and emotionally, externally and internally.

This is just one way that the authority of the educational system empowers the many teachers and other practitioners who claim to be educators to tyrannize students' identities and spiritualities. The fact of the matter is that the tenderness and vulnerability, the willingness to go out on a limb possessed by young people with "go-getter" personalities, even the motivation that students bring to the classroom—all of these valuable qualities are taken advantage of and/or repressed when students are not addressed or acknowledged as an integral, worthy part of society, schools, and classrooms. The latter is students' most crucial social space in society. The self-denial demanded in schools is already an action of cultural amputation; in and of itself, it interrupts the identity acquisition process. Only now do I understand that this was what was happening to me as an elementary school student. My doctoral studies allowed me to better grasp my oppression. On that, they constitute a great liberatory praxis.

More than ever before, students need to be recognized as "beings." I feel especially compelled to make this claim here and now because for many years I felt, but could not name, this need. When studying subjects related to culture and identity, largely because of blindness and minimal interest in human development, academia has the tendency to separate "subjects" and "objects" of study, ostensibly to better inform students. We are told by our parents that the struggles of life will pass if only we persevere in school, and that, if we do the right things, everything else will fall into place. Parents know that we fight a fight in this life, but it is an infernal fight. It is unfair before it even begins, because we cannot see the enemy.

What are we fighting? Who are we fighting? The entrenched forces that classify, judge and marginalize us based on class, gender, citizenship, "merit," race, and, more, including as hooks (2000) claims, state-sponsored, driven and perpetuated racism. In this battle, I sometimes had to put on armor—a nice, expensive suit and tie—to hide my true self (someone shaped by my own unique life), to "appropriately" present my "self," despite being a not-yet-societally-aimed being. This is because we forbid the past, which is where students come from. We negate their backgrounds, their relationships and bonds, their homes—the place where they were raised and acquired most of their empirical knowledge, refusing to acknowledge that each one is, and will always be, tied to these formative things until the day they die. The dominant educational paradigm—so bluntly evident in our neoliberal times—forces students to exchange their lived experience of activities, friends, family, rituals, credo, faith, celebrative moments, even ways of moaning and grieving, for an arbitrary sequence of present moments that entail being indoctrinated for the future, even though we are barely living in the present. I felt impeded from "being" while just existing.

Envisioning a better future, believing that their children will re-write their own stories in a better way, parents place their children in the hands of schools. And, sometimes, parents feel betrayed by schools. They generally trust teachers and believe that education is the best way to enhance their kids' chances of succeeding in life, yet, in reality, there are often huge disparities between parents' hopes and expectations and what actually occurs in schools. Is this type of education an attempt to dismantle the individual's identity? As Hall and du Gay (2012) warn about this very process of identity destruction, "once disassembled and no more a vector, time no longer structures the space. On the ground, there is no more "forward" and "backward"; it is just the ability not to stand still that counts" (p. 24). How is this applicable to life? My moments of reflection came under tremendous pressure.

So far, I have (a) examined my early life, as "in the beginning was the word," (b) described my first steps into education, while (c) unpacking the moments that began with my "un-schooled" happiness prior to kindergarten and the increasing deception and contested cognizance I endured as my education took form. After that, I stressed (d) the lack of relevance of my school and curriculum, along with (e) the actual struggle to make sense and to get sense out of the specific contexts imposed on me, emphasizing (f) the official knowledge imposed on students.

In the next chapter, I will turn my full attention to spirituality and its conundrums. First, however, I do want to be clear and straightforward about what spirituality means to me. I have mentioned before that I consider myself to be a spiritual educator, but not in the sense that I teach about, or advocate for, spirituality in education. Indeed, the core belief of my practice as a spiritual educator is that, according to my understanding, it is honest and fair to see and read the world through another lens—and I endeavor to do so. I do acknowledge the possibility that there are other ways of knowing, diverse interpretations of, and approaches to, education, existence, "being" as a whole, human rights.

Although this is a terrain I feel comfortable navigating, it could actually be quite dangerous for me to play with such a volatile and abstract subject, one that demands such stringent neutrality. Far be it from me to classify and scientify science and knowledge, but I want to take advantage of Tillich and Cox's (1952) words that "[c]ourage is self-affirmation in-spite-of" (p. 32). A "being" that understands, exposes, and challenges their non-"being" status can all the more actively affirm their existence and experience, thereby building strength for the aforementioned battle. Tillich (2000) claims,

> Courage as a human act, as a matter of valuation, is an ethical concept. Courage as the universal and essential self-affirmation of one's being is an ontological concept. The courage to be is the ethical act in which man affirms his own being in spite of those elements of his existence which conflict with his essential self-affirmation. (p. 3)

Looking back on my educational currere (Pinar, 1994, 1975), I cannot find a better way to define it than via the bottle metaphor. While there were so many realities that would have been crucial for me to interact and deal with—many of which I could actually see from inside the bottle—I was not able to grasp them.

So far, I have tried to "understand the contribution of my formal academic studies make to my understanding of my life" (Pinar, 1994, 1975, p. 19). It was "not necessarily a logic currere, but a lived one, a felt one" (Pinar, 1994, 1975, p. 20), which allowed me to lure transtemporally and transconceptually into the different currere in an itinerant (Paraskeva, 2011, 2014) fashion. My currere was a regressive, progressive, analytical, and synthetical itinerantology. A non-derivative currere as Paraskeva (2021a, 2021b, 2016) would put it.

I've opened up about part of my personal story to give a sense of why I am expressing my point of view and exploring the subject at hand in the ways I do, as well as to elucidate where I want to land and why. The question of who I am informs and justifies my endeavor and bolsters my specific goal of bridging, from this chapter to the next, the longstanding gap between education and spirituality. The latter is first and foremost an abstract matter, and yet I firmly believe it composes a highly important element in the formation of the self. Thus, in the next chapter, I will continue to unpack the impact of my formal education and my daily life as a spiritual human "being."

I thereby introduce spirituality into my discussion, in order to look into the undeniable and unmeasurable conundrums surrounding the correlations between spirituality, culture, and identity in a hermeneutical way. I will work to redefine spirituality, and to avoid misleading ideas conflating spirituality with religion or corrupting it via postmodern ideologies. In order to do so, I will posit a hybrid identity model, contextualized by the individual's cultural backgrounds, while unveiling my own perspective on being colonized and denied the freedom of thinking and expressing my own thoughts. I will embrace a back-and-forth exchange of ideas and experiences focused on multicultural backgrounds and education in order to explain the urgency of understanding and practicing what I mean by spirituality. The framework of my analysis is identity—who I am.

### Notes

1   By using the word "desert" I am acknowledging Apple's (1995, 2000) comment that life in itself carries and implies a great deal of suffering and struggle, along with scarce financial, emotional and spiritual resources, and that every day we are reminded that better days are still to come. In short, we can hope for what comes after crossing the desert.
2   The world I aimed for was, first and foremost, one of meaning: an understanding of my purpose in life, a satisfying exploration of my questions, and the accomplishment of my dreams as a student, as well as, potentially, my tasks in society.
3   My idea in using this word is to paraphrase Freire, not just because the quote in fact uses the word, but based on its etymology. I want to avoid going into terrains that make use of the term to define only an epikarsios (biased) and oblique position, such as religion defining purity, or differences in moral definition, although the term stands for goodness, virtuousness, righteousness, morality, integrity, dignity, rectitude, honor, respect, etc. Hence, I retain a common understanding that virtue might represent, too, the concrete aspects of what education and society are now desperately looking to see. As we discuss the effects of neoliberalism on the population and its role in the dehumanization of mankind, the backhanded position, i.e., the non-practice, of virtue is represented as disrespect, dishonesty, greed, and many kinds of wrongdoings that indeed are destroying humanity in all its aspects. If the Common Core was as good as it purports to be, it would decry the prison pipeline and define the labor force as a project to help all beings, especially Latinos and Blacks, to succeed fully in life.
4   In particular I cited Hursh (2012) because he brings to the dialog the significant attempt being made in order to reevaluate the factor gender-segregation in advancing women's rights through Islamic law. My initial idea is to bring to the dialog that such issues are currently under reevaluation with different lenses and international cooperation.
5   By saying that, I want to acknowledge that there is a general culture in schools, but there is a much more intimate one—the one students get to share in class when they feel they belong. So much so, that when students with different linguistic and ability needs are placed in another class rather than their everyday one, they often feel that they do not belong, therefore, holding the possibility of connecting their inner culture to knowledge.
6   The movie *Mad Max*, created by George Miller and Byron Kennedy, takes place in a self-destructing world. Survivors in this brutal environment become violent themselves, as destructive actions have become their lifeblood, their identity, their culture of survival. In

this text, I am referring to teachers who teach and grade in such a way as to intellectuality emasculate and dehumanize their students without knowing what they are doing, since they are just a mirror of the past, reflecting the separation of the self from identity as an epistemic culture reproduction.

7   I am referring to the barbarities perpetuated in the name of "modernity," clearly showing the deficiencies of the newborn republic of Brazil. The full realities of both the author and the rebellion are not presented in schools. The *Os Sertões* are presented just as a piece of literature, and not as a historical and social artifact, which makes it difficult for students to see the hidden messages the author intended to deliver.

8   In *The Matrix*, artificial beings are programmed to respond and interact in an identical fashion. No natural intelligence or common sense is involved. Humans themselves are being used as an energy source while their minds are imprisoned in an artificial reality in which the aforementioned artificial beings, in the form of humanlike robots, hunt down any digressions.

9   In these two pieces, Ellen Harmon White talks about the beginning of "educate" education—how it was metaphysically instituted before, and how, over millennia, education has impacted the lives of thousands of beings, driving many to an ameliorated state of life and many to the catastrophic end result of many years of indoctrination, human nature's deepest carnage. When it is necessary, she explains, these tendencies—which I believe are undeniable, not just because I have seen, but because I have lived through them—towards a metaphysical education may emerge again.

10  A quilombola is a resident of a quilombo settlement in Brazil. Quilombolas are the descendants of Afro-Brazilian slaves who escaped from the slave plantations that existed in Brazil until abolition in 1888.

11  With that specific word "why," I want to express feelings of outrage and dissatisfaction that began in my childhood but are not yet healed.

12  As defined by its etymological meaning to "bring up." Another Latin word "educere," means to "bring forth," meaning "*out of and to lead*," i.e., to educate means to "lead forth" or "to extract out" the best in man.

CHAPTER 2

# Identity Matters
*On (Whose) Spirituality!*

## 1   Introduction

This chapter attempts to unpack spirituality as part of one person's identity. My identity. In order to do that, I will define spirituality and, in so doing, reclaim it as a crucial component of contentious terrains such as morality and honesty. I will argue that such terrains convey a specific philosophy of praxis, which structures the individual in his/her/their forms of lived truth. I will highlight how my education created a state of permanent conflict with my identity by undermining my inner self, which, in my case, was profoundly spiritual. I will also argue that, given the current powerful momentum of neoliberal approaches to education, the challenges to integrating spirituality as part of the public school curriculum are gargantuan. I viscerally sense how vital this component is: I would argue that my Freirean (1979) conscientização—or, to use Nkrumah's (1964) term, consciencism—was profoundly spiritual, constituting, for me, my concrete truth, as Foucault (2001) would put it. And while I use my own being and experiences as the basis for this chapter, I also know I am not alone in this truth—and that the quest to bring spirituality to schools is therefore a profoundly worthwhile one. But before I delve into key issues, such as identity, morality, and honesty, let me right at the outset define what I believe it means to be a spiritual "being."

## 2   Defining Spirituality: A Possible Impossibility?

While a very fracture topic spirituality caught the attention of major Western Eurocentric intellectuals. As James Kirylo and Dryck Boyd (2017, p. 1) argue, the turn of the eighteenth century,

> sociologists and psychologists such as Freud, Jung, Weber and Allport found the study of religion and spirituality (often referred to as religious experience) to be a rich area of research. These early thinkers largely concluded that religion and spirituality are significant dimensions of human experience that can either contribute to or detract from fruitful

and healthy living. Historically, religion has helped individuals come to terms with the meaning of their lives, address questions of ultimate significance and connect individuals to their understanding of the Divine.

Joel Kovel (cited in Huebner, 1985a, p. 405) defines spirit "as connoting a relation between the person and the universe, while the soul is the more self-referential term connoting the kind of person who undergoes that relation." We may define the soul, Huebner (1985a, p. 405) adds, "as the spiritual form taken by the self."

Spirituality thus is a feature of "being," a quality embedded within the capacity for existing, a way of reaching for something bigger than ourselves, a moving force that gives life to life, a perpetual search for meaning. Unfortunately, it is quite often confused with religion, due to the abstract and/or undefined aspects of the term. Yet this abstract quality, along with its lack of affiliation with any institution, ensures that spirituality is not a religion. Nonetheless, spirituality can certainly be found in most religions. Religion can be defined in relatively precise terms: It entails following a set of beliefs and stipulated rules and practices encompassed by a specific affiliation. One can be a spiritual human "being" without necessarily following any "particular religion, religious institutions or set of beliefs" (Kirylo & Boyd, 2017, p. 2). And, by the way, while we all have a spiritual side (to be clear, in some of us, it's buried very deeply; in others it might be expressed more through art or work or raising children than through anything overtly "spiritual"), people may or may not become religious due to a multiplicity of factors. While "spirituality" has taken on a more eclectic and all-encompassing meaning, whereas "religion" refers to a formal set of beliefs and practices in and through which individuals live out their spirituality" (Kirylo & Boyd, 2017, p. 1). That is, £religion has taken on an institutional flavor focused on the adherence to certain beliefs, liturgical practices, and codes of behavior, whereas spirituality has taken on a more individualized and personal focus having to do with one's beliefs and experiences with God, a higher power, or a transcendent sense of purpose" (Kirylo & Boyd, 2017, p. 1).

The object of my investigation is neither religion nor its importance in public education and curriculum. I focus solely on the importance of spirituality in public education and curriculum. I attempt to grasp "what has this to do with education and curriculum" (Huebner, 1985a, p. 405). I argue that the importance of spirituality in education and in the curriculum is related to the true finite essence of the human being, as we flagged before a "finite temporality" (Huebner, 1975). Along with James Kirylo and Dryck Boyd (2017, p. 2) I argue that "spirituality causes people to be more aware of their inner life, the persons around them and the general state of the world. When viewed this way, the ultimate goal of spirituality is to help people find personal meaning and become more fully human, while serving the purpose of improving the lives of those suffering in the world." Spirituality has a real *Freirean* and *Nkrumahan* flavor—it helps one to humanize humanity.

The importance of spirituality in education and curriculum relies at the core of the true journey of life—of the oppressed and the oppressors—a perpetually incomplete journey.

> The moreness in the world, spirit, is a moreness that infuses each human being. Not only do we know more than we say, we "are" more than we "currently" are. That is, the human being dwells in the transcendent, or more appropriately, the transcendent dwells in the human being. (Huebner, 1985a, p. 404)

Such spiritual journey—"currere" (Pinar, 2004), non-derivatively as Paraskeva (2016) stresses—equips us and begs for a constant new language—"our" language—that confronts the reductive curriculum grammar and vocabulary, through which we have been forced to understand the world. Language is an identity matter. As Huebner (1985c, p. 313) argues, "we are at home with our language," and our language is also related to the language that we have been educated and schooled; a language that as been framed in "learning terms," and "learning is the cancer of curriculum thought" (Huebner, n.d., p. 1).

Spirituality, Shields (2006) claims, is an expression of how we understand and live our lives, ground our identities, and relate to the world outside ourselves. What amazes me the most in the spiritual sphere is that we cannot straightforwardly answer questions about spirituality in public education because the topic itself is so abstract, elusive, and even harder to define if not constructed merely through its attributes and etymology. But I would like to use a simple analogy, one we are all familiar with. It might sound simplistic, but the fact that I cannot see the wind or the oxygen I am breathing does not mean they do not exist; in reality, we cannot live without air. On this point, we can all agree—just as we can together acknowledge the existence and impact of the wind. Can we deny the aftermath of wind-related disasters? Things that cannot be measured can nevertheless be experienced (Jones, 2005). This brings us to a more personal dialogue.

Denying something just because understanding certain facts or events requires another mode of analyzing the subject, knowledge platform, or cognitive path, or believing that whoever speaks loudest speaks the truth—all of these undermine the possibility of other ways of knowledge, other truths, which is, at the very least, wrong and, further, implies a form of epistemicide (Paraskeva, 2018, 2021a, 2022). There is an abundance of knowledge in spirituality and so, within this multi-understanding of spirituality and its conundrums, it's important to define the objectives attempted by spirituality without stifling other possibilities. The absence of any such efforts in education and curricula constitutes a notable silence, one that in its very (non-) existence elicits questions about the root causes of that silencing. Yes, the modern Western curriculum (with its new[ish] Common Core face) is implicated in the dissemination and legitimation of a eugenic totalitarian view (Paraskeva, 2018, p. 86). Yes, this Western intellectual intersubjective configuration (Quijano, 2008) transpires denials, supremacy, legitimation of specifics, control of subjectivity and culture, and especially "knowledge and the production of knowledge under its hegemony" (p. 189). Indeed, spirituality has suffered even in its conceptual form via said hegemonic production of knowledge. The very words spirituality and spirit, especially in this century, have endured the devaluation of their postmodern linguistic and interpretive meanings to such a degree that no one can precisely define the word spirit or its fruits, i.e., spirituality, while still making the Greeks and Romans completely happy and unique in defining such word, not to mention present-day academics/theorists that given to postmodern knowledge, are in many ways, inhibited to pursue and push such definition into a postmodern channel of knowledge distribution. It is undeniable that academia—particularly certain counter-dominant vectors—fundamentally Eurocentric—feels very uncomfortable talking about spiritual affairs. There is an "academic spiriphobia" (Boyd, 2012, p. 760).

Since spirituality presents itself in interaction with "spirit," which is defined at times as an inner and untouchable phenomenon, I must start by addressing the meaning of spirit and only then jump into defining spirituality. According to the Etymology e-dictionary, "spirit refers to the animating or vital principle in humans and animals, and comes from the root from *spiritus*, meaning soul, courage, vigor, breath." The word is also related to *spirare*, "to breathe," from PIE *(s)peis- "to blow" (cf. O.C.S. pisto "to play on the flute").

The original usage in English comes mainly from passages in the Vulgate (a fourth-century Latin translation of the Bible), where the Latin translates to Greek as *pneuma* (πνεῦμα) and Hebrew as *ruah* (רוח), or breeze. Both *pneuma* and *ruah* bear undeniable metaphysical elements, with transcendence built into the very words themselves. *Ruah* can mean "breath, wind, spirit" and refers to our inner spirit, while pneuma can refer to "the immaterial part of the inner person" (e-Greek dictionary). In this light, the true meaning of spirit is "animating principle." Ultimately, it represents what has given us "being." In other words, spirit is life itself. Why am I pointing to these meanings and deconstructing a simple word using common sources? Because the endeavor each one of us, each spirit, aims for is to exercise with sovereignty the inner natural needs we have in order to fully exist, and thus "to be." I do mean simply to be: Our existence needs to count, not just as a number or commodity, but as a human, a person who carries the most important and transcendent thing, life. In this sense, spirit constitutively refers to *who we are and the sphere where the who we are is in constant unfolding, enhancing and enabling mode*, our unique inner essence and being that may be linked to a greater good and/or divinity. This relationship makes spiritual "beings."

Before the beginning of postmodernity, spirituality was not rearranged or turned upside down, nor were its inner-meta-cognitive-cultural dimensions redefined. The expansion and vulgarization process were romanticized, and the term then came to be used outside of its original context. Many agree that spirituality as a religious process of re-formation aims to restore the original state of the human "being" as oriented at "the image of God," as exemplified by the religious texts of the world. In modern times, the emphasis is on the subjective experience of a sacred dimension and the "deepest values and meanings by which people live" (Sheldrake, 2011). This is true not just because sacred means holy, but because what is the most personal and intimate part of a "being," i.e., their spirituality, must be highly respected.

Only in certain oppressive, dominant, materialist ways of thinking would this respect be jeopardized. Griffin (1988) debates how Western cultures force choices between dualism and materialism, anthropocentrism and relativism, supernaturalism and atheism, intolerance and nihilism, all of which can exist side by side. A multifarious non-monolithic group of intellectuals—what Paraskeva coins the generation of utopia swimming within a particular radical curriculum river (Paraskeva, 2011, 2016, 2021a, 2022) challenged such dichotomic approach. Both these dualities and their ensuing imposed selections are part of what Santos (2016) calls epistemicide, the Eurocentric way of denying one's habits, culture, beliefs, identity, or self, that is, those elements the individual really depends on to fully be. This human need for certain inner truths holds true across cultures, nations, classes, religions, and more. Perhaps that in part explains why, whether modern or postmodern, conservative or progressive, religious or agnostic, above or below the abyssal line, most theorists define spirituality with more similarities than disparities. This also indicates that there is something about this notion that is inexplicably felt and acknowledged by all people, be they individuals of faith or those who choose otherwise; this, too, underlines the separation between spirituality and religion. Griffin (1988), as just one example, examines spirituality in a context explicitly separated from organized religious institutions, and Waaijman and Vriend (2002) define it as the "inner dimension."

According to Tisdell (2001), spirituality and religion are *not the same*, and I must acknowledge that I hold a similar position. Although differences set these terms apart, we also cannot deny their interrelation and overlapping in our natural and cognitive processes. Why "natural and cognitive processes"? As far as the natural aspect goes, throughout life we occasionally feel the need to be fulfilled in ways that regular daily existence does not satisfy. For instance, we ask ourselves existential questions, often with the wish to somehow receive answers from someone or something bigger than us, especially when facing life and death situations, injustice, the absence of love, and so on. Cognitive, because faith is related to empirical knowledge as well, especially after comparing the aftermath of life events both good and bad. For example, digesting ineluctably factual information from a challenging experience requires a certain level of analysis, which may involve questions involving faith, beliefs, morality, commandments, covenants, and so on. In this sense, spirituality has the power to make religion more meaningful to the follower because it comes from the individual's inner processes and not from a written set of (religious) rules. Spirituality involves considerations about "inside vs. outside, here vs. there, near vs. far away, margin vs. center," which continue to concern people's minds every day—and the denial of these natural and cognitive deliberations is a "progressive spatial segregation, separation, and exclusion" (Bauman, 1998, p. 3). Religion, on the other hand, assumes a more institutionalized framework (Boyd, 2012; Elias, 2006).

Many scholars, such as Watson, Souza, and Trousdale (2016), Wright (2000), Palmer (1997), hooks (1999), Dantley (2005a, 2005b), and West (2017), agree that the perception of the need for spirituality in schools seems to be numbed, apparently in the name of intellectual integrity. To them, it is very clear that, given the multitude of benefits it offers, spirituality is a vital aspect of schooling and, at the same time, a fundamentally controversial issue. They know that in the academic sphere spirituality can balance a much-needed hermeneutic of nurturing with an also necessary hermeneutic of critical thinking, in essence integrating a quest for submission (being submiss to what the quest for belonging will naturally request) while aiming towards freedom. Here we have one explanation why many might deny spirituality. In the teaching-learning process, for example, spirituality refers to a deep connection between student, teacher, and subject—a connection so honest, vital, and vibrant that it cannot help but be intensely relevant (Palmer, 1999, p. 8). Such acknowledgment, such mutual honoring, has the power to form, ameliorate, and empower identities that never felt alive before. It is the exact opposite of what the capitalist, neoliberal approach endeavors to achieve. For many, spirituality is abstractly interrelated with a sense of wholeness and awareness, engendering a desire to honor that wondrous whole by exploring the deepest questions regarding all of existence, the mystery of what many refer to as life force. Many of us share a common understanding that there is something superior to our human way of understanding and explaining metaphysical matters.

Because we humans tend to interpret things, life in general pushes us to existential questioning, as Tillich (1952) claims in *The Courage to Be*. As a chaplain during World War I, Tillich faced many life and death situations, suffering, justice and injustice; he witnessed life fading away from many civilians and soldiers, including his best friend. His questions often concern the "courage" aspect of spirituality, as rooted in human indignation and our lack of satisfying explanations for certain life events, such as death, war, cruelty, and so on. In the face of incomprehensible things, where no argument can ultimately hold its ground, another way of seeing and analyzing life and its value may change the discourse. For instance, Tillich (1962) frames spirituality "as an ethical reality, but it is rooted in the whole breadth of human existence and ultimately in the structure of being itself" (p. 7). Within the same lens, courage is not just noble in itself, but, in benefiting others, it constitutes an act of giving yourself for the greater good. Stemming from the previous analysis, what can we call courage if not a spiritual act, wherein we negotiate principles and priorities? So here I will take the stand and acknowledge that having the courage to be (Tillich, 1952) is a spiritual act as well. There is an "invisible" force that animates this process and allows us to act courageously.

The notion of courage also facilitates the process of divesting spirituality from religion. Everybody has embedded courage, whether they are religious, agnostic, atheist, Buddhist, etc. In the same vein, we can cognitively frame spirituality as something universally much greater—yet related to human being's temporality (Huebner, 1975; Macdonald, 1974) than just an empty definition, as a feeling that accompanies reflection and may guide rational action when the subject, the "being," negotiates priorities based on their individual moral code. Within the context of courage as a trait, we catch a glimpse of how intrinsic our essence, our lifeblood, is in that negotiation process and how spirituality can expose the bedrock of the human "beings." Behind courage, there is a scale weighing priorities, knowledge, experiences, values, and timing via existential analysis. These factors are reflected upon, inextricably together, in light of the truth or what matters the most. Based on that reflection, the decision in question is made.

Tillich (2014) claims that, in our current social and global situation, only spirituality may be able to help us transport the physical, the seen, into a metaphysical view of life and its events, one in which we not only look into our many problems, but solve them as well. Tillich and Parrella's (1995) claim aligns with Santos (2008) in the sense that Eurocentric modern epistemologies have failed to provide answers to our societal questions. Positivism and postmodern ideologies do not have the capacity to acknowledge that there is something different from what we see. They disregard the possible existence of a truth or truths not imposed by sight or other empirical measures but inwardly felt. Eugenically, Eurocentric epistemologies have denied the existence and validity of other ways of understanding the functionality of the "being" and the world around them (Paraskeva, 2016, 2021a, 2022). The proof is in the growing number of people affiliating to religion, not out of curiosity but because they are looking for answers to their "most inner questions," as Tisdell (2005) claims. For instance, the pewforum.org states that the COVID-19 pandemic has strengthened religious faith in 28% just in the U.S. In this context, it's important to note that spirituality is fundamentally about meaning-making as well. That is one of the reasons why, most of the time, we allow spirituality and culture to co-evolve naturally. That is, the process usually doesn't entail enduring excruciating pain or confronting massive intellectual barricades, rather, we rely on honesty, thoughtfulness, and, ideally, inclusive multicultural vision to enhance our grasp of a volatile subject. For example, theorists who are explicitly interested in cultural issues are used to dealing with different viewpoints and cross-methodologically searching for other ways to interpret specific phenomena. Further, they rarely, if ever, delve into a topic without embracing parallel influences, such as cultural, economic, social, and many other factors, including, when relevant, religious and spiritual ones.

hooks (2009b), who places spirituality as an emancipatory praxis and towering within critical pedagogies, contends that such culturally holistic authors are trying to break mainstream cultural taboos (hooks, 2000, p. 82), thereby enabling us to name and define our cultures and helping to turn our passion for who we are into a counter-Eurocentric cultural force. On the flip side of the coin, positivism, as philosophically rooted in Comte (1798–1857), denies that there is something more than what we see—in contrast with those whose honest introspection reveals a deeper reality that "must" be acknowledged. Positivism claims that the only authentic knowledge is scientific knowledge—knowledge derived from actual sensed experience and "strict" application of the scientific method, as measurable thing. However, even ultra-positivist Comte (1822) created the law of three stages, acknowledging that human beings rely on supernatural agencies to explain what they can't explain otherwise.

As a matter of fact, even though he stopped believing in *god* (lower case, as he preferred), Comte did acknowledge that there is something greater than the scientized human "being." Believing that everything in this world had a meaning, he reasoned that meaning could be derived from a single source that had been divided, but could be re-assembled, reclaimed in positivistic humanism (Smith, 2004). We can understand his claim that divine will was damaging because it subsumed human rights, and so his beliefs were bouncing around looking for comfort on the shoulder of humanism, but

> humanism in itself shifts its foundation away from our inner knowing and towards the outcome of its fundamental doctrine: the belief that human "beings" possess the power or potentiality for *solving their own problems*, through reliance primarily upon *reason and scientific method* applied with courage and vision.

This, in turn, requires close study and definition of what "reason" means. Whose "reason" one is referring to? Who benefits?

To define reason, we need to look into what has been defined as "right" and "wrong," as well as who holds "the truth." My question is: If we live in such a multicultural society, how can one form of reason be the "correct" reason for all? Yet if we do broadly acknowledge the validity and equality of multiple forms of reason, potentially one for each and every individual person, we will end up with social chaos. I do understand that, in order to create a societal foundation that maintains a level of social equilibrium, there must be some generally accepted claims or agreements. Many will not bend to that "general/collective" agreement and reasoning, but here rests the difference between governmental/societal and individual acceptance. When these shared agreements rest on positivism, certain telling issues emerge. Lamont (1990) claims that humanism

> believes in an ethics or morality that grounds all human values in this-earthly experiences and relationships and that holds as its highest goal the this-worldly happiness, freedom, and progress—economic, cultural, and ethical—of all humankind, irrespective of nation, race, or religion. (p. 13)

Clearly, this approach has its compelling aspects, especially insofar as it allows for diverse ideas and beliefs. However, if we leave humankind to decide which forms of reasoning, ethics, and so on are valid, postmodernity facts proved that, driven by greed euphoria, people will take over every single thing their neighbor possesses, dismantling the ethics of sustainability.

We are increasingly self-centered, extremely anthropocentric. More and more, the hope for the future of our posterity is embedded in consumerism and radical ideologies, generating centrifugal forces that eschew the courage to do the right things, thereby separating nobility from obligation. We victimize others while being ourselves victims of a system that essentially denies our innermost soul. Genuine consciousness and conscientization (Freire's [1973] conscientização) are replaced by bifurcated "consciencism process(es)" in which "practice without thought is blind; thought without practice is empty" (Nkrumah, 1964, p. 78). Nowadays, thought embedded in practice is a hard thing to find in its purity. We instead substitute the very core of life with abstractions expressed through a hierarchy of sciences, such as mathematics embedded in sociology. Let's keep in mind that, as Freire (1979) claims, conscientization must be first and foremost an act of participatory action, the alignment between my conscience and the material expression of my consciousness; it inherently involves what we do with our consciousness besides just think. Nkrumah's consciencism and Freire's "conscientização" and inherent to human beings' temporality.

In *Consuming Life,* Bauman (2008) claims that we perceive reality based on the distorted assumption that we are free, and that everything we do is leading us to an increasingly free way of living, when, in fact, "those at one end experience space as a freedom; those at the other end experience it as bondage" (p. 35).

On the other hand, positivism denies the "concrete abstract," trusting only the empirical, observational and scientific quantitative endeavor, which in truth is no far from humanism's which does not believe in metaphysics, where this is the precisely terrain that deals with substance, cause, time, space and identity and possibility. So, repel the spiritual claim with such, is to destroy the possibility of the right of identity and the materialization of the conscience and its integrity process as cited before. Egolatric humanism eliminates the portion Theo (God) of man existence and/or metaphysic and/or spiritual certain abstract and metaphysical elements, but, if humankind fails to address its own issues as supported by humanism, the end is certain. Egolatric humanism and positivism can't indeed solve the problems we are facing at the current century. The very fact is that we are in desperate need of "beings" able to understand the context of individual cultures, identities and the conundrums around such, and the claim for a different curriculum, methodology and study guide and guider is qualitative and quantifiable undeniable. But both leave a significant vague space in existential matters unaddressed. Thus both can undermine spirituality within the terms explained previously, epistemicidically turning a blind eye to the subjectivity of the subject and lacking the instrumentalism suggested by a "being"-centered ideology. But together, both claims are unsustainable. To claim a world out of subjectivity is a conceptual and pragmatic impossibility. It is to claim a world out of human beings (Freire, 1973, 1975). The amelioration of society has to come from those who compose society and how democratically their identities unfold and coexist, which has to do with their inner "being." Together these two philosophies make our social and personal lives distant when it should be the opposite.

Tillich (1954) makes the following claim: "We are bound to the Ground of "Being" for all eternity, just as we are bound to ourselves and to all other life" (p. 34). Tillich is in fact saying that there is a platform, a foundation, or a specific point, a core, where existence begins—that where life emerges, the "being" emerges. To exist, in that sense and in the present tense, implies spiritus, spirit, and the living present tense means that living [existing] cannot be separated from spirit, spiritus, breathing, existence. So, the "being" (the human being, humankind) does not exist in fragments, in incomplete instances devoid of spirit, spiritus, the inner self; again, the "being" doesn't exist out of a concrete temporality. This leads us to at the very least contemplate the idea that "to be completely complete" we need our essential pieces. I am not attempting to describe what it means to be complete, merely to highlight what lack would surely make us incomplete. How can we be complete if we neglect, ignore, and abandon important pieces that surely are part of our whole "being"? Freire insists that knowing the world involves more than intellectual reasoning. True knowledge involves passions and feelings, past and present, our whole "being" in the world, our bodies and spirits/spirituality; as Freire (1994) declares, "I am a totality, not a dichotomy" (p. 30).

Our societies and, consequently, our educational and curriculum systems—the riverbed of brutal battles so eloquently grasped by leading historians such as Krug (1969), Kliebard (1995), and Schubert (2010), among others—certainly do not honor this wholeness, so we need to first acknowledge that we have repressed, denigrated, and denied spirituality in many respects.

To alienate spirituality from human and cultural development is to dehumanize the human "being." Since spirituality is part of human nature, students have the basic right to not have this fundamental element of being eviscerated from any part of their lives. We cannot leave ourselves, or part of who we are, behind in order to enter any given environment. Certainly, we should not be asked to do so by the very people entrusted with our growth. Why shouldn't students bring themselves as a whole to public schools, where places that by definition serve children and young people? The very "who they are" referring to students shouldn't be counted as core in education? I will call it "the right to be." However, the bill of rights is not allowed in schools in many respects, than we dare to teach democracy without essence, making democracy non-sense, confusing and undemocratically understood by the students. Then, I boldly would call education as unconstitutional by denying one's rights to be and the unchangeable and sacred essence. Such rights are often ignored in schools across the country in massive curricular exigencies.

In order to make schooling and curriculum just and fair then, an amalgamation of diverse philosophies (of course not just Eurocentric ones) are called to actively participate in the curriculum and beyond. As well, the integration of inclusive perspectives during these formative years of students' lives will reshape social perceptions and norms regarding what is right and what is wrong, turning who we are and what we have—our spirits, our cultures—into honored key elements of our endeavors for our world, and shaping unique ideas and growth as something to be aimed for, rather than imposing fixed qualities upon us. This will also lead to more creative expression, since "[s]pirituality is about how people construct knowledge through largely unconscious and symbolic process, often made more concrete in art format such as music, art, image, symbol, and ritual which are manifested culturally" (Tisdell, 2005, p. 29).

Spirituality moves the human mind to think and act proactively towards someone or something, correcting what is wrong and/or delivering what is good. When spirituality manifests solely in our consciousness, it remains just a thought. It is a form of inquiry; it is inherent to human beings' inquiry (Anzaldúa, 2002a). But, as Tinker (2008) notes, spirituality is not just reflection—it only reaches its wholeness when it is able to act, which occurs through our "being." As I have defined it, our spirituality alone allows us to see other knowledge, other possibilities; it enables us to see hunger, poverty, inequality, and so on. If it merely sees these things, but does not act, spirituality dishonors itself. Critical analysis of such perceptions is needed for materialization and expression. This result, the outcome of turning reflection into practice, can then be seen and coded as spirituality.

My claim is not that spirituality is just our conscience, but I do feel that, without spirituality, there would be no "complete" conscience. There would be no spirit in the recognition of injustice and need in the world without spirituality (again, as I have defined these two terms). If we argue that spirituality is what makes sense of life, both spirituality and conscience are truly interdependent, and naturally concomitant.

Although Tisdell (2005) intimates that spirituality happens by surprise, I would like to go a little further, based on what I have seen. Spirituality, in my personal view, is not just the result of spontaneous reflection, but may arise from an awakening of what is inside of us, despite the fact that our inner self often gets numbed or beaten down by life struggles, or by academic, social, familial denial of our "being." Naturally, this process varies from person to person. However, honoring the spiritual aspects of the "self" through the cultivation of good deeds and good habits, and the praxis and practice of humane deeds, helps those who nurture these habits flourish spiritually.

Being with the "self," through inclusive teachings and activities that celebrate all individuals, along with their community and culture, also helps students to reflect on other values that have not been previously acknowledged and shared. Spirituality is spirituality when the conclusions arising from my reflection and rationalization are passed on to a higher level of concrete expression and accomplishment. Spirituality is the volcano of "my struggles from within" (Pinar, 1974).

The word spirituality does not enroot with selfishness. Shifting from a dominant domain into a cognitive and affective (yes, involving affection) domain spurs spirituality to supplant selfish rationality, the most commonly criticized aspect of today's social injustices. Fowler (1995) claims that the use of this cognitive/affective domain might help students begin the process of nurturing their inner "spiritual" experiences, especially once these two domains are addressed culturally as well.

Spirituality does not have to be a religious term, but, when my students hear it, they often conflate it with religion. I try to explain to them that it has more to do with the connection between the other and the self, a form of expression that is not about reproduction but about understanding and creativity. In addition, it is important to acknowledge how spirituality is intimately connected to language, since the oppression of language is in a way the oppression of spirituality. As I have emphasized, spirituality and religion need to be grasped differently due to the institutionalized nature of the latter.

How do all of these factors coalesce in terms of pedagogical practices? Palmer (1999), while acknowledging the profound importance of spirituality, defined as the human quest for connectedness, argues that it is not something that needs to be brought in to or added on to the curriculum, but that, instead, *we need to open spaces in the curriculum for these specific practices*. I take issue with this stance, which is shared by a number of authors. How can we retain the same curriculum and also genuinely integrate spirituality if we don't formally, actively create spaces for it? More time to socialize? "Spirituality is at the heart of every subject we teach," and it needs to be explored, where it waits to be brought forth (Palmer 1999, p. 2). Spirituality, as the "human quest for connectedness," as Palmer (1999) claims, can be observed often in both youth and educators. But the educational process and curriculum as prescribed by the Common Core invariably deploy an anesthetization or distancing technicalization of knowledge and language, which bypasses the heart to the nonrational brain, engendering a silencing of body-politics. In many instances, this causes anxiety in students, who experience distress in their very "being" because they have been rendered non-beings (Janson, 2019) through being seen in society and schools as a commodity, a countable, measurable item. As I have stated before, spirituality inherently involves the morally necessary process of consciencism (Nkrumah, 1964) and/or conscientization (Freire, 1972, 1994).

One of my intentions in this work is to, by melding empirical, metaphysical, and autobiographical-philosophical approaches, point to a bigger picture wherein allowing/fostering spirituality in the educational setting enables and encourages the strong and healthy development of identity, morality, democratic democracy, genuine honesty, manners, and inner fulfilment. Without being integral to and continually and firmly built into the very core of education, the above spiritual traits become loose and ungrounded in adults and the society they perpetuate. Yet public education and curriculum are running away from massive public demand regarding the need for spirituality. Let me be clear that humanity is far from just humanism, despite the wording similarity, but humanism—as it has been defined and framed by the Western Eurocentric epistemological framework (Walsh & Mignolo, 2018; Escobar & Mignolo, 2017)—has failed humanity by being self-centered, removing the humanity from the humanities, marginalizing spirituality's transpersonal perspective as Macdonald (1965) claims, and celebrating self-contentment at the expense of other's discontent. Macdonald (1995) states:

> What this means is illustrated when we view man historically and individually. Rather than ask the question, "How could man have come so far in developing such technology and social life?" we are more prone to ask, "Wy has man failed so miserably in ridding the world of war, disease, famine and starvation?" Or rather than marveling at individual men and asking, "How could An Einstein be?" we may ask, "Why are there so few great Men?" it is because the answer must lie in the realm of what man and society do to the element of personal responsiveness that the questions are phrased differently. In other words, we are not concerned here with how man can condition, and has conditioned, himself to the present state, but how this very conditioning process has affected the creative, self-actualizing, personal aspect of his development. (p. 17)

In Macdonald's (1995) terms, education and curriculum are the political spaces where the "personal" should be groomed, and not via reductive notions of rationality undermining the inner self in which endless spiritual dynamics play an important role. Discrepancies between our curriculum/societal expectations and what's best for the process of growing into full human "beings" abound. According to Macdonald (1995), underlying the goal of becoming "characteristically human at all stages of development…is the urgent sense that the individual needs to be developed according to his own style of life that is self-aware, self-critical, and self-enhancing" (p. 17). This becoming/being is only possible through exercising/allowing/practicing spirituality, the sole way in which the individuality of humankind gets to be "infinitely beyond the puny individuality of plants and animals, who are preliminary or exclusively creatures of tropism" (Macdonald, 1995, p. 17). Without it, there is no room for personal improvement and identity formation. As Paraskeva (2021a) argues, as the spiritual struggle is a political struggle any wrangle for spirituality in education and curriculum is indeed a political struggle as well.

Public education is thus not providing a vital service that human "beings" require. Rather, education seems to be at the service of the treating students like animals—or worse. To talk about spirituality in public education but have one's own identity denied within the same system creates a clashing of realities that we can feel, but not make sense of. The same happens with language, the channel by which we spend most of our lives receiving information. We don't get to truly make sense of language unless we experiment with what words mean, in order to make it real, sensible, palpable, to experience its reality or essence, and develop a genuine, felt understanding of its abstract qualities. The opacity between public education and the necessary conditions for true growth produces unfortunate deviations in human development. We often talk about and justify the need for experimentation, but students are not actually allowed to experiment with their own individuality within the curriculum, and this dishonest ambiguity appears worded as standardized curriculum. Insisting on this unethical educational endeavor amounts to disdaining human "being" and individuality, and instead worshiping the dehumanization of infinite possibilities, exchanging intelligence for instinct.

So, for now, I will delve more into "consciencism" (Nkrumah, 1964) and "conscientization" (Freire, 1973) in order to underscore the importance of both the principle that must be developed, i.e., "conscientization," and the fact that must be acknowledged, i.e., "spirituality." As well, I will contextualize various battles for a coherent education, a curriculum and approach to learning that pays attention to spirituality, within the current neoliberal momentum. This struggle is, in my opinion, much more voracious than any other conflict in the educational/social terrain.

## 3  Coherence—*Really*—Matters: "Morality" and "Honesty"

Any discussion of morality and honesty is potentially contentious, as we are referring to concepts that frame a multiplicity of philosophies of praxis of both individuals and communities, both of which vary widely from place to place throughout the world. With this in mind, it is very common—and healthy, I would say—to be confronted with such questions as "Whose morality and honesty are we referring to?" It goes without saying that there is virtually no such thing as a neutral philosophy of praxis. Each one is classed, raced, gendered, and more. Even a superficial glimpse into current educational and curriculum policies allows one to perceive how subsumed its standards and policies—from high-stakes testing and budget cuts to the deskilling of teachers and pervasive use of the English language, etc.—are within a dominant conservative, capitalist, Western, positivist model that is driven by debatable notions of morality and honesty and actively reinforces and multiplies segregation, inequality, and injustice (Apple, 1982; Giroux, 2011; Saltman, 2014; Lipman, 1998). With that said, that road has been explored already by leading intellectuals in the field, and isn't really the subject of my study.

Within this cult of social engineering that colonizes formal education (Pinar, 2018), the person, the individual, the multiplicity of "selves" is sidelined. Following Santos' (2014) rationale, I would argue them that the pervasiveness a particular morality expressed by social Darwinist pedagogical forms renders a multiplicity of other notions of morality invisible. In my case, as with too many others, the social engineering curriculum in which I was educated minimized me as an individual and completely silenced my inner self, blocking me from understanding myself "from within" (Pinar, 1994, p. 10) and from openly feeling and expressing my spirituality as a moral value. I could not be honest. I could not be truthful.

Foucault (2001) and Nkrumah (1964) teach us great deal here. Foucault (2001) uses the Greek word *parrhesia* to stress the validity, and expand the meaning of, frankness or honesty. A *parrhesiastes,* someone who uses *parrhesia,* is one who speaks the truth. This very specific truth or frankness is very intimately related to honest interpretation, the sort of spirit-driven, proactive, self-perpetuating reflection we have discussed above. The risky act of conveying such truths to others involves, and is definitive of, a *parrhesiastes.*

Tinker (2008), referring to truth, states, "it must come to mean much more than that" (p. 151); and indeed, we must strive to cultivate genuine, often challenging or devastating truths in the face of a pervasive avoidance of deeper honesty with ourselves and others. Some hold that we can no longer manifest *parrhesia* (as originally defined) in our modern epistemological framework. I disagree, but doing so is harder than ever before. Why? In the process of colonization, not just words but social fabrics were gradually groomed to attend to the deconstruction of the meaning of words (and so much more) throughout the colonization of the curriculum. This implies that the first ones to be colonized were the instructors or teachers who somehow lost their ability to act as *parrhesiastes*. Foucault (2001) adds:

> The ability for the speaker to tell truths to herself, which can be part of the process of self-construction—is therefore of central importance... [a]nd serves as well as the bearer of true content for her own life and those around her. (p. 165)

*Parrhesia* can be seen not only as an honest engagement with others, but as a self-referential practice of telling truths to oneself. Without this dimension of *parrhesia*, its links to acts of self-transformation are tenuous (Foucault, 2001, p. 110). As Foucault (2001) often stated, *parrhesia* implies an innate harmony between one's speech and actions, an umbilical connection to self-mastering and self-governance.

Tinker (2008) addresses Foucault's topics of *parrhesia*/honesty/morality/truth with a more accessible, practical, but still powerful form of reflection, extending the implications of these notions to the average person, the masses, as well as the general educational setting, for two reasons. First, he calls upon Christianity to genuinely and honestly examine its influence on the educational process, and to reflect on how those who claim to have the attributes of morality and honesty should bring theories/ideas into the praxis level, using a critical approach. Praxis is not just the application of an idea or theory, but also entails the subsequent analysis of the ensuing practice in the effort to progressively continue doing better until all people's lives have improved. To know that someone is down, but close your eyes to their pain just because the majority of people shut their eyes, is, according to Tinker (2008), dishonesty. I agree with this assessment, but let me also acknowledge that honesty may also mean different things for different people. For instance, there are many people for whom being honest is not correlated with being spiritual.

To me, honesty means living and acting wholeheartedly, with non-derivative non-divisive ways to grasp "any truth" that I come to know being accessible, applicable, and open to all. No one should be left behind or be harmed by being neglected from the truth I know. Foucault argues that we need to discuss whether we share any common truth whatsoever in order to state, "I speak the truth" (p. 12). If we take his approach, specific truths may vary from one culture to another, even though we may all share a common "golden rule," a sort of intimate moral tenet that seems to make sense to all human "beings." Our "commitment" to something is, in itself, a matter of honoring our own theoretical view of honesty. If we establish the "right," as Foucault (1984) claims, it automatically means that we are further away from the "wrong." This notion adds fuel to the discussion of honesty and truth. For example, for a child who was raised to be a murderer, it is a matter of honesty to kill someone. However, that child would not want to be murdered. This demonstrates that we need help from moral coherence, where praxis comes to the game as a key component of honesty. With praxis, we learn the truth, and we realize that another knowledge is possible (Santos, 2007). With praxis, the lies my teachers told me (Loewen, 2018) become evident. I know now what it means to have been oppressed, denied, and silenced; therefore, to deny my students the opposite qualities is a matter of dishonesty.

The type of coherence Tinker (2008) refers to must not just make sense to me, but it must be amenable to concrete interpretation. It requires reflection in order to generate a productive meaning for both/all parties, thereby preventing any individual from being put into an unequal position. Honesty cannot be far from justice and equality, in fact, these terms or "actions" only exist if they coexist.

As for spirituality, an essentially contested term, I rely on Tinker (2008) to help clarify the need for wholehearted honesty about the role of spirit in education. Tinker is one of the few authors who addresses the subject of education from a religious and/or spiritual perspective through moral and intellectual reflection. Why do I use religion here? As I explained above, I intend to show the line separating one from another, in order to pinpoint the differences, but to do so, I must speak of both. Please bear with me. I do sympathize tremendously with Tinker (2008), especially because, although his genealogy speaks alone about the geno-ethnocide felt on his own skin, he delves carefully into the importance of praxis and praxism. He brings praxis and Christianity face to face, delving into what is preached vs. the materialization of those ideas and beliefs, interrogating both how the message is delivered and how reflections on justice are combined with concrete praxis, producing arguments about change and leading to "changes in the argument" itself. As Tinker (2008) suggests, praxis, praxism, reflection and knowledge cannot be alone in order to produce materialization, transformation. In the transformational side that suggests justice, justice will never happen without praxis, praxism, reflection and knowledge.

Nkrumah (1964) also recognizes spiritual factors (meaning traits of spirituality) as being primary (ordinary, as previously cited), and a matter held to be dependent on the spirit (or the existence of spirituality) for their very existence (p. 15). He celebrates the importance of, and connections between, knowledge, reflection, and materialization of the reflection to establish a direct connection with honest consciential analysis:

> If philosophical consciencism initially affirms the absolute and independent existence of matter, and holds matter to be endowed with its pristine objective laws, then philosophical consciencism builds itself by becoming a reflection of the objectivity, in conceptual terms, of the

unfolding of matter. When a philosophy so restricts itself to the reflection of the objective unfolding of matter, it also establishes a direct connection between knowledge and action. (Nkrumah, 1964, p. 92)

Paraskeva (2016)—which introduced Nkrumah's and other anti-colonial and decolonial reason in our field—argues how "consciencism" was the weapon through which the epistemic oppressed challenged "the close links between class and race developed in Africa alongside capitalist exploitation" (Krumah, 1964, p. 27). There is no way out of oppression with an epistemic oppressed out of "consciencism" (Paraskeva, 2016, 2018).

One of the great fractures among the various definitions of spirituality is in regard to abstracism contentment sole. Boal (2019) states that we need to stop being spectators and shift sides into becoming co-participants, through the process of "consciencism," (Nkrumah, 1964), in turning knowledge into action (p. 144). This indicates that spirituality is not a static quality that we "have," but instead a process that, over time, evolves and matures both internally and in external actions. Such crosses the pedagogical praxis. To this end, Huebner (1962) argues,

> [teachers] need to be free agents in order to realize moral and aesthetic values in the educational activity. It is in the teacher and in the teacher's education and continuing education that the major struggle between human being techniques and spirit is waged. (p. 111)

Tinker (2008) takes a slightly different path of reasoning that ends up pretty much on the same terrain. While Freire (1972) focuses on the higher states, "orders," and systems that systemize labor, production, oppression, curriculum, and education as a banking system, Tinker (2008) calls Christianity and Christians to task according to their own definitions of honesty and truth. He also discusses specifics around praxis and reflection on practice, along with the obligations they produce, both for individuals and for larger groups that might hold similar obligations, such as certain governmental agencies, or religious or spiritual organizations claiming to follow Christ's lived example. While Freire (1972) examines a giant system, Tinker (2008) hones in on the individual and appeals to our most intimate thoughts and reflections, calling each of us to think more deeply and honestly and pointing to the fact that changes must come from the individual. This seems to indicate that, at least from his perspective, the decolonization process should start from the bottom—meaning the colonized people—up and not wait for things to be initiated by the top, that is, government and corporations.

Another profound aspect of Tinkers (2008) work is his call for a reformation of praxis and practices for the average person, and, to that end, he uses accessible language to inspire as many readers as possible. This may sound basic, but many theorists write in words and modes that further marginalize the people they are trying to include, preventing those groups and individuals from understanding or reflecting on what is offered. They are unable to engage in what Boal (2004) calls, "listening to what we hear" (p. 110). This has been insightfully uncovered by Fanon (1961) when he argues that "everything can be explained to the people, on the single condition that you want them to understand." In addition, Tinker (2008) urgently calls upon Christianity to be truly just, fair and ethical, rather than anti-ethnic, exclusive, and "only" for specific people. Spirituality is a human right, something rightfully extended not "just" to Christians, but to all human "beings," including indigenous peoples, people of other faiths, spiritualities, religions, creeds, nations....

We so often debate teaching and the curriculum but negate the recipient of the teaching, the "being." So, to be honest, what matters most? I would argue the answer is honesty itself. Foucault (1981) related honesty to self-criticism, questioning oneself according to the principle of one's personal expectations from others. Furthermore, how one perceives the debate has to do with how honest one is with those who are part of an "educational" process that inherently demands ethical responsibility—whether or not that responsibility is indeed carried out. There is a Christian element here as well, since the U.S. constitution is based on a monotheistic belief platform, with a daily reminder on the dollar bill's "In God We Trust." Christians represent a large proportion of the teaching workforce, so I want to speak to the majority in the context of the responsibilities arising from our constitution. Justice and equality for all! As I have mentioned before, *parrhesia* (Foucault, 1981).

So far, I have been trying to explore the complexities and importance of spirituality in individual and social identity, and the related need for a coherent educational and curricular framework that respects and fosters the student's capacity to "work from within" (Pinar, 1974). Let me now turn to a biographical note to exemplify a contradiction—a potentially lethal one—between the enforced absence/presence of spirituality in our schools and what matters when one is experiencing a life-threatening, untreatable or terminal illness.

## 4   Within and beyond Life "as Is"

As a teacher and administrator balancing the job descriptions of my two-in-one career, I noticed that, like many others, I was slowly imbibing the tendency to oppress in exchange for power. I felt so uncomfortable negotiating the scars of my schooling journey this way. I felt I had to, with honesty, listen to the dark precincts of my soul (West, 2010). However, there was a day that I literally arrived to the conclusion that subjects like the ones I was teaching had low or no interest or value, and that—even more frustrating—the local institution's educational body was bowing to the hegemonic control (Darder, 2011) of the system-state-district.

Due to the nature of the subjects, students had to think in specific, concrete ways in order to process these academic requirements. One day William, one of my students at the high school, asked me, "What do we do with this [in life]? What is the meaning of this for us?" My student was implying and, at the same time, begging to have his living quest (Palmer, 2003a) acknowledged and validated. I was facing a *Freirean* question. I did not know what to do. Of course, I did not want to be ignorant and uneducated, yet I was beginning to sense that acting as I had been educated to do could be threatening intellectual freedom (hooks, 2003). The other students said, "Thank God one day we won't have to study anymore."

My school environment was a place that did not "cultivate humanity" (Nussbaum, 1997) at all, and, odd as it might be, most teachers did not seem to recognize that lack of humanity. As Macdonald (1995) insightfully argues, we must make the schooling environment more humane, which process is consistently is linked to larger cultural and social transformations. In fact, education is supposed to be an action giving every person access to the discourse that person prefers, to offer a path of personal significance (Greene, 1995). I confess that I went home that day thinking about what my students had said in class. William's question created discomfort in me and disrupted my life. It kept me from sleeping.

That same year, I volunteered at a hospital in my neighborhood. São Paulo, Brazil, is one of the biggest metropolises in the world. As in other such cities, public hospitals were packed. I had already graduated, but had never had a chance to actually delve into the chaplaincy field, one of my specializations, so I requested to be placed on the wing reserved for those with terminal and untreatable diseases. I knew the patients there would have one foot in this world and another in uncertainty. Questions about life and death have always haunted me—I've always tried to make sense of things and find the purpose of education and existence in itself—and working with this population seemed like both a good thing to do and a way to learn. In this endeavor, I truly wanted my innermost teacher to lead me towards a sense of meaning and purpose, and to, in Palmer's (1999) words, let my life to speak. So, I decided to get shoulder-to-shoulder with those who were happy to have just one more day of life, people who, at any moment, would have to say goodbye to those who they loved. These patients literally lived on the edge. I had no time to lose, so, while never being insensitive to their needs in the moment, I fully immersed myself in taking in the wisdom these very ill and dying people put forth. The environment was quite intense, and the doctors and nurses worked hard to manage the process of death 24/7. People were dying every hour. And what I noticed, as people got close to leaving this world, contradicted everything I had learned as a student in school. At the end, most of them held my hand, and I got the feeling that they (let me generalize by respectfully using the world "they") did not want to stop living life. Many held on to my hand very, very tightly—and most said, "I do not want to die."

I will divide what I learned from those patients into three main points. (1) They fought to continue living with all the strength they had left. They all said that they had sacrificed themselves throughout life in order to succeed and find happiness, but many had learned very important lessons too late. For example, one said he had finally realized what it takes to be happy, the things he should have said no to, the roads he should have followed in order to avoid addiction; another stated that he only now understood life and the side effects of an unhealthy diet and so on. (2) The majority did not express any regrets over not having invested their money better, or earned more—in fact, they tended to see money as the most degenerative gain. No one was worried about who would inherit their riches. However, they did demonstrate frustration about having procrastinated about or delayed opportunities to enjoy life, or not having taken the important things in life into deeper consideration. At the end of life, people shared a common sense that happiness is ultimately comprised of small things and positive attitudes towards the self and others, as manifested in precious time spent with family and friends. (3) Many expressed regrets. Again and again, I heard people saying, with devastating pain, "I should have followed my dreams." It seems terrible that anyone should live their out their whole life and then, at the very end, feel compelled to express concerns that should have been addressed long before their strength was gone. As was the case with most of the people I spent time with towards the end of their lives, school certainly did not prepare me for end-of-life realities—or any deeper, bigger questions—in any way. One root cause, according to Palmer (2003b), lies in the fact that "our students are told from an early age that school is not the place to bring their questions of meaning" (p. 4). Subsequently, throughout their lives people are forced, both by societal pressures and curricular negligence, to inhibit such questions.

To me, death seems to be the most important, generative thing when it comes to empowerment. When you have a real understanding that your life will end—especially if that end is near!—nothing can fool you. If you have no little or no time left, you are forced to evaluate the meaning of your existence. But we do not need to be about to die to reconsider things. There is endless wisdom being produced (and then, often, lost) around hospital beds. The way we feel at the end of life can tell us a lot about how we should begin it, starting now. My experience in that hospital wing taught me that I wanted to proceed the opposite way from how we usually do: I wanted to teach my students about the end...right from the beginning of the schooling process. I wanted to share with them what life is really about, according to those who have lost their lives. As research documents, schools—the ones I endured, those our children attend today—dehumanize students daily through their oppressive processes of selection and hyperbolic privatization of a curriculum that is already colonized and epistemologically redefined in order to fulfill the aims of consumerism and power (Apple, 1979; Giroux, 1981; Macdonald, 1975; Greene, 1978; Huebner, 1976). Such dehumanized students are produced through a dehumanized curriculum that ignores one's fundamental journey as "beings" in a finitude temporality. Schools are the very eye of a lethal epistemological hurricane coined as an epistemicide (Santos, 2014) or curriculum epistemicide and reversive epistemicide (Paraskeva, 2014, 2016, 2021a, 2022) that keeps being perpetuated.

Ignoring the very meaning of life has been deadly for our communities. Let's fight for a curriculum and pedagogy that voices the silences (Paraskeva & Janson, 2018) of crucial aspects of life that have been undermined and/or produced as nonexistent (Santos, 2014). My point is not to bring these realities to the classroom. In fact, such realities are already in classrooms. What I am fighting for is an educational and curriculum system that does not silence these vital realities, one that, instead of putting students through a self-extinguishing ordeal, celebrates and nurtures their whole selves. But the latter is far from what currently exists. In Macdonald's (1964) terms,

> We simply mean that the school does not exist primarily to inculcate our cultural heritage, not principally to develop role players for society nor primarily to meet the ends and the interests of learners. The school exist to bring learners in contact with reality, of which our society, ourselves, and our cultural heritage are parts. (p. 47)

Socially and psychologically, students are pretty much molded by reductionist derivative curriculum (Paraskeva, 2011, 2016, 2021a, 2022). And most schools express and inculcate the cult of the banking concept of education (Freire, 1990). They are thus designed and protected—as a real epistemological protectorate (Paraskeva, 2018)—to produce servants for an unjust system. This mode of education claims the authority of truth, sovereignty over what is right and wrong, moral and immoral, and honest and dishonest, and, last but not least, holds the arrogant position that it has all the answers (Postman, 2008). It also insists that we are all rational—and only rational—beings. While this might be accurate, it fails to understand that spirituality is part of any rationalized process. In this context, schools keep believing in the production of a non-spiritual "being," a "being" unable to hear itself Boal (2004), a "being" that denies the expectations of its own soul to commodify the definition of happiness as consumerism and the aggregation of things. It is quite a contradiction that, during the greatest challenges we face in life, and certainly by the end of life, we are confronted with the stark realization that we are not merely what the books (and schools, and teachers…) told us we are/should be. As Macdonald (1995) claims,

> what is consumed eventually is the student, the being, not in flesh and blood, but in living time, the act of consumption becomes a good in and of itself, a criterion of worth and "living." What is lost is the consciousness of everyday life in its active, creative, and productive vitality. (p. 115)

The capacity or possibility for hearing or understanding or talking with the inner self, the practice of spiritually engaging with my inner self was quite absent from my formal education. The *Freirean* leitmotiv "reading the word and the world" entails the spiritual—as I am framing it—too. The fact that a strong component of the human "being" cannot be fully expressed, debated, understood in particular moments of life—sometimes even the final moments of life—makes me speechless. It is interesting to notice that the same dominant groups—both hegemonic and counter-hegemonic (Paraskeva, 2016)—that have silenced and sidelined spirituality are at the front lines of certain emerging fields of study, such as "mindfulness." Such groups and social institutions, especially those that are "state funded, still act as major bastions of Western elitism and need to be decolonized as resources of knowledge production" (Smith, 2012 p. 129).

As an educator, I would say that we need to rethink education overall, but especially for the beginning and ending parts of life. But, right now, we—like so many others who have come through "the system"—exist. Let's just take a moment to observe where we are in this moment: an apathetic and indifferent world. In this context, elements of spirituality and dehumanization coexist, which shows me that spirituality is the fundamental element of conscientização. I didn't develop my need to look deeper and ask questions in church or graduate school or by reading any book. We do not need to go back in history to analyze the lack or need of something else. The object of study, the everyday meaning of life, as Macdonald (1995) states, shows us that

> society is not simply structures acting upon passive individuals, it creates a concomitant consciousness in individuals which then acts back upon society. It is the kind of modern consciousness that is being developed in schools through everyday life experiences...as ordinary events and encounters of his life with others. (pp. 112–113)

These ordinary truths are somehow "continuously bombarded with imagery ideas, and models of conduct that are intrinsically connected with technological production" (Berger, 1981, p. 40). Because of this reality, and given our current time and social context, technology, clashes, conflicts, and ideological battles, it is important to reflect on the global stage we are inhabiting. As I've argued before, this social reality is undeniably ordinary now, and needs to be considered as such.

Up to here, I have been examining the discrepancy between spirituality and current curriculum, as well as arguing for integrating meaning, listening, and inner self-development into public education and curriculum. For better clarification, let me delve a little into the global context in which education, human "beings," and spirituality are ensconced.

## 5  The Ordinary: A Global Context

The ruthless and bloody clashes between nations and regions, the entrance on the historical scene of doubts about the status of knowledge, the economy substituting for politics, the market replacing arts, truth being sought not in consensus but in dissent from what is true, massive production and dissemination of images and signs, human relations marked by fragmentation, pluralism (when exist to create confusion) and individualism (when is there to eliminate impose ego-ideological ways of living), simulation and virtual reality imposing themselves more and more in order to replace objective reality, the homogenizing and insatiable voracity of capitalism, technical knowledge, scientists at the service of systems of production—these are just some of the characteristics and conditions of contemporaneity, a selection of the elements embodying the ubiquitous machinery that serves the Eurocentric ideologies that dominate the world today.

These ideologies of power have deftly encouraged the social construction of a global population's blindness to a future that only seems promising, all the while sowing more division, sexism, oppression, and clashes between those who lead vs. those who are led, schools vs. students, school districts vs. teachers, in other words, a social classification of the world population, as Quijano (2000) would claim. Quijano (2000) frequently refers to Latin America as a stage for intellectual, physical, and spiritual savagery. These terrible, destabilizing clashes underline the fact that with such ideologies of power and oppression "came a caste system of sorts." The conqueror or the colonizer was at the top of the social hierarchy and the conquered and colonized was at the bottom" (Drisco, 2017, p. 113). As many social scientists point out, not just Latin America but the whole world is gaining momentum towards undeniable chaos. This is, as Paraskeva (2010) claims, the "normalization of chaos" (p. 10).

It might sound pleonastic, but I would say that the legality and functionality of knowledge and "ways"[1] of thinking are up for discussion. Further, a significant number of people from across social spheres are looking to have this conversation regardless of the language and jargons they might use. The message is felt alike across diverse social and intellectual groups. The language may change, but the experience cuts across intellectuality and all the way through to our empirical senses. Let's, just for an instant, meditate on what is going on in our social era:

> On the one hand our current time is marked by huge developments and thespian changes, an era that is referred to as the electronic revolution of communications, information, genetics and the biotechnological. On the other hand, it is a time of disquieting regressions, a return of the social evils that appeared to have been or about to be overcome. The return of slavery and slavish work; the return of high vulnerability to old sicknesses that seemed to have been eradicated and appear now linked to new pandemics like HIV/AIDS: the return of the revolting social inequalities that gave their name to the social question at the end of the nineteenth century; in sum, the return of the specter of war, perhaps now more than ever a world war, although whether cold or not is as yet undecidable. (Sousa Santos, 2005, p. VII)

Paraskeva (2021b) defines our current global moment as absurd. We live in an era of absurdism, and abnormality. From successive devastating economic and environmental havoc, the pandemic with a lethal footprint throughout the planet, the world is now facing the consequences of the war in Ukraine. Such sagas pave the way for a dangerous new political economy. Paraskeva (2021b) situates such absurdism as a defining feature of the colors of an intentional epistemological blindness framing the Eurocentric reason.

When we have political-academic discussions (like those we've had throughout recent politically volatile years), regardless of the language we use to explain the dominance and uniformity of knowledge and "scientificity of science" (Paraskeva, 2011, pp. 2–14), our opinions and ideas are deeply informed by our lived experiences, especially in the sense that we know that there are other possibilities for addressing the problems we are currently facing. We have already spent a long time persisting with Western modern Eurocentric epistemological approaches to problems, especially the ones we are facing right now, such as immigration reform, education improvement, racism, politics and its macro and micromanagement and results and gender. The latter has increasingly become an explosive topic that cuts across religion, education, sociology, and psychology. Moreover, the problems we have as a humanity are mostly created by such Eurocentric reason. As Lorde (2007) argues, "the master"s tools cannot deconstructs the masters house." Furthermore, the dichotomized understanding and acceptance of this term is shaking the theo-political platform, causing U.S. jurisprudence on gender equality (Kohm, 2008) to be one of the most bombastic and avoided topics in education. Kohm (2008) notes that "[t]he Supreme Court of the United States has tried to remedy gender disparity in education by affording women a quality military education," which, while not remedying the problem, did massage liberal expectations. Military education for women has essentially functioned as a social band-aid for a major injury, which gives us an idea of the fear and obstacles surrounding gender equity. As I finalize the preparation of this volume, the battles against critical race theory in our society and schools reach a delirium momentum.

Despite the absurdism (Paraskeva, 2021b) that we facing as humanity, it is puzzling to see the very same avoidance present in the face of claims around spirituality, with these two equality-seeking "problems" taking a similar journey with similar outcomes. The Western modern Eurocentric epistemological platform is obsolete and outdated and cannot handle the confusion generated by questioning; rather, it explains—sells—modernity as bright and shiny, thereby hiding its shadow and darker side (Andreotti, 2014). Mignolo (2000, 2011) argues that modernity is generally defined in relation to the brilliant shine associated with concepts such as seamless progress, industrialization, secularization, humanism, individualism, scientific reasoning, and nation states, amongst others. Eurocentric epistemology does not have the tools to explain what is going on in society, and so, with no legitimate response to offer to the questions asked, it simply denies and categorizes such queries, doubts, and challenges as non-knowledge, dismissing them as invalid, inferior subject matter that lacks the proper scientific base. As Paraskeva (2016) claims, this is the epistemicide at full blast. Lazzarato (2011) points out that the nucleus of this force that fights against so many others in the name of retaining global control is not without myriad and diversified approaches. It uses every single possible avenue to, "if" necessary, spin, and storm the near environment, forcing an economic claim for a different agenda wherever a new economic ideology is offered by the colonizer.

Similar to the saying about the hand that rocks the cradle, Paraskeva (2016) claims that the need for a "sanguinary" hand approach (p. 4) creates catastrophes or alienates one country from another through sanctions to ensure that the subjectivity of the subject (students) and subjectivity of the curriculum (what it really wants to teach) stands its ground as part of a broader overall agenda; this force is ideologically presented as "legal" law. In a more critical analytical claim, Paraskeva (2016) calls this "concrete epistemological cleansing" (p. 3). No one is allowed, never mind encouraged, to proactively think differently from Western Eurocentric theo-political official/valid pathways to knowledge and scientific functionality. To be clear, in Western science, professors are the authority of knowledge production (Ndlovu-Gatsheni & Hira, 2018). One cannot forget that the responsibility of the banking praxis of education also relies on teachers—specifically those who persistently refuse to understand the brutality of such praxis. As a result, the validation of knowledge is rendered particular to such circles of intellectuals, leaving no room for the existence of other knowledge. Whether it occurs on the global scale or in university departments, I am forced to agree that there is a constant fight for the dominion of the human mind, a pervasive effort to turn a long-free "being" into a servant of the global system, an entity empty in itself and full of confusion and ideologies that strip its life sense away and exchange it for a basic existence in which it is forced to consume and compete in order to have a social orgasm and sense of fulfillment. But, when death approaches, our sense of frustration and the need to redefine what truly matters in life almost invariably arise. Why? In this social sphere, we are encircled by an environment that we have no control over and subjected to evil agendas stemming from terrible ideologies of greed and domination. Dying people come to this realization when they face death. Yet spirituality in public education and curriculum could enable students to live fully throughout their whole lives. This is why I contend that spirituality in education is a human right just as much as education itself is—maybe even more so. Incorporating spirituality into the curriculum is vital to elucidating what permeates true "being" in this world, while religion and culture must also be taken into consideration in order to separate spirituality for the object of study. Thus, since we have unraveled the complexities of spirituality, let me go back a bit as I feel that it is also necessary to reflect again on religion in order to clarify the differences.

Dewey (1934) defines religion as "any activity pursued on behalf of an ideal end against obstacles and in spite of threats of personal loss because of its general and enduring value" (p. 43). As a chaplain listening to the stories of those facing death, I was acting as a religious figure in this vein, yet it was not religion but rather spirituality which allowed me to reconsider my path in life and to delve into questions about the spiritual education that some benefited from and most others missed. Tillich (1964) explains that "[r]eligion is the state of being grasped by an ultimate concern, a concern which qualifies all other concerns as preliminary and which itself contains the answer to the question of the meaning of life" (p. 58). He boldly centers such concerns as an ordinary priority. Others frame religion broadly, as something shaped by—but also consisting of much more than—social, empirical, and philosophical observations. McNamara (2007) allows religion to be what it needs to be, i.e., more than just a definition: "Try to define religion and you invite an argument" (p. VI). Such a tremendous truth. Internal attempts and metaphysical self-definitions can never be measured or precisely shared. Idleman (1993) states that not even judicial law has a settled definition of the institutionalized word: "The dividing line between what is, and what is not, a religion is difficult to draw" (p. 464).

Various intellectuals approach religion as a cultural system, as behavioral practices, or even as a supernatural, transcendental subject. Some see religion as humankind's needs and practices vis-à-vis a superior "being," or as people's relationship with that superior "being." In many tribes with well-established, socially organized rituals and rites of passage, religion is not coded as religion per se but as part of the culture. Many times, religion involves a detailed system wherein humankind establishes its understanding of transcendence and how individuals should operate under a certain set of rules and regulations, beliefs, creeds, and rituals, in order to impress/please a greater "being," or God.

Spirituality is the practicality of the praxis when religion is voluntary and self-directed, without any required affiliation. Tinker (2008) warns of potential misinterpretations of these two terms, stressing the necessity of applying "moral coherence" to their differences—lest we perpetuate the status quo. Our theology (meaning our ethical and religious concepts, along with related personal feelings and ideas only) can no longer be constructed in alienation from the Global South, nor in a context in which religion claims (colonizes) spirituality. We need to put social justice, empowerment, and commitment at the heart of our own thoughts about religion and spirituality. And we must extricate spirituality from being both subsumed in religion and marginalized by the educational system.

So far, I have sought to unravel the essence and processes of spirituality in society and public education. I've attempted to hold education accountable for veering far away from its own purpose and definition. If education is to inform, allow, guide, promote, enhance, and reflect, education must be seen as a social, ethical, and moral process that is primarily enrooted in conscientização (Freire, 1972). Such a process stimulates and promotes intellectual vitality as well as human growth and fulfillment. I have tried to unpack how we face a very complex historical moment as a humanity that triggers new herculean challenges to those committed to "spiritual inquiry" (Anzaldúa, 2002a). I have argued how the reason undergirding such absurdism is exhausted. It is prat of the problem and cannot alone promote any positive transformation. I also took the opportunity to once again reiterate the difference between spirituality and religion. Let me now dedicate the next section to unpacking my claim that education is not only rooted in spirituality but that spirituality is an educational meaning-maker that leads to the healthy unfolding of identity.

## 6 "Consciencism" and "Conscientização": A Spiritual Call

There is no disagreement or mystery around the fact that critical theorists, social scientists, and many other scholars are now advocating for the need for concientization or conscientização, much as Freire (1972) promoted it almost six decades ago in *Conscientizing as a Way of Liberating*. As for consciencism as it was framed by Nkrumah (1964), that theorist's concepts were actually only brought to the "eye of the curriculum storm" via the recent works of Paraskeva (2011, 2014), who championed the need to engage in battle against curriculum epistemicides (Paraskeva, 2011, 2014, 2016). Nkrumah's consciencism blends with Freire's conscientização. As I explore these concepts, it is equally important to understand the importance of spirituality in the ways we envision new alternatives to thinking about and debating the curriculum. They both frame spirituality as a critical call crucial in the struggle against of domination and segregation.

Let me now briefly unpack Paulo Freire's spiritual footprint. The work of James Kirylo and Dryck Boyd (2017) teaches great deal here. To begin with normally, Freire's spiritual vein is undermined as the political angle gets overemphasized. As hooks (2001), and others argues, the "spiritual is political." Drawing on Sternberg (2011, pp. 609–610), James Kirylo and Dryck Boyd (2017) stress that "those of us who espouse critical pedagogy and embrace Paulo Freire's visions of praxis and conscientization work out of a tradition, often unknowingly, with deep ties to religious faith." What attracted me in the work and thought of Paulo Freire was precisely the "political of the spiritual" vis-à-vis the spiritual of the pollical right at the center of his praxis of "conscientização."

"Conscientização," in Freirean terms, relates to "a truly liberating education" (Freire, 1995, p. 35) through a permanent critical awareness in interpellating—dialogically—the socially constructed political, economic, and cultural contradictions and oppressive dynamics of reality. His dialogical commitment to the human being's temporality deflates the dynamics of dialect interpellation.

> Conscientização is not based on consciousness on the one hand and the world on the other; for another part, does not intend a separation. On the contrary, it is based on the consciousness-world relationship. Taking this relationship as the object of their critical reflection, human beings will clarify the dimensions obscurities that result from their approach to the world. Conscientização, as a critical attitude of human beings in history, will never end. If human beings, as beings who act, continue to adhere to a "made" world, they will find themselves submerged in a new obscurity. (Freire, 1979, p. 1)

That is, "conscientização" is a "process of political literacy" (Freire, 1979, p. 2) a praxis that announces and denounces oppressive and dehumanized structures situated in a concrete historical time; a way of existence and thinking, a way of being that materializes the endless utopian possibilities of radically transform the world. "Conscientização" is "precisely the human praxis, the unity indissoluble between the human being and his/her reflection on the world" (Freire, 1979, p. 5).

Freire's work talked eloquently to me, to my own inner self in such powerful way. His spiritual development is deeply related to his Catholic agency/praxis "particularly concerned about the poverty conditions among the rural campesinos, who in essence were tenant farmers on lands owned by large and powerful landowners" (Kirylo & Boyd, 2017, p. 4). Such praxis was quite transformative as "experiences caused his spiritual sensitivities to become intricately and intimately related to a commitment to social change and a fight against oppression" (Jeria, 1984, cited in Kirylo & Boyd, 2017, p. 4). The human being's spiritual-political existence, Paulo Freire (1979) argues, is not a-historical, quite the opposite, as it interfered in the course of history and humanity. That is, Freire's spiritual approach deeply political and he maintain that "human beings, not God, made changes in the conditions of society" (Freire, 1970)—and not as they pleased. In here one can vividly see Freire's full blast jouissance—as Paraskeva (2016, 2022) would put it—of a Marxian spiritual take. That is, the sublime capacity to seek spiritually the transcendent while not denying Marx on the worldliness (Kirylo & Boyd, 2017). Here relies "conscientização" as praxis, a social capital, a social resistance, a way through which once read the world and the world. Like Marx, he fully advocates that one can transform the course of history, not only according to his/her circumstances. In doing so, Freire taught us—like no other—the beauty of finitude. Freire adamantly defended that

> people needed to work to change their circumstances and could not simply wait on God to change people or their circumstances. God's role consisted of providing the vision of what human completeness and social justice looked like. "[God's] transcendence over us is based on the fact of our knowledge of this finitude. For man [sic] is an incomplete being and the completion of his incompleteness is encountered in his relationship with his creator, a relationship which by its very nature is always a relationship of liberation." For Freire the purpose of both education and social justice work were to move toward this vision of completeness. (Elias, 1976b, p. 41, cited in Kirylo & Boyd, 2017, p. 4)

Leveraging on Althusser's rationale, Paulo Freire (1979, p. 45) emphasizes that conscientização "is also a cultural action committed to the freedom of human beings, a political act that does not surrender to ideological mystifications, nor is it limited to a simple moral denunciation of myths and errors." Conscientização, he stresses,

> undertakes a rational and rigorous critique of ideology. The fundamental role of those committed to an action culture for awareness is not exactly talking about how to build the liberating idea, but to invite men and women to capture with their spirit the truth of their own reality. (Freire, 1979, p. 45)

Conscientização saturates the immanent and the transcendent dynamic of the human being in its dialogical nexus with history. The commonalities between Freire's "conscientização" and Nkrumah's "consciencism" are evident. Such commonalities are so clear that we found intriguing the absence on Nkrumah's matrix in Freire's reason—an issue that is worth to be explored in future research. The spiritual dimension of Freire's argument is quite undermined in our field—exceptions noted in the work of intellectuals such as hooks, West, Darder, and others—find the same profound political latitude in Nkrumah's rationale.

If philosophy is to provide the foundations of knowledge and theoretical existence, as we can see in Platonism, then it entails careful inquiry into the essential and ontological dimensions of the real world. In the process, we must overcome the thoughtless opinions of common sense that remain captive solely to empirical reality and sensible appearances, and use philosophy as a wise interlocutor between knowledge, empiricism, science, and more. In this way, Kwame Nkrumah (1964) sees philosophy's origin in "theological speculations" (p. 29), embracing natural rights and providing "principles to inform any political theory and law" (p. 30). Putting this all together, philosophy becomes the "conscientização" itself, which Nkrumah calls "philosophical consciencism," therefore,

> If philosophical consciencism initially affirms the absolute and independent existence of matter, and holds matter to be endowed with its pristine objective laws, then philosophical consciencism builds itself by becoming a reflection of the objective, in conceptual terms, of the unfolding of matter. (Nkrumah, 1964, p. 87)

This is a process that becomes, not a process that is. Such processes ameliorate what is, leading me to conclude that the similarities with Freire's (1974) conscientização, are once again embedded in cultural identity and spirituality. This process leads to inner enhancement, but also to a transformation from a stage of ideological-being to one of analysis and transformation of the inner state of "being" as it responds to the external environment. Nkrumah (1964) adds,

> It is evident at least that philosophical consciencism cannot issue in a closed set of ethical rules, a set of rules which must apply in any society and at any time. Philosophical consciencism is incapable of this because it is itself based upon a view of matter, as caught in the grip of an inexorable dialectical evolution. (p. 88)

Such processes promote evolution and progress, acting as road map to the decolonization of intellectual terms and discourse—for colonized African peoples, especially, but also in the Global South and beyond. They find fertile ground in dialectics and seek to change the dialectics of a specific matter to bring about desirable and necessary change. According to Nkrumah (1964), "consciencism" has no room for parallelism, rather it claims both a mind-body problem and its resolution. Dialectics need to evolve into action, wherein ethics predict and insist upon the worthiness of each individual. This philosophical approach seeks to ensure that the cardinal principles of ethics are effective, which generates the clear edict that education should be an attempt to enhance, protect, and amplify the inherent value of every human "being." Such philosophical concepts as "consciencism" and "conscientização" are interdependent with spirituality. Spirituality is the force that awakens and impels the conscience into the modes of conscientização and/or consciencism in the fight against the realities of "colonialism, imperialism, disunity, lack of development" (Nkrumah 1964, p. 98), not to mention neoliberalism and its quasi-omnipresent tentacles.

Freire's "conscientização" and Nkrumah's "consciencism" elucidates the other's point of view; it shifts our thinking to the deep structures that each individual naturally contains, thereby exalting humanity, generosity, selflessness, and benevolence. Both concepts are right at the epicenter of counter hegemomic liberatory praxis of the epistemic subject of the Global North and Global South—as Paraskeva (2022) would put it. In *Critical Pedagogy*, Freire (1972) emphasizes the need for self-consciousness, not to reflect on what we ourselves think, but to interrogate how/why we and others might think what we do—and thereby enables us to avoid thoughtlessly ingesting the unilateral, ideologically biased thinking that is imposed on us by social systems, including those involved in education. Freire echoes Anzaldúa's (2002a, p. 4) advocacy for the recognition of spiritual intimacy as a form of inquiry. Moreover, both Nkrumah (1964) and Freire (1972) paralleled Keating's (2002, p. 8) proclamation that "radical change—material, spiritual, personal, political—is possible." The struggle against coloniality and its oppressive matrix, couldn't be successful out of the autochthonous epistemic yarn, one of the enzymes of such yarn relies on the spiritual inquiry of the world. Such inquiry fosters spirituality as a critical dynamic (Dantley, 2005b). Dantley (2005b, p. 655)—who places spirituality at the center of the African American struggle against racialized segregation—argues that the "African American experience is both spiritual and esoteric with two major structural aspects; one that consists in a critical reflection and the other based on performative creativity." Spirituality, he (2005) adds, provides African Americans with "inner strength to critically reflect upon the rituals and forms of life in the U.S. that are often grounded on racism, classism, and sexism."

As I was able to examine earlier, Kirylo and Boyd (2017) further developed Freire's concept of "conscientização" to acknowledge the lived message he advocated by challenging the church to shift from individual piety to prophetic action, a shift that clearly relates to (what should be) the primary mission of education. Classic philosopher Socrates helps sustain this line of thinking with his focus on enabling the individual to become conscious of the self.[2] This process has to do with emancipation, liberation. Yet, in *Education*, Harmon (1952) claims that education in itself should be more than just emancipatory—it should entail the coalescence and development of one's inner-outer true "being." Given this internal-external/holistic aspect, I have no alternative than to boldly argue that "consciencism" and "conscientização" constitute a spiritual call, a call that materializes through what West (1998) terms as prophetic pragmatism, that a concrete spiritual footprint with the political battles to confront and smash inequality, oppression, segregation.

There is substantial self-studies and scientific work that gives voice to the silent, claiming the need for the subject to have context. The separation of the context from the one subjected to the context is often silenced, too. With its biased policies and teacher training programs, public education and curriculum has become permeated with the *creative destruction* wisely articulated by Harvey (2011). To argue that there is a scientific cure for our current social problems is to underestimate the powerful claims of students and those who have endured the system previously. Nowadays, our policies are based on information generated by think tanks and lobbyist groups aiming at "political support" (Saltman, 2016), and representing a global agenda of human exploitation via the corporatization of schools. The more technicfied education become—under the fallacy of scientific management ideologies—the more difficult becomes any attempt to engage in the spiritual/metaphysical dimension of human being's temporality.

It is now undeniable that, more than ever, the "highest" endeavor of our current educational guidelines is to deploy a curricular enterprise that distances humankind[3] from its rights. This system ignores people's/students'/children's desperate pleas to be decolonized. But this can't happen through yet more scientific and theoretical analysis. It must be driven by consciencism and conscientização. To that same end, we also need to decolonize research, in order to look for genuine justifications for returning to primary sources, the context where silenced voices can teach us the hermeneutics of life. There is no tutorial for educators to address such everyday life events and the heretofore silenced personal thoughts and experiences of students in the classroom. But it is clear that we need an education for life, meaning for life as individuals, as "beings"—and not as mere commodities. Decolonization of words, research, concepts, and curriculum can begin to engender "being"-centered solutions.

Here, we have the opportunity to discuss spirituality in education again. If we look at the mess we are in, we must agree that the current functionality of schools—insofar as they only transfer certain limited, "scientific" knowledge to students—will not be sufficient to foster (or even accommodate) the necessary advancements of technology and society, not to mention the student-"beings" themselves. We might find ourselves as a society becoming less positivist and humanist, but the educational system is still the most obvious place to measure the forces working for the new world order to which we are subjected. No concrete—dominant or counter dominant—methodology or rationalization process can lead us out of this chaos. All of the potential Eurocentric solutions humanism has to offer have been exhausted.

Janson (2015) claims that examining spirituality may help us come to understand the trap we are in, and that it will probably lead us to not just think about and fight against the dominant discourse, but to act beyond the bounds of what is imprisoning us as "beings." Similarly, time spent in reflection, analyzing our attitudes and thoughts and the outcomes of the same, will certainly lead us to a better, more emancipatory, inclusively systematic hermeneutics of education. As previously stated, Tinker (2008) defines spirituality as a process to be followed towards liberation and emancipation. Isn't that what we are looking for? This practice is at the core of conscientização and consciencism. It is thus impossible to separate spirituality from reflection. As I have argued, spirituality is a form of inquiry (Anzaldúa, 2002b).

Spirituality does not arise or flourish out of nothing, even though many think it does. It comes embedded in a lot more than we realize. Let's not forget that it is a fundamental element of the essence of who we are. It exists and grows in the gap between theory and praxis, as Tinker (2008) so strongly stressed. This gap is where reflection and responsibility must be the torches that elucidate the purity of spirituality. This certainly holds true for Christianity, as a co-participant active in this process since the beginnings of Western recorded history. At the end of the day, spirituality ends up representing the "truth" that we believe and enact. As I believe Socrates has something to say to us, so, let's delve into the self for a moment.

Socrates was a watershed figure in ancient philosophy, so much so that the philosophers before him are traditionally called pre-Socratics. Indeed, Socrates brought a significant shift in discussions about truth and knowledge. The early philosophers were concerned about finding the foundation (arké) of all things. Socrates, for his part, was more interested in our relationships with others and with the world. Strangely enough, Socrates wrote nothing. All we know of him is thanks to his disciples, particularly Plato. From what was recorded by his followers, we know that Socrates' ideas were very much inspired by the inscription at the entrance to the temple of Delphi: Know thyself.

To understand the meaning of this phrase, Foucault (2006, p. 197) suggests we must inscribe in it a more general strategy of self-care, because taking time to turn inward in tranquility often allows an individual to gain access to the truth. But what kind of truth? And, what is truth? Whose truth? Who has benefited historically? Obviously, we are not speaking of just any truth, such as the chemical formula of water, but of that truth which is capable of transforming the subject into its own true "being."

Socrates, in those ancient times, recognized how time spent with yourself, in reflection, is a way to not just examine "your own" self but also to discover how others look at you. He recommended this solid and dependable method to promote consciousness/awareness/knowledge of the self, but it also inspires intellectual and spiritual growth. It functions as a sort of psychological fertilizer, bringing clarity, improved attitude, clear decision-making, and honesty. It leads to better outcomes, because you understand your limits, abilities, and needs, along with those of others. So, borrowing from Socrates and Foucault, I would like to dig a little deeper into the ideas of "truth" and spirituality, and the correlations between them. As I argued before, these two aspects—knowing/trusting oneself and knowing/trusting/following one's conscience—provide the foundation for being intellectually honest, precisely through the concept of "whose honesty."

The journey to have access to truth, however, is by no means a purely intellectual act. It sometimes requires certain sacrifices, renunciations, purifications, of which Socrates provides an example. Socrates claimed to have a mission from God to exhort the Athenians, whether they were old or young, to stop taking care of things, and instead to take care of themselves. This "calling" made him devote himself entirely to philosophy and to dialogical practice (a special form of dialogue, called maieutic),[4] through which he made his interlocutor perceive the inconsistencies of his discourse and self-correct, thereby producing self-consciousness/awareness.

In other words, the "truths" that lead us towards a state of enlightenment—quite an epistemicidal stage (Paraskeva, 2016, 2018, 2021a, 2022)—are not the product of study but the fruits of a practice, one that involves constant reflection on actions and attitudes as well as how to modify them to become a better person. It is as if life is a work of art in which we are shaping and perfecting ourselves over the course of our existence. Pinar's (1998) "not ready yet question" comes to mind, since we are always in a process of amelioration, constantly searching to grow as "beings." Eventually, as we develop our humanity, we ask ourselves why we accumulate the types of knowledge taught in schools, and we realize the answer is simply to infinitely increase our knowledge. It becomes apparent that we—early on!—entered a race, an endless race, in which we never questioned whether our efforts would result in the promised benefits.

Socrates, however, saw the search for truth as a path of personal and social self-mastery, because, when we take care of ourselves, we change our relationships with others. Many say critical thinking is easily mistaken for just having an idea in the head, as if it was the same thing as ordinary thinking, rather being rational, comparing, analyzing, and having an opinion. As mentioned above, Tinker (2008) argued that "it must to come to mean much more than that" (p. 151). That is, the search for truth, to really matter, must bridge the internal and external, linked by the forces that impel us to reflect, grow, and live our best impulses.

For example, we sometimes see how artists externalize what is inside of them in such a way that their work becomes even more than the simple expression of cultural fact. Such art expresses who they/we are as "beings"—and is perceived in turn by us in much the same ways as the artwork itself was produced, since "how we make meaning is also cultural and thus connect us back to our cultural selves" (Tinker, 2008, p. 43). In other words, cultural expression and consumption/perception, too, are rooted in spirituality, so it makes sense to define culture in order to understand how spirituality and culture circulate around identity.

So far, I have argued that spirituality is a matter of honesty, call, activism, and inquiry and as intrinsically a human right—as freedom. I delved into the "consciencism" and "conscientização" processes and the complex aspects of spirituality as path towards liberation and emancipation of the identity. In doing so, and along with West (1988) and Dantley (2005) I advocate spirituality as critical consciousness and prophetic pragmatism to accurately grasp the social construction of "truth," one that cannot ignore Pinar's (1998) "not ready yet" punctum as Paraskeva (2022) would put it. As I have argued, spirituality is an ethical and identity matter. Next, I turn to a vigorously debated discussion of identity and the ethics around this contested term.

## 7    Whose Identity!

For many years, we have been seeing a "complicated conversation" (Pinar, 2004)—although not necessarily just (Paraskeva, 2022)—in social science/cultural studies about the possibility (or impossibility) of defining identity, as well as how it can best be studied and analyzed. Theorists wonder whether identity can be negotiated to such a degree that it genuinely changes, or if it is a shadow that follows the individual everywhere they go, continuously unfolding independent of place, culture, and language. Discussions about this subject are clearly volatile and full of abstract elements (including spirituality), but it is still worthwhile to endeavor to understand identity, since it carries an ocean of arguments, knowledge, and feelings, and both represents and contains the uniqueness of the individual's response to their cultural and geographic worlds and everything within them.

Since the content under discussion is dense enough, I will focus on the essence of identity. As spirituality is an identity matter it is crucial to ask if identity can be altered or fragmented through external attempts to impose change? If so, what are the implications of that alteration and/or fragmentation, especially within the educational sphere, in which social structures, at the very least, can presumably be reengineered? Hall (1996) posits that everyone needs identity, but departs from the idea that every person is an "individual" carrying and enacting their "oneness"; instead, he sees people and their identities as "never singular but multiply constructed across different, often intersecting and antagonistic, discourses, practices and positions" (p. 4). What we do know is that this "inner core which first emerged when the subject was born continues or identical with itself—through the individual's existence" (Hall, 1996, p. 275). In this model, the essence of the self is the identity that, over the course of its life, will be unfolded and continuously enhanced, not autonomously and self-sufficiently, but formed and readjusted in relation to others and the social environment. The classic sociological view is that identity is formed in the interaction between self and society, the inside and the outside:

> The notion of the sociologic subjected reflected the growing complexity of the modern world and awareness that this inner core of the subject was not autonomous and self-sufficient, but was formed in relation to significant others, who mediated to the subject the values, meanings and symbols—the culture—of the world he/she inhabited. (Hall, 1996, p. 275)

There is no question about the importance of identity for the spiritual individual and the social world. However, given the scope of this work, I aim more to delve into my concerns about why identity, for uncountable decades a stabilizing factor in society, has now devolved into a matter of research defunding, absent from curriculum platforms and not valued by the educational system? Why is it that while identity is clearly embedded within social culture "where everybody is," and in spirituality "where everybody reflects," we have not yet constructed its inner intellectual/educational topographic boundaries and protected it as a form of self-ownership akin to sacred sovereignty?

As I stated above, for thousands of years, identity was "the" key factor that defined the individual and gave society its principles around both individuality and interactions/relationships. With the expansion and advancement of Western Eurocentric modernity, the attempt to pluralize identity is visible. Note that I am censuring the pluralization of the identity. Identity is unique, uno-inner-individual. But for what reason, if identity is a socio-constructed label (Pinar, 1974) that identifies the individuality of the individual? I'll address this more precisely below, but, for now, I want to articulate the reasons underlying pervasive attempts to destabilize identity, which, as Hall (1996) claims, fragment the individual by disrupting, moving, and removing the stable anchors that tether us to ourselves and our communities. Hall (1996) argues that identity is increasingly in danger, not because it is no longer important to inner development and social well-being, but rather because we are subsumed in a culture of disruption and fragmentation that continually shifts and redefines the anchors we need to ground and build our lives. This disruption is deeply hidden in the curriculum, a stark example of what Santos (2018) points out in his "the sociology of absences."

Please allow me to express myself as part of society, as someone who observes and interacts with the social world. I believe that never before have the issues of gender, race, immigration, ethnicity, class, and other differences reached such a social boiling point, regardless of the turmoil and chaos we have seen over the course of history. As I have highlighted, we live in a moment paced by absurdism (Paraskeva, 2021b). Today, a graduate student in the social science field is already aware of the myriad major conflicts occurring all over the globe. Massive waves of immigration, the pandemic, climate changes and the recent war in Ukraine, has exacerbated many of these divides. Culture often has been supplanted, liberty and freedom forced to incline over the political debate as new normal. The cultural identity that frames the so-called postmodern era is not the same as the cultural identity that framed societies a century ago. The perception of identity has evolved, but not, frankly, in such a way as to ameliorate most people's lives. I am not debating the greatness of modernity or the struggles of the past. I do contend, however, that a curriculum that prepares, produces, and certifies social zombies (Giroux, 2011) is deeply and inherently connected with a particular form of cultural politics (Apple, 1995); by philosophically justifying, creating, and perpetuating a curriculum designed to "improve" humanity, this system produces particular forms of identity while crushing others. As the world faces uncontrolled waves of immigration, one sees the attempt to put policies in place that pave the way for the brutality of the identical (Han, 2019). Despite such social havoc, it seems that our field remains lost in irrelevant minutia to help address the global social malaise. Such social insensibility was identified by Huebner (1976) decades ago when he proclaimed the moribund state of our field. Unfortunately, decades later, it seems that Huebner prognosis was accurate.

Returning to where we started in this section, Hall (1996) describes how identity typically unfolds and takes its various forms and then continues to be shaped, from the very beginning and then throughout life. Relationships with others, conflicts and their resolutions, voluntary and involuntary cultural exchanges and experiences—all allow an individual's identity to take a unique form that is nonetheless full of commonalities. We need a social atmosphere to become individuals, to make space for identity. But to identify ourselves with whom? The very word identity implies the social/cultural aspect through which ethnic, racial, linguistic, religious, and other common/shared cultures are internalized and negotiated; hence, lived identity is where the sense of *belonging* naturally flourishes. In contrast, postmodern education attempts to produce identities as volatile and malleable, instead of anchored. The fragmentation of culture starts with this neglect of the backbone of identity, the social piece. For years, particularly in schools, our capacity for dealing with other's ways of "being" has been depleted because of stressful, noisy, environments, even while our socialization time has been reduced. The sites where negotiations around identity occur have been transformed, due to, in Hall's (1996) view,

> the fragmentation of the cultural landscapes of class, gender, sexuality, ethnicity, race and nationality which gave us firm locations as social individual. These transformations are also shifting our personal identities, undermining our sense of ourselves as integrated subjects. This loss of a stable "sense of self" is sometimes called the dislocation or de-centering of the subject. This set of double displacements—de-centering individuals both from their place in social and cultural world, and from themselves—constitutes a "crises of identity" for the individual. (p. 276)

This dislocation can be attempted/inflicted in many different ways, as, over the decades, modernity has been reshaping and replacing the myriad catalysts of individuals' lives. Interaction between the self and society is fundamental to the "inner core of essence that constitutes the real "me" (Hall, 1996, p. 33). Somehow, this vital interaction—heretofore a continuous dialog with the cultural world—is redefined, refined, and implemented in schools via a one-way monologue of repetition and standardization, deploying a one-size-fits-all methodology designed to produce one "right" type of person. In this context, the friction between the self and society prevents the free, natural, and continuous unfolding of the self that is so necessary to healthy identity formation. We do know that the unfolding and establishment of one's identity depends on shared experiences, so when environments, relationships, symbols, and specific cultures, such as educational systems and curricula, are manipulated to affect the process of identity formation and prevent deviation, both natural interactions and people themselves are sidelined. This is the hallmark of the quest to achieve ever more "modern" population. Modernity is not just the simple replacement of hardship with the ease of technology, nor is it just about the amelioration of transportation, science, and so on. Modernity,

> is not only defined as the experience of living with rapid, extensive and continuous change, but is a highly reflexive form of life in which social practices are constantly examined and reformed in the light of incoming information about those very practices, thus constitutively altering their character. (Giddens, 1990, p. 37)

There is not much to say about identity without taking its exterior aspects into consideration. The multitudes of people, events, things, and symbols that constitute our social world, the "modes of life brought into being by modernity have swept us away from all traditional types" (Giddens, 1990, p. 21) of social-personal identity constitution. This shift, driven by oppressive modern Western Eurocentric forces, has produced unforeseen and unprecedented changes, extending into the core of even the most intimate and personal elements of our existence. From one decade to another, modernity has ripped apart the time-honored conditions humans have lived under and within for centuries. These traditional lifeways offered the individual certain key, integrally linked, formative personal-social traits—originality and belonging, meaning and understanding, worthiness and respect for others. Now, as Harvey (1989) claims, the social sphere engenders "a never-ending process of internal ruptures and fragmentations within itself" (p. 12), displacing the individual and distancing them from their relationship and their communities. In this way, "the "being" is constantly being de-centered or dislocated by forces outside of itself" (Laclau, 1990, p. 12). Modern society, and specifically the postmodern education it produces, has no basis or precedent for identifying/connecting the individual with any intimate and personal feature of his/her/their self or his/her/their past. This displacement and de-centering of the subject entails the denial of one's oneness in the guise of a claim for modernity's advancement. It produces a curriculum that neither allows students to look into their "selves" nor enables them to seek or return to whatever can anchor/answer their daily questions of existence.

I contend that it is impossible to touch upon spirituality without delving into the undeniable and ordinary truth of identity. I also argue that any attack on identity matters is an attack on the human being spiritual dynamics. It ignores the spiritual reason that structures the human being's existence in the world. Fraser (2000) offers a compelling rationale in this respect, one she frames in terms of recognition and redistribution. A full and just debate on identity needs to recognize spirituality as a major category for a massive proportion of individuals, crossing class, race, gender, and other social dynamics. In turn, any policy directed towards recognition and redistribution (Fraser, 2000) must also integrate matters of identity and, thus, spirituality. As she argues,

> struggles for recognition can aid the redistribution of power and wealth and can promote interaction and cooperation across gulfs of difference. Everything depends on how recognition is approached. I want to argue here that we need a way of rethinking the politics of recognition in a way that can help to solve, or at least mitigate, the problems of displacement

and reification. This means conceptualizing struggles for recognition so that they can be integrated with struggles for redistribution, rather than displacing and undermining them. It also means developing an account of recognition that can accommodate the full complexity of social identities, instead of one that promotes reification and separatism. (Fraser, 2000, p. 119)

In Fraser's (2000) terms, we can either absolutely, consciously, actively understand that battles for recognition and redistribution must honor the enormous importance of key aspects of the inner self, such as spirituality, or we can resign ourselves to both battles being unquestionably compromised. The quest for social justice is also a quest for identity. And the struggle for recognition is also metaphysical.

Identity thus "is centered author of social practice, or to restore an approach which places its own point view at the origin of all historicity—which in short words, leads to a transcendental consciousness" (Foucault, 1990, p. XIV). In this sense, spirituality is central to identity, similar to a suture wherein both parts of the abstract "being" are stitched together in order to give essence to the individual's existence, and without which there would be no "being." Without this synchronic entanglement and interconnectivity, there is no totality of the "being" in itself, which is then also expressed in that "being's" total and proper fit in society. I do not intend to affirm that each identity "is" the proper fit as a final completed and sealed individual, but that the current process of "never being a proper fit" attempts to lead us to uniformity, when we are in truth all different from one another. The proper fit can only contribute to human "being" when it is an ongoing, evolving mechanism. It needs to happen as we exist and grow, with our environments—including, above all, schools—cultivating rather than pruning us as we do so. Only then can we experience freedom and authenticity.

Hall (2000) claims that "identification is, then, a process or articulation, a suturing, an over-determination not a subsumption." This process involves constant flux and transformation, along with careful attending to the inner demands of the human being, so as to foster self-awareness and improvements in life and relationships. It directs us all towards the valuable traits of rationality and intelligence. At the very moment that we disallow such processes or standardize the proper fit between the individual and society, we begin to oppress by preventing the "being" from attending to the claim of its oneness. The proper fit for me is a stage of "being," the capacity to be on the road towards completeness simply by "being"; on this journey, I can be a "being" who is "not ready yet," but who knows I have my entire life to become ready. This stage is what allows the individual to absorb, accept, interiorize, exchange, and carry on in his/her/their ways of being identified.

Although collective identity also grapples with societal impositions, Appiah (2005) claims that the labels society has inscribed on the group play an even bigger part in the identification process of the individual; from this social identification, individual identity descends from or emanates from the larger "whole" in a structural way, so that "the label plays a role in shaping the way the agent makes decisions about how to conduct a life, in the process of the construction of one's identity" (p. 66). He argues against the idea that the process of unfolding identity happens to the individual alone and independently (Appiah, 2005). Instead, we should operate on the principle that individuals identify themselves via already existing terms, and, from there, tend to align themselves with the aims of those terms; further, these same terms also determine how the individual will be identified by society:

> It requires the availability of terms in public discourse that are used to pick out the bearers of identity by way of criteria of ascription, so that some people are recognized as members of the group—woman, man; blacks, whites; straight, gays. The availability of these terms in public discourse requires both that it be mutually known among most members of the society that the labels exists and that there be some degree of consensus on how to identify those to whom they should be applied. (Appiah, 2005, pp. 66–67)

The divisive nature of our curriculum forms and their ultimate goal of cultural uniformity—based on one size fits all pedagogy—torpedoes any identity that challenges such eugenic uniformity and maculates our schools and curriculum's social justice mission (Huebner, 1975; Macdonald & Zaret, 1975). I do sympathize to some degree with Appiah's interpretation and certainly it is well-dissected and grounded in many aspects of the social and biological fields where my concerns are raised. Appiah (2005) brought me a great deal of understanding about why the postmodern world endeavors so assiduously to fragment society's coherence and fog identity's inner meanings. Taking Appiah's approach, the main channels where society is already inscribed confirm the completely corporate origins of neoliberal education—and the "labels" society deploys have been entirely formulated according to corporate desires in order to remove the safe anchors that would otherwise ground the "being's" ongoing, unfolding identity. Such "labeled" identities have been erroneously aggregated to individual identities, leaving an open field for individual identities to be misunderstood and vulgarized. Identity thus now depends on whatever the current volatile social culture is presenting as style. The rhetoric of diversity has hybridized new cultural identities, wherein most of us have something in common, while we leave behind what we originally were in order to belong or fit in. We cannot move away from the social cultural piece. Indeed, if we remember that it is the suture that unites culture to the unfolding of identity, we must recognize that we intrinsically need our communities and societies. Separated, there can be no proper fit, no belonging whatsoever.

Thus, if culture is constructed via the fragmentation of the natural, then the oneness of each "being," which is the metaphysical piece, will be fogged, obscured. As the aim of this work is to delve into what happens when the human right to spirituality is denied to us, I must ask how a "being" can be conscious of the self if the self has been clouded from his/her/their sight? This prevention of self-awareness is surely a matter of "controlling the destiny of civilization," as Pinar (2019) claims. We only need to look around us to see that our culture has traded spaces and time previously dedicated to community practices (*language, celebrations, rituals, family traditions, community exchanges, communitarian approaches, humanitarian feelings*, and *respect for human life*) for technology.

I am not condemning technology as a potential enhancement of human life. The essence of such traditions and community exchanges has been changed and recolonized obscuring the self-awareness of who am I for who should I be. However, I am not totally rebuking technology. After all, many of the greatest benefits and freedoms in modern civilization arose from technology. It seems to me, however, that the saved turned on the savior. Pinar (2019) notes,

> Not in the remembrance of things past or at risk taken in the name of the future, social action is replaced by proceduralism in the field of curriculum studies conveyed simplistically in the so-called Tyler rationality, wherein the implementation of objectives is constantly evaluated, creating s self-referential set of cul-de-sacs reiterating what is already. Because proceduralism leads nowhere but where one began, the objectives-evaluation axis tends towards intensification, creating, a cult of efficiency. (p. 100)

Pinar pinpoints how and why such advancement snowballed, impacting not only the battlefield of identity formation but the very roots of this battle itself. In this vein, Hall (1992), too, brings our attention to the fact that identity is constructed within the play of power and exclusion. Pinar (2019) explains that freedom as a state of "being" has been changed into the capacity to possess products and consume services:

> In the private sphere, however, freedom is recast as choice of consumer goods; in the public sphere, it converts to control, the demand that freedom flourish so that whatever is profitable can be pursued. In new products and increased productivity, technology and capitalism conflate. At the same time, in its tendency toward intensification, technology undermines freedom and efficiency, submerging us in minutiae, tying us to the present moment, and interminable atemporal present in which we become preoccupied with the next sensation, the next "bit" of communication or information, focused on the expectation that momentarily "something" will happen, a new website will stimulate. (p. 100)

When people enter such a state of alienation, it is only through the exercise of spirituality and the practices of "consciencism" and "conscientização" that they are able to reflect upon their lost "freedom" as a state of "being." We often exchange the state of "being" for the acquisition of material possessions, thinking that such things can free us from exclusion. But it is more than that. Technology as a representation of modernity, "not only structures how we apprehend the world, it becomes a "mode" of "being" that "transforms" how "we know, think and will" (Pinar, 2019, p. 100). Let me exemplify this state of postmodern intellectual and emotional malnutrition. Imagine you deliver a speech about an endangered species to a specific group of people and, at the end, the only thing they can think of is "What zoo can I see that animal in?" In this mode, none of your audience will think about how and why such species are going extinct or what can we do to prevent such tragic extinctions.

Such a state of intellectual anemia transforms the exterior environment into a stage for mere subjective observation. Now, let's at least be honest. Given this situation, what do we expect in the classroom? What should be the task of the pedagogue and curriculum theorists? (Huebner, 1999). Or, how do we expect our children to leave the classroom, when done "learning?" Minds "nurtured" in this context are unable to understand what democracy means, as their teachers are not able to offer a democratic education in this context. To be clear, the student is not the problem. Neither am I pointing at teachers. Instead, I am looking at the curriculum.

The curriculum—what is to be taught and how it is to be taught—represents the most fertile terrain for student growth. If the teacher is allowed to sow a healthy seed (what) in a healthy environment (how), it will germinate and grow mightily, thereby significantly improving both the individual being's life and community, along with society as a whole. Pinar (2019) quotes Grant on what constitutes a good society: "one in which as many as possible came to the liberation of the soul. Society existed to promote the education of the persons, not vice versa" (p. 1).

Above, I claimed that the exterior social becomes "me" or the "I am" within subjectivity. To have the expected subjectivity within, we need to depart from the exterior, which happens with the teaching and the cultivation of what we need to be fruitful. Pinar (1999) overtly claims that educators have shied away from power and politics in their thinking, perhaps because of the unfortunate connotations of both words. But the curriculum is the ground where teachers have to enact their politics and exercise power. Tillich (1954) argues that in "any encounter of man with man, power is active, the power of personal radiation expressed in language and gestures, in the glance of an eye and the sound of the voice, in face and figure and movement, expressed in what one is personally and what one represents socially" (p. 87). Such power can indeed be transmitted to the students via such curriculum and classroom relationships. However, educators need to use the appropriate language with those who will receive the information in order to, through language, reach the maximum deliverance of knowledge so the maximum of outcomes and rationalization might be produced. A noneffective communication-relationship will generate a narrow or limited intellectual outcome. How can teachers communicate anything to students if they don't have the power of the right words to empower the deliverance and exchange of the knowledge? That lack alone should enable—even force—teachers to run away from the formal/traditional curriculum. It should help them understand that, throughout the educational process, the goals, purposes, and objectives of and for life itself are a crucial part of the existential journey of their students. As consciousness of existence over time emerges, temporality arises. Human temporality (personal history, memory, the whole life) is integrated into education when students are allowed to study and analyze aspects of life through language (spoken and non-spoken) and its meanings. This brings vitality into Freire's conscientização and/or Nkrumah's consciencism and "spiritual" self-development. In Freire and Nkrumah's proclamation, spirituality unfolds within specific contexts. Bringing the past into the future brings continuity and essential rootedness, as students emerge from yesterday into the future. Learning is not just today's forecasting of tomorrow's many possibilities but also threading the historicity of goals, purposes, and objectives as a claim for continuity—and a scaffolding for building the changes necessary for tomorrow:

> All of these categories are concerned with society's existence "in time" refer to man's concern for historical continuity which gives his social forms and institutions some kind of stability, yet vitality, as they emerge

from yesterday into tomorrow. Unfortunately, the educator's too easy acceptance of the function of or the necessity for purpose or objectives has replaced the need for basic awareness of historicity. (Pinar, 2008, pp. 238–239)

If teachers actually allow students to dive and submerge themselves in their own and others' historicity, the resulting modes of thought and learning may well lead to powerful tools that will be enormously useful in curriculum design. But the neoliberal curriculum is quite aware of humanity's temporality and is designed to obscure it from the daily educational process. The social conditions that one depends on can provide vital frameworks for personal development, yet, within the current prevalent system, they become disruptive instead of constructive, dehumanizing rather than uplifting, depleting rather than informing. This is because, in Macdonald's (1995) words,

> In order to become minimally human, an individual must learn how to interact with others and must operate through the prevalent symbolic system; and in the process, he must learn to "see" himself and his world as others see him. His basic quest is toward mastery of common understanding about status and roles, objectives and ideas, himself and others. (p. 19)

The curriculum eliminates a just social time and space in which a multiplicity of identities organically rub against each other, instead increasing pro-system/pro-"success" activities, claiming that modernity has no place for those who don't know how to multitask or don't condone the exigencies of the future. Giroux (1981) frames such curricula as formed and perpetuated under the yoke of positivism. As I argue before, under such yoke there is no space for "spirituality" (Huebner, 1985b). Learning, "is a trivial way of speaking of the journey of the self" (Huebner, 1985b, p. 405).

These deterministic curricula reshape and patrol the boundaries between past, present, and future by reconstructing history and stories so that students' concerns for the past, for their whole selves, are alienated by a sold-out, artificially engineered hope for the future. This process castrates the very terrain where students would have the chance of finding themselves, where they might otherwise reflect upon and pursue their most essential questions about the meaning of existence. When this absolutely basic quest is negated, the personality-identity continues to be unfold—according to the social conditions provided. In this context, the personality-identity will be bent to the will of the industrialized modern Eurocentric positivist and capitalist curriculum.

This curriculum socializes the individual, blocking out multiple social aspects and centering others, thereby molding students into a certain type of human—while never nurturing the "being." As Macdonald (1995) explains,

> The manner by which the individual is "socialized" is also of a great importance. The degree of understanding, love, acceptance, recognition, hostility and aggression, for example, will have deep consequences upon his personality formation. So, the content of his world and the process which he encounters will be set by his particular social conditions. Social conditions are minimal conditions. They provide a framework by which the individual becomes human. (p. 19)

Such social processes regularly occur in schools, where students spend most of their lives.

Macdonald (1995) discusses how certain activities foster becoming, describing the ordinary, necessary process of becoming as creative realization (p. 21), the root of true satisfaction. While such becoming is clearly the heart and soul of identity, the curriculum supports only a very limited simulacrum of becoming. Without the true inclusion and self-reflection that are part of full becoming, there will be no proper fit (as explained above), and, furthermore, there will be no human development, no becoming a "being." Without becoming, there is only fragmentation. Curriculum thus lacks meaning for most people:

> When experience is meaningless, living is a state of general anxiety in the sense that present meaning schemes do not promote ego integration at higher levels, but reflect a process of disintegration which most often causes the ego to restrict its functioning in controllable areas. (Macdonald 1995, p. 20)

A curriculum without meaning—one that obliterates endless diverse and different epistemic forms—puts students in a state of shock and anxiety, blocking their creativity and human potential. No wonder, then, that the public educational system now has a devastatingly high proportion of students with emotional problems. At a very young age, children's human potential is incarcerated.

Without the benefit of exercising their spirituality and "being," students are forced to settle for materiality, further distancing them from vital dialogic encounters with their teachers and classmates. Pinar (2016) claims that, in modernity, "faith in technology has replaced religious kind (compassion), severing us from historic spiritual aspirations for human excellence" (p. 64).

The resulting displacement or de-centering of the subject has been just one brutal outcome of the postmodern curriculum. Curricula based on serving the labor market have sacrificed many human beings, both physically and metaphysically, "distracting students and teachers from the dialogical encounter-subjective presence through face-to-face communication and diverting us into screens where we are forced to comply with programs created by commercial entities with profit, not freedom in mind" (Pinar, 2015, p. 64). As I have claimed before, life's aim needs to be aligned with the process through which we want to achieve results—and with the outcome we actually hope for:

> If we want these children to have a deeper understanding of themselves, and a better comprehension of their own epoch, it will be necessary to introduce curriculum materials which are consistent with these ends. And, in addition, the curriculum materials must provide the opportunity for children to express attitudes, feeling, beliefs, interests, purposes, aspirations, and to discuss their activities, in and out of school. (Macdonald, 1995, p. 29)

The exchange of relevance for the ideology of achievement has filled our society with people who have lost their sense of themselves. Our educational and curriculum processes is conceived and enacted via the quantification of metaphysical-spiritual "beings"; this is justified and promoted as a valuable and productive effort to assess quality. Monitoring students and their development in numerical terms directly contradicts—and overtly hampers—their intelligence and freedom. Achievement is indeed pivotal to human beings; we are intelligent "beings" who are constantly creating. But, in the current educational system and curriculum, a terrible inversion of values occurs, wherein the product—and not the individual "being" and their creativity—is the goal. But my argument regards what is done with the hours students spend in class. If students are taught and allowed to acquire relevance and explore the meaning of life and their humanity in school, let home deal with the achievement aspect. In cases where students are not motivated to explore such relevance at home, the meaningful, kind and open-minded relationship in the classroom will allow such students to growth freely and accepted leading to at least a meaningful school life. In other words, what might students actually achieve once they know how to be reflective and generate relevance and real value in the world? The creative application of such tools of "being" would bring amazing gifts and progress to society and humankind.

I've intentionally allowed my discussion about spirituality in education and curriculum to meander through specific channels, such as social influence, curriculum, the act of exchanging experiences within and beyond the school landscape, in order to approach the subject from myriad angles. How is this process of unfolding identity fragmented? How are the anchors that ground and nurture learning and "being" fragmented? We need to first understand that an almost infinite number of attempts have been made to justify the current educational system, framing it as a crucial force for humankind's amelioration. The curriculum has enormous potential as a site for hope, transformation, and justice but, aside from its enforcement in schools, it has become merely an object of study, bereft of spirituality, personal history, dialogic interactions, and more. The areas of the curriculum wherein such needs might be reconstructed and addressed are increasingly left behind as model for curriculum design. In Huebner's (1966) words:

> It is possible, now that we are partially freed from vision-hindering busywork, that we can begin to make efforts to grasp the overall design of curriculum and to see how man's evolving techniques can be made subservient to man's evolving spirit? Educational environment and activity in the schools are symbolic of what man is today and what he wants to be tomorrow. The design of these symbols is a great art. The study of curriculum should be a preparation for this artistry. (p. 112)

Huebner (1966) clearly emphasizes the inner dynamics of the self when he references humanity's "evolving spirit." Over the years, our visions of curriculum and instruction have been colonized. Our intellects have been deprived of animation and sustenance in the perpetual, ruthless indoctrination of education that purports to fulfil the aims of the future. Yet we might well ask: Who has been in the future while also existing in the present? We have two ways of answering this query. Obviously, one response is: no one. Alternatively, we could argue that someone who has, in a certain sense, control over and knowledge of time spans the now and what is to come.

Let me delve into this matter a little bit. We educators have certainly been known to advocate for a more coercive and future-oriented curriculum on the grounds that it could advance students' possibilities for a better future. Indeed, for many decades, we have been promoting just such a curriculum, all along increasing technology's contributions, time in the classroom, and subjects covered, while reducing subjectivities and social attention. To void/avoid any dialog about transcendence and eternity, and maintain a "neutral" environment, "the transcendental" is not allowed in schools. As schools amplify coercion and future-orientation and actively discourage becoming, "being," and interconnection, we advance inexorably to...what, exactly? Education, according to

IDENTITY MATTERS                                                          145

Huebner (1985a), is only possible because humans are "beings" who can transcend themselves (p. 345) on a daily basis. Huebner (1962) helps us great deal:

> Man's confrontation with man is also a vehicle of transcendence through conversation, argument, love, economic conflict, and cooperation, even war and hate, and simply by comparison. That is "to be face to face with a man who speaks differently, wants other things, has other ways of life, or who sees the world differently is to be confronted with the inherent questions: "Who am I?" "Who is/she?" and "Why are we the way we are?" ... "if the questions are not dealt with honestly and openly, then they are eventually forced upon the confronters by conflict of interest, as is happening today in the integration baules, and the political and economic conflicts in our world. Inherent in each human confrontation is the possibility of growth and transcendence, for as man meets man, he meets the other; someone who differs and consequently someone who manifests other qualities of life and human value. The thinking, feeling, and seeing of others points to the way that I think, feel, and see, and suggests that the world that I think is out there is not the same world that the other thinks is out there. The inherent tension which exists between people because they do differ is, or can be, the source of new life and possibility. The question that must be asked is not How can man learn to make social encounters vehicles of human transcendence?" but "What are the barriers in today's conditioned world, in the world of technique and necessity, which prevent man's realization of his temporal nature?" (Huebner, 1962, p. 104)

To create a program, device, or plan (or curriculum) for future amelioration is indeed transcendent, as it entails looking into the past, projecting on the present, and implementing for the future; it implies to understand the human beings intricate temporality. this transcendence necessarily integrates the whole "beings," internal and external, of students. In so doing, education is able to fulfill its true aims, offering students an informative developmental process embedded in a spiritual-transcendent approach that allows teaching and learning to take place as an integral part of the journey of the self. In this context,

> [r]eligious language could be used as metaphor to look and speak about educational events and phenomena...in fact, that very process of transferring religious language to education strikes me as being foreign to what I am about, and in part would distort the story of my own life as educator... most of my professional career has been a search for more adequate and powerful ways to describe education. (Huebner, 1985, p. 358)

Throughout my analysis of the literature on spirituality, identity, and religion in the context of my educational experiences, I have seen many honest and bold statements. However, with Huebner (1985), I came to understand the principles and practices that naturally follow from the facts that, first, the majority of the world population is somehow religious, and that, second, no matter where these citizens go, in any hemisphere, any country, their identity will unfold within a society that is connected to some extent with religion. This undeniable fact is pivotal to the process of teaching and learning. For example, when encountering the abstractions of natural science, the process of deep thinking can become both an adventure in speculation around the (political, social) sources of/forces around the knowledge being imparted, and an opportunity to turn to elements of religion and religious language to delve with more certainty into the unseen, thereby integrating the transcendency of the human being as already dissected early in this work, since, in Huebner's (1985) perspective, "religious or theological language helps one to do that" (p. 358). Note that I sustain the claim that one *helps the other* in integrating transcendency but I do not sustain that; alone, religion or theology are the sole way to integrate the nurturing and transcendency to the "being." However, as cited above, the language used with traits of theology or religion must perfume the dialog between those who have such religious or theological background with the kindness, love, understanding and inviolability of one individuality and identity. Mirroring this learning approach, the process of conscientização is itself transcendent (in the sense discussed above). There can be no such transcendent processes—educational or personal—without profound reflection on subjects that are in a very real sense empty of the ways we usually think about time, space, and conclusions, all of which are generally pondered vis-à-vis mundane consequences that reside in and affect our future. Huebner (1985) states:

> Education is the lure of the transcendent—that which we seem is not what we are, for we could always be other. Education is the protest against present forms that they may be reformed and transformed. Education is the consciousness that we live in time, pulled by the inexorable Otherness that brings judgment and hope to the forms of life which are but the vessels of present experience. (p. 360)

The timelessness of certain spiritual concepts does not mean we do need to think about the future in order to grow intellectually and technologically. As a matter of fact, the chronology of time and space is what enables science to keep looking into new discoveries, specific phenomena, possibilities. We humans are always attempting to transcend our limits, whether via by such knowledge or through religion, love, power, and so on. These efforts are actually, to some extent, expressed in our curricular conundrums. On a practical level—and given all we've learned so far—using a hope- and being-promoting approach would in my opinion mean avoiding benchmarks and comparisons, as well as integrally linking growth with transcendence. Let's look into one view of curriculum planning that takes a similar stance, wherein:

> the process of arriving at these objectives, goals, or purposes involves inspection of the past; identification of forms of existence or aspects of life considered worthy of maintenance, transmission, or necessary for evolution; and the projection of these valued forms into the future. Basically, the determination of objectives is the search for the bridge between the past and the future; it is an argument over the degree of community necessary for change, or the amount of succession and duration. All of these categories are concerned with society's existence "in time" and refer to man's concern for historical continuity which gives his social forms and institutions some kind of stability, yet vitality, as they emerge from yesterday into tomorrow. Unfortunately, the educator's too easy acceptance of the function of or the necessity for purposes or objectives has replaced the need for a basic awareness of his historicity. (Huebner, 1999, p. 132)

As Huebner (1999) claims, the future is humanity facing itself in anticipation of its own potential for "being." The very core of "being" is a precondition of a full future. The inner questions humans ask themselves involve attempts to find their place—not in the present, but in their yearning for the self in the future, their dreams and hopes of what the purpose of the self will be; without this, there is no human "being," only a human who is barely "existing." It seems that there can be no existence without being tied to time and space—the past, where we came to exist; the present, who we are right now; and the future where our lives end...death. Such temporality can be explained if we but acknowledge, with Huebner (1990), that

> [n]o act of man is possible with reference solely to the past or solely to the future but is always dependent on their integration. Thus, for example, the future may be considered as the horizon against which plans are made. The past provides the means for their realization, while the present mediates and actualizes both. Generally, the future represents the possibility, and the past the basis, of a free life in the present. Both are always found intertwined with the present: in the open circle of future

and past there exists no possibility which is not made concrete by real conditions, nor any realization which does not bring with it new possibilities. This interrelation of reciprocal conditions is a historical process in which the past never assumes a final shape, nor does the future ever shuts its doors. Their essential interdependence also means, however, that there can be no progress without a retreat into the past in search of a deeper foundation. (p. 137)

Human identity unfolds in temporality, forged by social relations—which are not just physical—the conditions of the environment in which one lives, and how one accepts and interacts with oneself and other selves. During this process, the human being is always growing. And most people envision their end of life holding a certain dignity and satisfaction. For this to happen, everyone seeks to achieve success in different aspects of life. People may immigrate to another country, as I did, to improve their social and material or educational conditions. Throughout the course of their lives, many people's identities are reworked, adapted, proven by different social situations and conflicts. An important detail to consider is that, when people immigrate, they lose neither their identity nor their spirituality. However, the postmodern curriculum and school setting attempts to undervalue these travelers souls and reevaluate students as unfinished "beings." These travel with them, as do most of their customs, memories, language, religion, etc., which comprise their inner luggage.

The United States of America is, not the most, but a powerful, diverse, and inequal country, and certainly it has significantly influenced global society and education over the last hundred years or so. Anything that affects society, impacts education, and vice versa. As I am examining the roles of spirituality and its related notions of identity, community, and personal historicity, I would like to acknowledge the hybrid cultural identities (Bhabha, 1994) of those who immigrate to this country and must adapt to a new and different culture. Originally, this term was used in biology; in 1994, Bhabha introduced the concept in the social sciences, particularly in the areas of language and culture. Hybridity arises from the relations between colonizer and colonized, wherein dynamic interrelations and interdependencies generate the construction of (colonized) subjectivity, unfolding a hybrid cultural identity that is expressed in—and seen as—mimicry and ambivalence. Bhabha (1994) argues that all cultural statements and systems are constructed in a space called "the third space of enunciation" (p. 37), in which

> It is significant that the productive capacities of this third space have a colonial or postcolonial provenance. For a willingness to descend into that

alien territory...may open the way to conceptualizing an international culture, based not on the exoticism of multiculturalism or the diversity of cultures, but on the inscription and articulation of culture's hybridity. (p. 38)

It is important to understand that this term "the third space of enunciation" was used in postcolonial discourse and is still commonly used to describe cross-cultural exchanges, in which I would include cultural amalgamation. Struggles over identity representation are a daily experience for the hybrid individual. The fundamental questions are turned upside down, becoming about how one is seen, rather than how one sees oneself. The focus point is situated within the politics of the representation of the self, and not within the ways in which one's identity is produced and how one has externalized it. In the same sense, such identities are very much negated within the curriculum by not just the formation, production, and teaching of the contents but also in how these identities are expressed. Why do I say that? Even the ways non-native students answer questions and absorb knowledge are different from those of native students. They were taught with different techniques and methodologies, and their minds tend to follow the patterns of that teaching. Such teaching-expressions can be beneficial to students, yet the so-called postmodern curriculum uses labels to nullify and demonize such hybridity:

> Hybrid hyphenations emphasize the incommensurable elements—the stubborn chunks, as the basis of cultural identifications. What is at issue is the performative nature of those differential identities: the regulation and negotiation of those spaces that are continually remaking the boundaries, exposing the limits of any claim to a singular or autonomous sign of difference—be it class, gender or race. (Bhabha, 1994, p. 313)

The vast majority of immigrants leave their native countries behind to improve economically and otherwise by endeavoring to climb the social ladder. The desire/need to leave one's origins can be, too, a result of what colonization has done by empowering a single culture with the ultimate worth. In what is both a dispute and a reflection of hope and admiration between the colonized and the colonizer, the colonized tend to mimic the colonizer, existing in-between and in flux:

> The stairwell as a liminal space, in-between the designations of identity, becomes the process of symbolic interaction, the connective tissue that constructs the difference between upper and lower, black and white. The hither and thither of the stairwell, the temporal movement and passage

that it allows, prevents identities at either end of it from settling into primordial polarities. This interstitial passage between fixed identifications opens up the possibility of a cultural hybridity that entertains difference without an assumed or imposed hierarchy. (Bhabha, 1994, p. 5)

Without such dual practices, without expression of the original/home culture, the ever-growing identity can be severely affected. For immigrants and other multicultural humans, socialization in both/multiple cultural spaces is vital for this process to unfold to its fullest. Bhabha (1994) claims that immigrants can end up in between cultures (p. 313), and, as result, they develop hybrid cultural identities, enabling them to navigate doubly, amidst two or more separate yet coexisting cultures. Through such processes of inclusion, "new sites of identity are initiated, and innovative sites of collaboration and contestation take place" (Bhabha, 1994, p. 1):

> The migrations of modern times...have transplanted themselves according to some social, religious, economic or political determination, or some peculiar mixture of these. There has therefore been something in the removements analogous in nature to religious schism. The people have taken with them only a part of the total culture...The culture which develops on the new soil must therefore be bafflingly alike and different from the parent culture: it will be complicated sometimes by whatever relations are stablished with some native race and further by immigration from other than the original source. In this way, peculiar types of culture-sympathy and culture-clash appear. (Bhabha, 1994, p. 54)

The negative aspects are often seen in the partial or complete dismissal of one culture/ethnicity, followed by the marginalization of that ethnicity/culture, as seen especially in recent decades with Latin Americans. When the dispute is over IQ, grades, and other metrics, the impact goes even deeper. The learning deficit goes up when biometrics are taken in such populations, since the tests used are not measuring students' real IQ or potential intelligence, but rather looking into their immediate response to meaningless exercises in memorization. The effects of such students' inevitable hybridity are misunderstood by many of those in charge—who should know better, but have a lack of multicultural understanding or exposure. The immigrant or multicultural student, while often not "measuring up" according to the system in place, is, in fact,

> not only double-voiced and double-accented...but is also double-languaged; for it there are not only two individual consciousness, two voices, two

> accents, as there are socio-linguistic, consciousness, two epochs...that come together and consciously fight it out on the territory of the utterance...it is the collision between differing points of view on the world that are embedded in these forms...such unconscious hybrids have been at the same time profoundly productive historically: they are pregnant with potential for new world views, with new "internal forms" for perceiving the world in words. (Bhabha, 1994, p. 58)

Furthering the discussion, Hall (1996) claims that,

> actually, identities are about questions of using the resources of history, language and culture in the process of becoming rather than being: not "who we are" or "where we came from," so much as what we might become, how we have been represented and how that bears on how we might represent ourselves. (p. 4)

For du Gay (1996), the concept of identity has been a problem since its inception. Identity never reaches a palpable or physical stage where it becomes graspable, rather it is "disembedded or unencumbered" (p. 19). Usually, we hear such a claim when someone is lost emotionally, or want to claim a type of belonging, or attempt a proper fit. But, in fact, it du Gay (1996) is describing what it actually feels like to be in the process of absorbing and acculturating:

> Identity is a name given to the escape sought from that uncertainty. Hence "identity," though ostensibly a noun, behaves like a verb, albeit a strange one to be sure: it appears only in the future tense. Though all too often hypostasized as an attribute of a material entity, identity has the ontological status of a project and a postulate. To say "postulated identity" is to say one word too many, as neither is there, nor can there be any other identity but a postulated one. Identity is a critical projection of what is demanded and/or sought upon what is; or, more exactly still, an oblique assertion of the inadequacy or incompleteness of the latter. (p. 19)

In this way, I perceive identity as a—social constructed—"background" obligative force: From birth, it becomes a task the human being is striving to engage in/accomplish in order to find its "self," and to claim its oneness. In the political sphere, the ways identity is produced, unfolded, and matured are often questioned, and, as Hall (1996) points out, the matter is often taken up through practices of representation (p. 90), through which we basically avoid the cultural sphere. Given the abstract and volatile aspects of the term, this makes the subject of identity all the more vulnerable to speculation and hypothetical approaches in the political arena and elsewhere. However, the collective abstraction and sheer force of identity, culture, and spirituality make the trio the most unquantifiable and ungraspable combination in the social sciences. What is undeniable is that without addressing these three interrelated human elements—the fundamental aspects of "being"—we will never achieve personal, mental, social, or spiritual vitality. When any or all of these three are denied, human beings are bent into a miserable condition of mere existence. In this context, as Greene (1978) writes:

> The theme has been developed through the years as technology has expended, fragmentation has increased, and more people have felt themselves impinged upon by forces they have been unable to understand. As time has gone on, various writers and artists have articulated experiences of being conditioned and controlled. Contemporaneous with the advance of scientific and positivist thinking, therefore, an alternative tradition has taken shape, a tradition generated by perception of passivity, acquiescence, and what Thoreau called "quiet desperation." It is what may now be called the humanist tradition, if the human being is understood to be someone always in search of himself or herself, choosing himself or herself in the situations of problematic life. (p. 162)

In the same sense, it is only honest to say that, even if we were able to completely dissect everything about the inwardness and transcendency of humankind's thoughts and abilities, such comprehension and analysis are essentially meaningless without understanding that in order to *be someone* we need to ceaselessly search for the "self"—and that this ever-new search itself, in tandem with the resulting practices and actions, is what constitutes "being." Similarly, spirituality is where abstract words take form and become the essence of one's life. This intangible force moves the individual towards its oneness, the perfect self-fit. For example, the word "courage," mentioned at the beginning of this work, cannot be understood if not through a lived experience of what the essence of the word means, as expressed in deeds. I am not insinuating that we are lost just because we are constantly looking for our oneness as spiritual-metaphysical "beings." I'm stating that, by looking for our oneness and striving to protect our individuality while it unfolds, we find ourselves. The importance of this uniquely human activity is unparalleled:

> Only the preforming and specially the working self is fully interested in life and, hence, wide-awake. It lives within its acts and its attention is

exclusively directed to carrying its project into effect, to executing the action of its plan possible. This attention is an active, not a passive one. Passive attention is the opposite of full awareness. (Greene, 1978, p. 163)

On the other hand, education and curriculum are responsible for allowing and promoting a just environment wherein students are taught to move into a state of critical awareness, and, consequently, to develop a sense of moral agency as a fundamental part of their identity. Greene (1978) urges that "only under the rubric of arts and humanities such aim can be constructed" (p. 162). How can identity develop if the very core of the curriculum is immoral? Why immoral? Because it is immoral to remove the students themselves from the central aims of education. Education is for human beings; and humans are made for holistic learning and growing. Therefore, to remove the central piece, which in any curriculum should be the student as a whole "inner being," is to do the opposite of what is moral. Without centering students, we cannot even discuss democratic education. It is imperative that education not disconnect students from their forms of living, their history, their stories. Each student's life has significance and carries a special and unique intersubjectivity that must be honored by, and integrated into, their education. When students are encouraged by their teachers, and teachers are backed up by a just curriculum, these inclusive pedagogical practices provoke crucial questions about meaning that directly spur inner growth.

So much has been said about the fact that education is in collapse right now. Teachers are looking into any and every alternative in an effort to make things better, but the situation has become chaotic. Individuals seem to be losing who they are; moreover, they are losing their ability to live fully and becoming accustomed to merely existing. Loss of identity has deprived people of perspective for the future, and, as Greene (1978) claims, "when complications increase, the desire for essentials increases too" (p. 74). This is one of the many conundrums of identity mismatch, and just one facet of the venerable aims of postmodern corporate education. On the other hand, it fosters a most laudable and noisy silence, wherein, more than ever before, essential questions are clamoring to be answered.

So far, I have dissected and deconstructed the notions of identity and culture by theorizing the absence of certain essential stages of "being." In so doing, I was able to clarify a bit about what both the absence and presence of identity and cultural interdependence and intercompleteness would represent to humankind. I argued how spirituality is an identity matter and how our curriculum forms are a blunt attack on identities that dare to not conform to eugenic criteria of uniformity. However, from here, I would like to delve more into the terrains of neoliberalism and conservativism in order to better explain where, when, and why disputes of power occur, and why such sociopolitical disputes are the primary battle site for the curriculum.

### Notes

1. I am noting the word "ways," since many "ways" of thinking are not considered valid according to Eurocentric scientific parameters, which hold that there is no "correct" knowledge beyond what is Eurocentricly defined. This subject was dissected by Boaventura de Sousa Santos in *Epistemologies of the South*, which I've often quoted in this text.
2. In this specific moment, I want to use "self" to open a small and new dialogic pocket. My intentions in posing the "self" involve facing not just what it means and is to itself but, furthermore, in putting the self, "me," in my own place as a human being. No better than others, but equal in rights and potential, sharing the same planet, breathing, experiencing the most inexplicable gift ever conceived of by human beings, "life." By looking inside myself, I can see my needs, potential, existential questions, ideology, culture, and how I identify myself within and beyond this world. I guess I could say the "self" represents the point in time and space "in life" where I—including all of my inner and outer parts—am right now.
3. Here, I am actively implying that the global postmodern education currently on offer contains the intrinsic intention to embrace, even if the result is bloody, the social and ideological enslavement of all humans, beginning in their youth.
4. Denoting the Socratic mode of inquiry, which aims to bring a person's latent ideas into clear consciousness.

CHAPTER 3

# A Conservative Neoliberalism or Neoliberal Conservatism?

## 1     Introduction

In this chapter, I will situate the battle for integrating spirituality into public education and curriculum within the framework of the current neoliberal moment. A I argue, under the neoliberal consulate—which emerged at the end of the 1970s and has, ever since, impacted public institutions, especially education—difficulties in producing curricular and pedagogical forms sensitive to the spiritual dynamics of the inner self have become even more entrenched. I will briefly outline the history of neoliberalism, identify its key features, and dissect its connections with the absence of spirituality in public education. It goes without saying that spirituality was a noisy silence in public curricula and pedagogies well before the emergence of neoliberalism. My argument is that under neoliberalism the degree and depth of its absence have escalated to a dangerous stage. I will then examine how conservative neoliberal attacks on the humanities and liberal arts provide solid ground for the consolidation of treacherous so-called neutral educational forms—deterministic, objectivistic pedagogies, curricula, subjects, and modes of teaching and evaluating students that are overtly detached from the organic indeterminacy of the personal component and the inner spiritual self. I will dissect how curricular knowledge—a process of selective tradition (Williams, 2005)—is responsible for spiritual absence.

I will begin this chapter with a personal anecdote from my time as a school administrator, in order to contextualize how neoliberalism is embedded within an ideology that excuses negative outcomes in the name of a conservativism that abuses and denies cultural identities, bending the generative possibilities of creativity and imagination into a culture of surveillance and oppression as authentic leadership ceases to exist. In so doing, I intentionally allow the abuse of power to be exposed.

## 2     The Absence of Authentic Leadership: Framing Dropouts

In 2012, I was nominated to be the principal of a private elementary school in Massachusetts. I will omit the name of the school out of respect for my colleagues who still serve the institution. Upon accepting the position, I was finally content: For the first time in my life, I would be able to overcome the bureaucracy and mandatory curriculum apparatuses that dominate most schools, and thereby push back the cult of positivism that pervades the educational system (Giroux, 1981, 2001). I initially thought that somehow I would be able to engage in curriculum and pedagogical forms more progressive in a private institution. I was naïve. I was sick of state impositions on public education. With the personal understanding I had of education, I thought I was going to be able to at least create opportunities above and beyond the curriculum, and offer teachers a sort of freedom in their teaching. My dream was to empower teachers to create spaces for a more meaningful education and deeper teacher-content-student relationships. At the time, I felt the palpations of neoliberalism, but had yet to learn of its theoretical definitions and real-world effects. However, as I came to define and theorize it, I began to understand it as a global norm. In my attempt to evade curricular imposition, bureaucracy, and mechanical teaching-learning, I slowly discovered that there is a force acting in all of our educational and societal conundrums.

The school itself enjoyed a rich ethnic diversity, with 90% of its students coming from Brazil, Portugal, Cape Verde, Guatemala, Mexico, Puerto Rico, Costa Rica, Belgium, and Russia, and the remaining 10% being white, native-born citizens of the United States. We heard at least five languages fluently spoken in the school corridors every day. I oftentimes had to shift from one language to another in order to effectively communicate with students. At the time, my school was a vivid example of a diverse and multicultural community. Yet, I felt my students were fighting to survive in an environment where their identities were under threat. Later on, when I read Fine (1991) in my doctoral program, I realized that this was exactly the case in the school I led: These students were "about-to-be-the dropouts" and the incarcerated in the adult-making process. How could it be otherwise when,

> [i]n the United States, public schools, particularly secondary schools, were never designated or low-income students and students of color. And they have never been very successful in this work. Relying upon dropping out as a crude indicator of educational inequity, historic data confirm consistent patterns of relatively high dropout. (Fine, 1991, p. 22)

It is no secret that the dominant curriculum framework and school culture are at the service of a small racialized and classized minority, not in the sense that such minority groups are taking over chairs in classrooms across the country, rather that such a curriculum/culture creates an environment where only a minority of students will succeed, given such an inhospitable environment, to which so many come entirely unprepared (Darder, 2012). This, then—of course—leads to the majority, which largely consists of minoritized students, to edge closer to dropping out. This unjust cycle is perpetuated indefinitely, as it is seen by those in power as a good format and disciplinary system with which to raise soldiers of the system. These factories of success and failure (schools) are in charge of creating and cultivating a rigid brand of excellence in individual achievement and developing money-oriented aspirations, undermining genuine development and flushing the human being as a whole down the toilet, all the while driving students to obtain a false conception of humanity and presenting society as more important than the human being. Fine (1991) adds,

> What distinguishes the situation today is not the dropping out but the consequence of being denied a school diploma, [where it would perpetuate the effects of a more stable financial, social and emotional life. However] the alarms the claim is more preponderant on what facts push the students over the edge. Some schools seem to be saturated with the institutional compulsion to smooth and obscure these social and economic contradictions. (p. 31)

No matter what, the institution has an obligation to comply with state regulations and policies, as do teachers and administrators. Some internal behaviors around these comprehensive bureaucratic regulations make the school environment even more bitter than it already is. In fact, those who are in charge of overseeing the daily schooling process end up serving as bastions of the system, framing dropouts via the colonizing Eurocentric positivist benchmarks put forth by that system, and blaming the students themselves for such "lacks" as on low IQ or low language proficiency. However, such students actually have depreciated knowledge exchanges with teachers, through which the state and the economy vindicate the state's attitude. Needless to say, "institutions can deflect responsibility for the creation of social problems" (Fine, 1991, p. 159); that is, school administrators and principals normally walk away from this social saga free of personally or societally enforced guilt. While I am not placing the blame on school leadership, I honestly think that a radically different kind of leadership, one that is its committed to authenticity (Anderson, 2009), will help to mitigate such social anathemas.

Back in the corridors of my school, the representative from the superintendent's office was frequently around. She would often ask me, "Why do you communicate with the students in their language instead of English?" She was manifesting linguoracism (Darder, 2012; Valenzuela, 1999) by implying that these languages should not be accepted as a way of communicating in the school setting. Dominant modes of "being" and knowing (Santos, 2018) are legitimized by diminishing and vanishing forms that are deemed incapable of producing valid knowledge. Both my students and me were subhumanized as incapable of transferring knowledge while speaking another language. But the true incapacity involved the ways in which my superintendent representative and others were unable to understand how powerful biculturalism is (Darder, 2012, 2014) and how curriculum eugenics deny it (Paraskeva, 2016).

Clearly, I was faced with a total absence of an authentic praxis of critical leadership, as Anderson (2009) would put it. In Anderson's (2009) terms, authentic leadership focuses "on turning bureaucratic institutions into caring communities in which all of the school professionals develop a strong sense of belonging" (p. 37). Needless to say, the absence of authentic leadership provokes an absence of belonging. Therefore, engagement, liberty, social and cognitive justice, and equality—everything my students and their relatives came in search of—were denied to them in the very environment where such crucial values should be advocated for, promoted, enhanced, and shared. When the latter occurs, Anderson (2009) observes,

> teachers, students and administrators are more productive professionally in schools where norms of collegiality and trust are cultivated. In schools of business, public management, and education, the field of leadership and organizational theory have tended to view authenticity as an important element of effective leadership and of a productive work environment. (p. 37)

According to my superintendent representative, when pressed on her criticism of my use of other languages, she explained that using any other language besides English within the school would constitute a failure to deliver a quality education. So, I asked, "But who defines what a quality education means?" And, also, "whose English?" Apparently, schools have a requirement to colonize the students in order to commodify them as English speaker students. She claimed that my use of other languages would slow their process of learning English. I argued, forcibly, that they need help in order to feel comfortable in school and express themselves better academically. Although I was finally in the "freedom" of the private sector, I found myself struggling unsuccessfully to liberate my students and make school engaging and meaningful to them (hooks, 1994). In the minds of the superintendent representative to speak more than one language is a deficit. Unfortunately this eugenic view pervades dominant curriculum, pedagogy and leadership forms.

# A CONSERVATIVE NEOLIBERALISM OR NEOLIBERAL CONSERVATISM? 159

In contrast, when those in the classroom, both teachers and students, "recognize that they are responsible for creating a learning community together, learning is at its most meaningful and useful" (hooks, 2018, p. 11). We can actually let the fact that we all "long for loving community" (p. 154) resolve most of the problems we have in the process of teaching and learning. A loving community indeed helps to substantially diminish dropping out. Furthermore, our capacity to live purposefully by learning how to experience satisfaction in whatever work we do is especially fruitful in the teaching/learning process; it will indeed enhance the well-being of students, even while they take ownership of the setting and knowledge that they are immersed in.

Despite cultural and linguistic differences, understanding and acknowledgment materialized in actions promotes a sort of invested feeling and learning for both, teachers and students, creating a sense of mutual respect and "cooperativism" in which critical thinking flourishes. Together, sincere understanding and the "bending down" to the student's level lay the grounding for another and higher way of learning and teaching.

But instead of honoring these vital qualities, the superintendent representative was squeezing me to commodify the students as soon as possible: "We have a due date!" (meaning the test day). She was deploying deadline-oriented neoliberal agenda which frames the curriculum as designed to prepare the students for tests (Hursh, 1988) that are based on anti-knowledge theories of education, not knowing that

> Inauthenticity, then, whether at the individual, organizational, or societal level is linked to this growing gap between our cherished ideals and the realities of our lives. In many cases, ideals like liberty and equality have come into conflict with each other as well, with equality often losing out to an invigorated belief in individual liberty. (Anderson, 2009, p. 50)

I would contend that such a stage of inauthenticity forces students to stay in modes of "being" and learning that perpetuate their position as abyssal citizens. This emotional and physical curriculum oppression, imposed on teachers, educators, and students alike, leads students especially to a stage of spiritual pressure, which, I argue, is deeply depreciative, a rape of their emotional and intellectual vitality. Such impositions are visible in the so-called postmodern curriculum via its claims for achievement through obedience and discipline, instead of through freedom and the wholeness of the student's genuine aims. It unquestionably sets the scene for chaos, wherein depression, not "success," is the natural outcome:

> Depression began its ascent when the disciplinary model for behaviors, the rules of authority and observance of taboos that gave social classes as well as both sexes a specific destiny, broke against norms that invited us to undertake personal initiative by enjoying us to be ourselves…the depressed individual is unable to measure up; he is tired of having to become himself. (Han, 2015, p. 9)

In this sense, we are very much forced to acknowledge that such a struggle to "be" describes late modernity's endeavor as a setting in which "to be," often means "to be a failure," specifically when language is used as a colonial and hegemonic tool wielded to deny one's possibility of building attachments. The pressure to be a "failed" colonized "being" can be defined as systemic violence (Han, 2015, p. 10) that is expressed and experienced through pressure to achieve standards on tests, language expression castration, and or impaired social relations.

In Hursh's (2015) terms, high-stakes testing has become a pedagogical cult that frames the neoliberal agenda in education. This cult is manifested in action as a weapon used for political purposes, blaming schools and teachers for the crises in public education and transforming its very mission. In my case, it was inflicted as an issue of ELA (English Language Arts) performance; achieving better grades was required—no matter the human cost—in order to have the school classified as a top private school in the district. This was just one materialization of a biased endeavor aimed towards certain students who could not "perform" and as a result would (and, according to this system, should!) drop out of school (Fine, 1991). Even though I was at the helm of a private institution, where parents paid top dollar for an exclusive education, there were many cases in which students—rightly recognizing that they deserved a better approach in respect to their rights to learn and be themselves—decided they just could not take any more of the denial my school imposed on them. How could it not have done so, existing as it did (and does) inside a pedagogical machine in which students must be able to read certain texts in certain ways and then perform in certain ways on certain tests to feed the requirements of Eurocentric modernity. It is clear that the number of specific required types of performances of this sort has grown since the 1980s, along with the quantity of high-stakes tests students must face (Hursh, 1988); at the same time, knowledge of literature, which in itself is a requirement of this very system, has declined. "This presents quite a contradiction. One might argue that the massive quantity of tests in play should enlarge students' grasp of literature, but the slope goes in the opposite direction."

As I attempted to guide my school and students, I finally understood what Macedo (2003) meant when he said, "possession of two languages is not a matter of having two tools, but actually means participation in two physical and cultural realms" (p. 80), a fact which, sadly, is not perceived, never mind honored, by many in the educational field. I had to come to terms with the fact that administrators are yet another part of the perpetuated condition that reinforces the collective need for a standardized curriculum. As it did in my case, any real reflection in this context forces us to recognize our complicity with a system in which the "race to the top" implies that American public schools have been at the bottom of global education and that, with a corporate approach, American schools will finally lead the world.

We didn't technically have a full standardized curriculum. However, private schools cannot run away from the requirements imposed by the department of education. Indeed, with other private schools throughout the state, we still had benchmarks that were intended to demonstrate our success. We had graphics to show parents our students' growth in comparison to the previous year, as well as various other "evidence" of "success." We had to prove to parents that our school was "good enough," meaning rigorous enough, to deserve their dollars. The school acted like a marketplace in which our job was to "subordinate educational value to economic value" (De Lissovoy, Means, & Saltman, 2014, p. 41). By the end of the day, the vision and mission of that institution was forgotten in the face of powerful external competitive pressure. The vision and the mission was stamped with the market impulses. First, the school condoned communication between human beings only if framed in an evolving culture of "subordination over the minority speaker" (Macedo, 2003, p. 15). Second, the school denied students' language as culture acting as a "collective memory bank of people's experience in history" (Elliott & Weaver, 1998, p. 12), thereby rendering its definition of education a fallacy. Instead of honoring and developing each student's unique personhood, their local context was ignored, their very "being" oppressed. The process/mission was simple: prepare students to enter into better, elite schools, instead of helping to develop them to live their lives with a deep social and spiritual connectedness. Furthering this marginalizing approach, discipline in the school corridor was essentially militarized. Today, with the critical lenses I have developed through my doctoral studies, I understand that "knowledge is no guarantee of good behavior, but ignorance is a virtual guarantee of bad behavior" (Nussbaum, 2010, p. 81). Yet I remain devastated to have been closely involved in an institution where, despite my best efforts to the contrary, there was little love and affection but rather an absence of cultivating humanity (Nussbaum, 1997). Some environments almost invariably suffer from a caused anomaly: the absence of a sense of democracy and the lack of human-centered philosophy to enhance teaching practice.

My point is that what educators and schools truly stand on must be transparent in the teaching practice and class environment. This is exactly what

I argued before, that is, when we understand the whys behind education, as well as for whom and by whom it occurs, our practices change. Schools cannot talk about democracy and then punish students for acting on it. Schools neglect students' real needs, such as development of humanity, affection, and love, while shoveling information into the hippocampus and expecting it to satisfy them as "beings." Human beings require companionship, not just quizzes, tests, and books. The balance of both, according to Nussbaum (2010), will move students and teachers towards the true exercise of their democratic and educational citizenship. Furthermore, Nussbaum (2010) argues, "The presence of the other, which can be very threatening, becomes, in play, a delightful source of curiosity, and this curiosity contributes toward the development of healthy attitudes in friendship, love, and, later, political life" (p. 100).

At my same private school, we had a 10-foot poster at the main entrance that read, "Love your neighbor as yourself." This love was absent when a student was late because his mother had to bring her baby to daycare before heading to our school to drop off her other son. Instead, discipline was implemented, just as in public schools, in the form of the well-known detention. Really? Detention? Shouldn't we lovingly rush this kid to a classroom, so he could feel a part of the group and understand that he had finally made it to school, and it was worth it? The neoliberal agenda has a firm grip on education, whether public or private, but also on changing the fabric of it leaving no other option of saying, if not; that neoliberal agenda keeps shaping education more and more.

At the time, we remained a private institution—ostensibly one in control of its own values and procedures—and yet, without noticing, we condoned extreme neoliberal practices by isolating students, literally dragging the abyssal line into the classroom. Our classrooms, curriculum and pedagogies were/are the carburators of a divisive reason (Paraskeva, 2021a, 2016). In Santos' (2007) terms, modern Western thinking as an abyssal mode of thinking (p. 45) consists of

> a system of visible and invisible distinctions, the invisible ones being the foundation of the visible ones. The invisible distinctions are established through radical lines that divide social reality into two realms, the realm of "this side of the line" and the realm of "the other side of the line." The division is such that "the other side of the line" vanishes as reality, becomes nonexistent, and is indeed produced as nonexistent. Nonexistent means not existing in any relevant or comprehensible way of being. Whatever is produced as nonexistent is radically excluded because it lies beyond the realm of what the accepted conception of inclusion considers to be its other. What most fundamentally characterizes abyssal thinking is thus the impossibility of the co-presence of the two sides of the line. To the extent that it prevails, this side of the line only prevails by

exhausting the field of relevant reality. Beyond it, there is only nonexistence, invisibility, non-dialectical absence. (Santos, 2007, p. 1)

Such "abyssality," Paraskeva (2016) argues, frames not only the daily life of our schools, curricula, and pedagogies, but also, the way we think about education and pedagogy. When I was told to impose English as the main language, the importance given to one's cultural background was presented as non-valid in the context of the validity of the required knowledge and dominant language. On "our" (i.e., the school's) side of the abyssal line, their language was not considered a valued language or deemed inappropriate for instruction. No matter the private or public rubrics, we, perhaps without knowing, produce sons and daughters of the meritocratic system through valuing behavior and test performance over the well-being of the individual.

Nusbaum (2010) claims that "education should provide the necessary elements to develop ourselves effectively in the multinational dialogue as world citizens" (p. 50) without depriving students of learning and opportunities to share their experiences, which would in fact generate knowledge fluency. As mentioned, my school did not have an extreme standardized curriculum per se; however, I noticed that the teachers' de-intellectualized (Giroux, 2011) mentality involved proving themselves academically rigorous enough to impose respect as "good teaching." Another point that dumbfounded me was that some parents showed a preference for such teaching. I have to confess that, until then, I did not realize that there was something influencing and changing the fabric of education, and, even more so, the fabric of society. Teacher education, conferences, meetings, etc. are not enough to dissect how pernicious and infectious this is. As shoppers, parents do look at the job market, and they see what kind of openings there are. They have a comprehensive sense of what it takes to be a candidate, and that is one of the reasons many parents require schools to be tough on their children. This was the period during which I started to pay attention to how modernity and neoliberalism have shaped the social fabric of our society, creating both the venom and the antidote to their own poison. In the advancement of capitalism and modernity, parents show themselves as indoctrinated, hooked by modernity's consumerist status quo—and willing to introduce their own precious children into the same system.

Present-day consumerism—one of the dangerous features of the cult of presentism (Pinar, 2016) or momentism (Paraskeva, 2016, 2017)—though, is no longer about satisfying human needs, not even the more sublime, detached (some would say, not quite correctly, "artificial," "contrived," "derivative") needs of identification or self-assurance as to degree of "adequacy." It has been said that the spiritus mavens of consumer activity is no longer the measurable set of articulated needs, but desire—a much more volatile and ephemeral, evasive and capricious, and essentially non-referential entity than "needs," a self-begotten and self-propelled motive that needs no other justification or "cause".... "Despite its successive and always short-lived reifications, desire has itself for its constant object, and for that reason is bound to remain insatiable, however high the pile of other (physical or psychic) objects marking its past course may rise" (Bauman, 2018, pp. 74–75). If current education does not promote and provide this kind of expectation to students and parents, with "some exceptions," the embedded expectations of a modern world will not satisfy either students or parents. Bauman (2018) deciphers how modernity is able to permeate the conundrums of school and curriculum: "The rationality of the ruled is always the weapon of the rulers" (Bauman, 1998, p. 142). The ruled would do anything to reach the temporary fulfillment which comes throughout consumerism; in part they do so via exchanging their true "being" and real learning for an education that is advertised as "modern education."

The language and illusions of the job market is mistranslated to the average population. "As neoliberalism highjacked the language and perception of what social justice is…it redefined the perception of the schools and society, emptying the notion of social" (Saltman, 2015, p. 95) from schools and related considerations and questions. Thus, the idea of "quantification" is welcome. Parents and students aim for good grades, lending support to the neoconservative argument which promises intellectual growth for expansion and maximization, adapting into a 21st-century globalized curriculum that supplies the needs of the market. It's a supply and demand curriculum, exactly the opposite of what "beings" need, with knowledge of literature incessantly decreasing. As the greed for developing hard skills and quantifying learning by testing/grading grows, human development fades. How can schools guard our children's lifeblood and individual emotional, spiritual, and social potential from these cunning attacks that are masked within neoliberal and neoconservative hegemonic power?

Now, I would like to delve into a subject, namely, neoliberalism, that will help me to structure my arguments and address many of the questions that I myself have raised throughout this text. In so doing, I will dissect its influence in economic, social, educational, personal, and political terrains in order to help me build a more solid claim, while connecting the various parts of this chapter to my main point: that spirituality is a human right.

## 3    On Neoliberalism

As I mentioned at the outset of his chapter, there is a perfect symbiosis between the rise of neoliberalism, its consolidation for over five decades, and the absence of spirituality in public education. While spirituality was overtly absent in public education well before the emergence of neoliberalism, it is undeniable that, with its meteoric ascent 1980s, that absence re-escalated and assumed eugenic impulses (Santos, 2018; Andreotti, 2011). This process underlies my contention that, under neoliberal educational policies and the concomitant commodification of teachers' work, curriculum, pedagogical forms, and students, spirituality—so crucial in the lives of countless students—became a "nonexistent" dynamic.

Let me now turn my focus to a critical examination of neoliberalism to help clarify my claim. Needless to say, studies of neoliberalism have yet to include an exegesis on spirituality. Yet interrogating neoliberalism enables me to understand and demonstrate why spirituality has been rendered "nonexistent," as Santos (2014) would put it. To be more precise, my critical examination of scholars such as Harvey, Bauman, Giroux, Darder, Saltman, Macrine, Paraskeva, and others helps me better comprehend my own battles with a dynamic that is an integral part of my identity, while also allowing me to apply a critical lens to the distinct and heretofore unexplored subject of spirituality in education.

Given the complexity of the word and concept of spirituality (as addressed in Chapter 2), its entanglements with neoliberalism are complicated and far-reaching. The latter might be conceived as an octopus with visible and invisible tentacles, its many arms embracing all of the spheres of our daily life. So, naturally, it is hard to define neoliberalism in a chapter, never mind a section of a chapter. At the most basic level, neoliberalism can be framed as an ideological, political, and philosophical pathway. Some authors, such as Saad-Filho and Johnston (2005), find it "impossible to define neoliberalism purely theoretically" (p. 1). Neoliberalism does not overtly direct political organizations to function in a certain way. Neoliberalism does not take a stand in defining where and for/with whom democracy and the free exchange of political ideas and goods should happen. Because it is a global phenomenon, neoliberalism does not self-proclaim, rather, it creates conditions and conflicts enabling itself to be implemented anywhere, even in autocratic regimes. Harvey (2005) defines neoliberalism as a "values market exchange," and as

> an ethic in itself, capable of acting as a guide to all human action and substituting for all previously held ethical beliefs. It emphasizes the significance of contractual relations in the marketplace. It holds that the social good will be maximized by maximizing the reach and frequency of market transactions, and it seeks to bring all human action into the domain of the market. (p. 3)

In brief, Harvey (2005) calls it a "neo-liberal regime of power" (p. 189). In the United States and the United Kingdom of the 1990s, neoliberalism was defined as the "answer to global problems" (Harvey, 2005, p. 93). Such a definition exerts an enormous influence over the rest of the globe. As Harvey (2005) states, neoliberalism,

> is particularly assiduous in seeking the privatization of assets. The absence of clear property rights is seen as one of the greatest of all institutional barriers to economic development and the improvement of human welfare. Enclosure and the assignment of private property rights is considered the best way to protect against the so-called tragedy of the commons. Sectors formerly run or regulated by the state must be turned over to the private sphere and be deregulated. Competition—between individuals, between firms, between territorial entities—is held to be a primary virtue...Privatization and deregulation, combined with competition, it is claimed, eliminate bureaucratic red tape, increase efficiency and productivity, improve quality, and reduce costs both directly to the consumer through cheaper commodities and services and indirectly through reduction of the tax burden. (p. 65)

In Harvey's (2005) terms, neoliberalism is a radical and perpetually evolving revolution at the very core of civil society—and its most fundamental undertaking involves transforming the very mission of its public institutions, such as schools. From Macrine's (2016) point of view, neoliberalism is the dominant ideology shaping our world today, making it the most successful and ruthless ideology in history. She adds, "neoliberalism is also about the exertion and distribution of political, economic and cognitive power and discourse" (2016, p. 6). Neoliberalism is the evolution and/or continuity of liberalism. Not so long ago, liberalism was a very "influential" political ideology, if not a fully social one. Over the years, it evolved into a more modern and broad way of thought, so much so that it gave space to a new version of liberalism: neoliberalism. As Hall (2011) claims, "neoliberalism is not one thing or one concept but something that continuously evolves and diversifies" (p. 12). Bauman (2008), in dissecting neoliberalism, reached the conclusion that it is/acts like an invisible hand that is "able to guess or predict, let alone direct and correct, its moves; a "hand" which any poker player dreams of, rightly expecting it to be unbeatable" (p. 144).

Neoliberals believe that the market economy is efficient enough to redistribute resources in the "proper" fashion. In neoliberal philosophical terms, the market, not the state, is the great equalizer (Apple, 2001; Giroux, 2018).

Paraskeva (2010, 2012) maps neoliberalism as the root of what he calls neo-radical centrism. As he argues "the dichotomy of the weak state vs. the strong state, one of the leitmotivs of the neoliberal hegemonic bloc, misrepresents the central tenet of neoliberalism" (2012, p. 702). In fact, it is the state that is paving the way for the market (Paraskeva, 2007) in such a way that the neoliberal state makes no mistakes in overtly walking out on all its responsibilities, suspending its powers—what Agamben (2005) calls a state of exception—if and when it is necessary to allow the totalitarian desires of the market to flourish (see Paraskeva, 2010). Public education is one of the social apparatuses that has been suffering the rapacious consequences of a *capitalisme de connivence*, as Samir Amin (2008, p. 50) would put it. Public education was and is still a real obstacle to fanatical marketers. Neoliberalism is the riverbed of a global crisis, a

> global crisis with a local face (or local faces) represents the emptiness of participatory democracy as an endless social treasure, while simultaneously creating "natural" conditions for a deranged attack on public teachers, public education and everything that is public by definition. Such attacks open the door for a set of social and educational reforms coined by the market, as if these marketers, who are now philanthropically rising to the top via education, had nothing to do with the financial disarray the global community is currently facing. (Paraskeva, 2012, p. 703)

Neoliberalism is against state interference—such as market regulation, establishing rates and international regulations on trades and exchanges, or international tariffs—in the economy. According to Apple (2001),

> Neoliberalism is a hegemonic bloc framed and led by neoliberals, incorporating neoconservatives' new middle class and authoritarian populists—which include a huge percentage of evangelical groups. (p. 59)

Apple's (2001) framework accurately predicts and describes the recent alt-right turns that many nations, including Brazil, Hungary, and the United States, are facing, expressed by bizarre alliances in which populist authoritarianism is being aligned with radical religious conservativism. While religious-right impulses pervade such new-right coalitions, the truth is that they do not help to create conditions conducive to the production of educational policies more sensitive to, and inclusive of, issues of spirituality. The reasons for this paradox are three-fold. First, evangelicals constitute a tiny minority within these hegemonic blocs; second, they ferociously fight and lobby to impose a very specific religious cult in our schools and society as the sole acceptable religious dynamic, vs. framing spirituality as an abstract way of being within the world; and, third, neoliberal commitments focus on market fundamentalism, superseding any other impulses. Neoliberalism is a powerful and complex economic, political, and cultural system that transforms and injects the market into all aspects of life. It is fair to say that neoliberalism is like a dust that infiltrates all of the underlying intentions, as well as the production of, knowledge, goods (food, products), ideologies, and social constructions, having its tentacles also in the application of the laws and policies. Its normalization of individualistic egoism is undeniable, and promotes a way of existing that collides irreparably with spiritual existence.

Moreover, as Apple (2000) argues, "the entire project of neoliberalism nationally and internationally is connected to a larger process of exporting the blame from the decisions of dominant groups onto the state and onto poor people" (p. 60). This definition explains the ruthlessness mentioned above (see Macrine, 2016). Further, this transference of blame to those already vanished as sub-human is the root of the epistemological denial (Paraskeva, 2016; Santos, 2016) and absence of spirituality now guiding human actions.

Giroux (2017) defines neoliberalism as

> an ideology and politics buoyed by the spirit of a market fundamentalism that subordinates the art of democratic politics to the rapacious laws of a market economy that expands its reach to include all aspects of social life within the dictates and values of a market-driven society. (p. XXII)

Although they dominate the majority of the public sector, neoliberals diminish the efficiency of public institutions and look to private ones for efficiency, justified by its self-created argument of the necessary good and necessary bad (Apple, 2000). A simple way of understanding is by looking the venom and antidote anecdote. By having one creating destruction and disgrace, the one that might remedy the situation becomes fundamental, it becomes salvation. Rather than destroying the threat, we need the threating creature to produce the remedy, the band aid or the salvation of the mega capitalism endeavors. Over the decades, neoliberalism as an ideological party has divided into two factions: conservative neoliberalism and neoliberal conservativism.

According to Saltman (2014), conservatives break down into two categories. "[F]iscal conservatives tend to justify education predominantly through an economic lens" (Saltman, 2014, p. XXIII); they generally believe that public schools are bad or inferior simply by virtue of being public. The cultural conservative, on the other hand, "emphasizes memorization, submission to authority, and a hierarchical view of culture and knowledge, valorizing individual submission to moral codes and good character" (Saltman, 2014, p. XXIV). Fiscal conservatives are driven by finances and tend to be market fundamentalists. They defend corporations as something proactive in education. Even the jargon is conservative, with explicit nods in favor of corporations pushing corporate school reform. They aim to justify education through the lens of corporate-leaning economics and to generate money-hungry kids by exposing them to an unmatched reality where "only" hard skills are valued—and those who have "the material resources denied are forced to want things they cannot have" which is a summarized concept extracted from (hooks, 2009a, pp. 50–53). This is how neoliberalism empowers itself, provoking the continued poisoning of society while also offering the "antidote." Many fiscal conservatives are well-known sons and daughters of neoliberalism. They frame public education as a subspecies of private service, contractable to the "best" bidder and primarily intended for the working class, portraying parents as shoppers and teachers as mere service providers. Neoliberalism is intimately connected to the a perpetual state of

> This global crisis with a local face (or local faces) represents the emptiness of participatory democracy as an endless social treasure, while simultaneously creating "natural" conditions for a deranged attack on public teachers, public education and everything that is public by definition. Such attacks open the door for a set of social and educational reforms coined by the market, as if these marketers, who are now philanthropically rising to the top via education, had nothing to do with the financial disarray the global community is currently facing.

The very conception and mission defined by neoliberalism—individualism, determinism, mechanization, objectivity, standardization—collide directly with the spiritual dimension of the individual. In spiritual terms, education, curriculum, and pedagogy are in fact prayerful acts (Macdonald, 1974), with the focus on autobiographical, and thus political, impulses. The cult of individualism, pretentious objectivism, and standardization blends beautifully with the dominant positivist-determinist-mechanistic vision of education, curriculum, and pedagogy, which union—as escalated under the neoliberal consulate—nullifies any possibility or hypothesis of the spontaneity, authenticity, originality, and introspection so central to spiritual "being(s)." The denial of spirituality in public education settings is an act of cognitive cleansing, and it carves a major dent in the struggle for social justice, since there is no social justice without cognitive justice (Santos, 2014).

Under the yoke of neoliberalism, teachers are more vulnerable and likely to be disposed of, towards educational products that are offered to the parents through public-private institutions, where the stress of knowledge assimilation is a burden to students' natural emotional, physical, and social growth. In these institutions, perceptible to the naked eye, we see epistemicide committed at full blast (Paraskeva, 2016; Santos, 2014). This manifests not just in the denial of students' knowledge, but also in redefining a "suitable" reconstruction of spirituality itself by claiming validity only for that spirituality which is acceptable to, and approved by, neoliberal definitions and aims. Let's keep in mind that for many, including me, spirituality is a question of inner fulfillment. Neoliberalism reproduces an artificial fulfillment via consumerism and the possession of material things, mixing these concepts with religion as well to produce an "allowed" conception of the spiritual as a certain sort of "pursuit" among others. As Frankfurt School social theorists, such as Horkheimer and Adorno (2016), documented, consumerism anesthetizes social consciousness so that the human being sees him/herself as the beginning and the end of history. The resulting truncated social consciousness (one of many related effects) is responsible as well for a putrid absence—or "nonexistence"—of spirituality in public schools. Seeing as education is about the welfare of the human being, and given that spirituality is essential to human well-being, any education that violates this fundamental element of our existence denies the common good of the population being educated. Any pedagogical formation that negates the power of the person—their unique experiences, their spontaneity, their "being"—by framing both the learning process and the individual as neutral is a frontal attack on the spiritual dynamics at play in the inner self.

Such a curriculum, as molded by and, embedded in, the self-perpetuating neoliberal ideology (for its own needs), creates a never ending desire for fulfillment that gets even worse when there is little or no financial ability to buy such satisfaction through "consumerism," thereby introducing crime as a profitable, "satisfying," "fulfilling" alternative (hooks, 2000). When individuals become afflicted by life events, whether because they are in dire need of self-esteem or affirmation, looking for prosperity, or in search of strength to overcome the difficulties caused by their personal consumerist behavior, they tend to repeat self-defeating behaviors in order to quiet the life questions that arise in this context. They live with more technicality than humanity. More products than real freedom of choice. They buy more to attempt to feel satisfaction. In a nutshell, that's how neoliberalism produces the temporary fulfillment of one's inner desires, while spirituality, in contrast and in opposition to the capitalist system, questions both these sorts of priorities and their fulfillment. Neoliberalism, as argued before, has remodeled our social expectations and it works daily and ceaselessly to reconstruct our social fabrics via education.

Neoliberalism aims to construct a new "being," a "being" who supplies the demands of those higher in the hierarchy. To that end, the consumers of said ideology must be produced in order to enable neoliberalism to continue to be reinvented, to such an extent that it is now clearly and ubiquitously imposed to the point that human beings automatically become invested in its capitalist, consumerist ideology. Complete domination of the educational terrain is the only way to achieve this. Changing how people act starts with changing how they think; the endless repetition of how one should think, enacted in our very own educational systems, leads to changes in how society as a whole will ultimately act. And so, the wholeness of the act of teaching is removed, replaced by a culture of overcoming crises by creating crises—as falsely advertised by a mechanical curriculum—and the democratic imposition of socialism-slavery-by-consumerism, all put forth as propaganda for remedying socio-economic needs. Indeed, Williams (1966) saw ahead of time what the future channel of deliverance for these substitutions would be: "the use of tragic text to formulate a socialist theory of tragedy in which revolution would receive a literary justification and society would become more important than the individual" (p. 113). For this reason, I feel it is important to delve a little deeper into the conundrum of the politicism and ambiguity of the aforementioned false claim of spirituality, an empty neoliberal gesture that purports to be pro-humanity, when in truth it is predicated on the absence of spirituality.

## 4 Everything But Spirituality and the Humanities

Since the beginning of the 1980s, neoliberalism has profoundly reconstructed the educational landscape as a whole. In this endeavor, public schools are both the terrain and the laboratory of the battle. Let's revisit the antidote anecdote. In the U.S, a democratic country, we agree that what the people decide is what should be. So, by tricking the "people" into wanting and then turning that "want" into a commonly claimed necessity, neoliberalism creates a diversified "formation of groups to pressure the state" (Apple, 2000, 2001, 2004), thereby justifying the need for privatization, i.e., for "corporations to take control over the schools/industry" (p. 90). As argued before with Bauman (1998), the invisible hand "manipulates" the public sector by adding a "rupture" or "breakage" or "problem" in order to offer a privatized, better articulated, competitive market solution (Hursh, 2007). It privileges the private, leaving no other "valid" choice besides privatization. The state then leaves the crime scene and allows the private corporations to take over the terrain of education, surrendering to a better promise, promised as promissory. In this scenario, one we and our children live every day, students are seen as consumers. Therefore, schools are forced to compete among them in order to deliver the "imposed knowledge" more efficiently, as based on consumer ideology. In this sense, high-stakes testing has been concomitant with curriculum standardization, and the manipulation of the ensuing data has undeniably given the impression that knowledge is the greatest commodity neoliberalism has taken ahold of. This can easily be perceived in how teachers and schools are required to numerically quantify the consumption of knowledge (teaching/testing) by student "consumers" (Saltman, 2015). Neoliberalism's pedagogical forms constitute the supreme example of the banking concept of education (Freire, 2017). As Nussbaum (2010, p. 18) argues, education "is not about the passive assimilation of facts and cultural traditions, but about challenging the mind to become active, competent, and thoughtfully critical in a complex world" (p. 18). Instead, however, the eugenic banking concept of education (Freire, 2017), which frames passive pedagogical forms (Nussbaum, 2010) as ideal, has been able to thrive—despite resistance and challenges—because it has been identified (By whom? By itself!) as the best way to propel progress and intellectual development.

Nusbaum (2010) urges us to observe how this type of education came to supplant the old mode: "This model of education supplanted an older one in which children sat still at desks all day and simply absorbed, and then regurgitated, the material that was brought their way" (pp. 17–18). Clearly, the prior educational model also had its issues, and students do not now sit in military formation, but they still do not have the freedom or the right to learn anything else other than what is democratically imposed. And even while students may not be aligned a certain distance apart in rows, the social distance between them increases when their teachers regurgitate disconnected curriculum knowledge.

The production of such knowledge, Saltman (2015) states, is enacted only by "experts," and it is then delivered by teachers "taking advantage of the genuine education, and consumed by students" (p. 15). Embedded in this process of indoctrination, education and its contents become private property, entities that in themselves have the power to decide what is valid and non-valid knowledge. The privatization of knowledge and schools makes neoliberalism screen its consumers in order to diversify a market niche so as to satisfy the aims of the neoliberal agenda. Schools are categorized as good and bad schools. Numerical classifications raise flags for schools whose students perform lower on testing; these schools are then disqualified. According to Saltman (2015), what makes this process very efficient is the way it ties performance to state and federal financial disbursements. The lower the students' grades are, the less financial support. Schools with better cultural capital, predominantly located in white communities, are at a greater advantage than schools composed of a majority of Black, Latinx, and immigrant students. Our schools, Saltman (2014) argues, "are imagined like factories and the aim is to streamline production to speed up efficiencies" (p. XXII).

In the process of privatization, teachers have no control over the curriculum or teaching process. This modern educational system leaves no room for a closer relationship between teachers and students and banalizes the inner development that is so vital to all "beings." Concern is solely devoted to the development of hard skills. Because of the mechanical schooling process, teachers are seen as mere instruments, machines that use what should be a genuine educational process to deliver corporate-validated knowledge.

Let's observe that, before, teachers were respected professionals who represented knowledge, decency, and respect, honored educators who aided and influenced students and parents (Giroux, 1998, p. 125). They were known as intellectuals, opinion-formers. Today, education is more related to a supply-and-demand labor market than to developing citizenship and character. Education nowadays is not interested in the development of the individual and the "being's" inner experiences, ideas, feelings, or battles. Neoliberal education is not concerned with forming the individual as a citizen, because if it were to develop individuals as such, all cultural, social, and spiritual aspects would be observed as ordinary—and integral to the process of education. This mercantilization of education has clearly contributed to the total absence of a true spiritual dimension in education. One can see that this lack existed before 1980, but neoliberalism has strongly and continually reinforced it. Through the deployment of neoliberal politics, educational reforms made it impossible to practice our original praxis and practices, as well as disqualifying teachers and institutions that condone thinking about students' subjectivity as part of the educational process. The absence of spirituality—or the production of spirituality as "nonexistent" as Santos (2014) would put it—that we feel in schools has been accentuated even more via the neoliberal agenda. Thus, these days, it is ever harder to infuse any educational environment with spiritual issues. And while I completely understand that schools should encourage reflection on spiritual issues with subtlety, decorum, and respect, I am also aware that even such a tactful approach becomes almost impossible under the reign of neoliberalism.

Neoliberalism does not work on people per se, that is, it does not enhance their inner "being." Rather it enhances the value of commodities—and the transformation process of the subjectivity of the "being" is the ultimate commodity. Detaching students from their realities, from their inner selves, is indeed a process of dehumanization. In fact, the classroom is the perfect environment for neoliberalism to promote its agenda of stripping humanity from humans, leaving only one option for fulfillment: consuming goods for personal pleasure. Neoliberalism unleashes a commonsensical commonsense of greedy material impulses, deterministic and functionalistic ways of being, thinking and existing which is at odds with the human rights spiritual sense and sensibility. Neoliberal pedagogy is not a call for introspection and reflection. Neoliberal pedagogy is a pedagogy of debt (Paraskeva & Macrine, 2015).

The more technical the curriculum becomes, the more the essence of education and humanity fade away. Liberal arts were always the channel through which the inner "being" of students could be accessed and addressed. Today, this channel has been minimized or removed from the curriculum, despite being a crucial way to reach for, and deliver on, humanity's concerns. As Nussbaum (2010) explains:

> Higher learning can offer individuals and societies a depth and breadth of vision absent from the inevitably myopic present. Human beings need meaning, understanding, and perspective as well as jobs. The question should not be whether we can afford to believe in such purposes in these times, but whether we can afford not to. (p. 124)

If we only look into the current moment in which we are living, there will certainly be nothing to lose if we analyze the consequences we are facing by abandoning the liberal arts model. It appears we are already sifting through decades of deep quantitative and qualitative research in our attempt to solve the problems that such distance from the liberal arts model has caused. Exchanging it for a market model has been at the core of teachers' actions and students' reactions and attitudes in a myriad of ways. Most of these results express diminished health and emotional wholeness, along with a large decrease in "intellectual vigor," ostensibly education's most desired outcome.

Whether propelled by conservatives or neoliberals, there is a satanic double standing in for humanity when such an agenda is permitted and genuine education is forfeited. The idea that "morality should reign supreme" (Apple, 2014, p. 67) is somehow translated into cash for power, in order to gain participation from the main political parties—both of which are dominated by the same force—in control. Teachers fear losing their jobs if they do not abide by the "good" "teaching" practices and curriculum that put forth the "only" "correct" knowledge. As Nussbaum (2010) contends, "we have become captive of the immediate world we serve" (p. 124): teachers are no different from the rest of us captives, and the market model has become the fundamental and defining identity of higher education.

Among the policies being proposed under this ideological position are national curricula, national testing, a "return" to higher standards, a revivification of "the Western tradition," and increased patriotism, and more recently, the shameful brutal attack on critical race theory. Yet what is underlying some of the neoconservative thrust in education and in social policy in general is not only a call for a "return." Also, behind it—and this is essential—is a fear of the "other" (Apple, 2014, p. XXVIII). Daily, teachers are reminded of the tenuousness of their job. If students do not perform well on standardized tests, their results are considered as indicative of a low-quality teacher—a situation I would call forced indoctrination. Apple (2013) would claim this as emblematic of the call for return, wherein low-performance schools are endlessly seen as part of a failed public system. Such messages are broadcast regularly in school districts, making teachers and administrators even more insecure and vulnerable. The value-added ideology that holds that teachers' and administrators' jobs depend on students' performance on high-stakes tests forces teachers to condone a fast-food education, forcing the entire school system to bend to the neoliberal agenda. Schools and curriculum for jobs is not about reform; it is a bout deform—individuals and society. Schools on the way to failure are offered a comeback plan, achievable through yet more value-added programs (Saltman, 2015, p. 17).

The school reform that has been promoted in the name of cost efficiency and higher turnover rates for teacher and student success demonstrates a highly articulated corporate ideology of cost and efficiency denominators (Giroux, 2014). The privatization of public education into subdivisions, including charter schools, vouchers, and infiltration of private groups purporting to help schools turn around (Smarick, 2010), has been paid for with public money and yet has effectively distanced current corporate schooling from the traditional educational model (completely public, "low pressure on students performance"). The corporate model of schooling has "overtaken educational policy, practice, curriculum and nearly all the aspects of school reform" (Saltman, 2012, p. 1). In this privatized system, teachers are constantly targeted and evaluated from a fiscal viewpoint in an attempt to weaken their strength, whether the latter is gained via personal reflection, teachers' unions, or some other positive element. If that was not enough, teachers are de-intellectualized (Giroux, 2001) as a figure of respect, because real knowledge instigates critical thinking. The school environment has changed into a flow of instruction intended solely to promote good grades and test results, all endorsed by a Common Core that standardizes education as if human beings are not all different from each other, with a deep need to be treated as unique "beings." As Saltman (2015) argues, "de-intellectualizing teacher's jobs to refashion school helps corporate-profit-making initiatives and burn out experienced teachers at even faster rates" (p. 18). Paraskeva (2012) pushes the debate to a more radical avenue and challenges the field's anti-intellectual cult. Drawing on Santos (2014) and others, he states that "anti-intellectualism needs to be understood as non-naïve naïveté, a notion in which the media plays a key role" (Paraskeva, 2012, p. 710).

> One major battle that neoliberals have been winning, although not without severe resistance, is the attack on intellectualism. This construction of the desensitized intellectual as nonexistent and the cult of particular forms of literacy produces realities beyond a specific western white-male supremacist platform. If any one social field has been deeply engaged in such quarrels, it is education. Unlike early in the last century, when public institutions supported and promoted intellectualism, and intellectuals "engaged in ongoing public conversations about political and cultural issues that were of great social importance [were] able to comment critically and broadly on a number of issues [and] exemplified a mode of writing and political literacy that refused the instinctive knee-jerk reflex of privileging plain-speak over complexity," our current era devalues intellectualism. (Paraskeva, 2012, p. 710)

There is an intentional idea here: economic and social oppression lead citizens—who are as part of this process groomed to be sub-citizens—to think that capitalism and freedom (Friedman, 1964) cannot exist separately. As Chomsky (2006) states, both freedom and capitalism work conjoined with the hypnotizing idea that "profit-making is the essence of democracy" (p. 9). The misunderstood idea presented by Friedman (1964) is profoundly biased; it entails, as he notes, "the political freedom that under some circumstances promotes economic freedom, under other inhibits economic and political freedom" (p. x). One way or another, neoliberalism gets the people, the profit, and the social conditions under its control via another face, here, capitalism. Citizenship ceases to be acknowledged, therefore, inner and spiritual development has no "plus" in the economy. Freedom stops being a condition of making choices or an abstract/physical state of "being," and is instead turned into a quest for possessions. Freedom means the ability to "buy" things, as representative of power, satisfaction, fulfilment.

The true quest for fulfilment is annihilated by neoliberalism and reintroduced to humankind reconstructed and psychologically reinvented in the curriculum and all other structures of society. I call this domination through freedom. Now, a significant number of top-tier universities are recognizing that their soft-pedaling of liberal arts in the curriculum is clearly implicated in a lack of creativity, critical thinking, and broad understanding (*especially in the social and technological sciences*) of history, economics, global citizenship, cultural, and concerns about humanity in general. Many of the latter, including epistemologies of the Global South, and the cultural identities of minorities, are riding a growing wave of interest:

> Outside the United States, many nations whose university curricula do not include a liberal arts component are now striving to build one, since they acknowledge its importance in crafting a public response to the problems of pluralism, fear, and suspicion their societies face. I've been involved in such discussions in the Netherlands, in Sweden, in India, in Germany, in Italy, in India, and in Bangladesh. As I have observed, it is precisely in the Indian Institutes of Technology and Management—at the heart of the profit-oriented technology culture—that instructors have felt the need to introduce liberal arts courses, partly to counter the narrowness of their students, but partly, as well, to cope with religious- and caste-based animosities. (Nussbaum, 2010, p. 125)

Paradoxically, as Geary III (2013) insightfully argues, the so-called scientific, Eurocentric curriculum doesn't "entirely deny" the need for contemplation. Discussing Palmer (2003a), Geary III (2013) adds that

> secular education is already a covert type of spiritual formation, and he offers contemplation as a form of research encouraging individuals to go beyond first appearances. Simply put, if things simply are as they initially appear, education itself would not be necessary; all would be readily apparent, without further research. The purpose of these disciplines is to see through and beyond the appearance of things, to penetrate the surface and touch that which lies beneath. (Palmer, 2003b, p. 59)

To be more precise, scientific analysis aims to break the world into parts, while contemplation (or prayer) aims at relatedness (Geaary III, 2013, p. 23); yet both "prayer and analysis seek to make the world transparent" (Palmer, 2003a, p. 59). But to what end? A clear view to more consumerism and capitalism does not help human beings flourish, while personal reflection may bring enormous compassion and insight.

Such waves of interest reflect the need for re-implementation of liberal arts in the curriculum, directly counteracting/contradicting what neoliberalism has aimed for. The right hand of neoliberalism, capitalism, has admitted that there is an urgent need to pay attention to the liberal arts. The heart of modern business is innovation, claims Nussbaum (2010), and "there are reasons to suppose that a liberal arts education strengthens the skills of imagining and independent thinking that are crucial to maintaining a successful culture of innovation" (p. 53). The cultural and societal lacks caused by the absence of the liberal arts[1] in the current curriculum is becoming unsustainable, undeniable, too big to hide,

> Again and again, liberal arts graduates are hired in preference to students who have had a narrower preprofessional education, precisely because they are believed to have the flexibility and the creativity to succeed in a dynamic business environment. If our only concern were national economic growth, then we should still protect humanistic liberal arts education. (Nussbaum, 2010, p. 112)

But even the liberal arts have been colonized by neoliberalism, not to mention the Eurocentric, objectivist, western leanings of modernism. Crouch (2011) aptly discusses the stages of neoliberalism and the astronomic capacity for transformation and adaptation it presents. Its representatives in social thinking were slowly introduced by politicians, bureaucrats, economists, business leaders, journalists, and intellectuals, bringing forth questions that made conservatives think (forced thinking) about the possibility of conforming to the neoliberal approach to the economy, much as neoliberalism creates personal/educational catastrophes and, afterwards, seems to bring the solution.

Most people cannot fully understand how neoliberalism has been toxic for the world without understanding what preceded its implementation; if we are to be transparent about the cost of it, we must acknowledge that there have always been forces promoting spiritual denial, as well as emotional and economic slavery. In our age, however, spirituality has been almost entirely replaced by greed to the point that we, and I must include myself as well, don't sense how greedy and how self-centered we are on our attitudes of buying, selling, teaching, leaning, testing and reflecting. Our self-perception lenses have been obscured by the speed of neoliberalism and to revert the process we need severe maintenance on the way we sense and reflect on things. As I stated before, neoliberalism appears to have tentacles, not just controlling social events but also guiding individuals to a fallacy of freedom, even while their citizenship is exchanged for bondage. Going further back, let's just take a moment to acknowledge and respect the real owners of the American soil, the indigenous people. How many genocides were committed in the name of modernity's expansion? These "beings," their descendants, their realm...all were literally vanished, in many cases, forever.

Today, we read history that brings us a so-called "real knowledge" that has actively, intentionally "forgotten" the truths of the ancestors of students who are descendants of the original inhabitants of the Americas. Over time, both political blocs are to consume the same curriculum, with students from all sorts of families—indigenous, immigrant, conservative, liberal...—turned into consumers of this commodity. So, what difference does it make? Political-ideological promiscuity is needed to enable conservatives to aggregate power to govern through policies. To be sure, that there are good elements in both political and ideological standings (Williams, 2007). Rorty (2003) claims that it all comes down to a "very disputed terrain, education as ground to do politics" (p. 430). Note that each one is disputing the terrain to disseminate its understanding of how education should operate. Dominion over curriculum and educational endeavors has become a "competition force acting in legitimating knowledge and what is counted as good teaching and learning and what is a just society" (Apple, 2000).

In any case, there is no time for anything besides preparing students, receptors of this mechanical information, for testing. What is absent is the time for, and interest in, human development. In the name of competing with other international systems, the modern educational framework preaches that we should put more effort and time into testing-memorizing-grading. The sagacious economy says that it will give you more if you drink more from the ("correct") knowledge fountain. Therefore, the commonly held beliefs about "helping" students increasingly involve bringing them to a space of loneness and absence from their own selves. Their essential and ordinary culture, their humanity, is permeated with spirituality. But there is no time to address the cultivation of humanity, which entails, first and foremost, critical thinking and self-examination (Boni & Walker, 2018; Nussbaum, 1997). It means learning about being a citizen of the world, and the related development of the narrative imagination, [which] only can occurs if time and effort is dedicated so we can develop the idea of critical examination of our self, life, traditions and habits, testing ideas for "consistency, correctness and accuracy of judgement" (Nussbaum, 1997, p. 10) as an art process.

In this section, I frame the exclusion of spirituality and humanity through the system of knowledge transference. My point here is that neoliberalists know the implications of addressing the "being" through a more humane curriculum. The castration of spirituality implicates neoliberalism's pervasive, astute attempts to hoax human nature by forcing human beings into an inadvertent process of premeditated confusion wherein changing the physical into the metaphysical seems unnecessary, and the denial of the transcendent for the temporal seems quite scientifically valid, epistemologically speaking. This, in turn, makes humans work and live in a completely dysfunctional mode, rife with depression, anxiety, anger, aggressiveness, behavioral issues, and so on. Such dysfunctionality is immeasurably profitable. It promotes the ongoing recreation of the job market as people search for more opportunities to fund ever more empty pursuits and products, and it enriches the pharmaceutical companies and healthcare industries treating this premeditated emotional dysfunctionality. And so I ask: What values and whose knowledge is public education promoting?

## 5   Reflection on Whose Knowledge!

At the end of the day, political battles are biased and based on claims shaped by personal preferences, life principles, beliefs, and, most of the time, battles to obtain power. Indeed, there is a fight on both sides of the aisle. Needless to say, the absence of spirituality in public education is overtly visible in the essence of the knowledge that is transmitted and how it is produced, taught, and evaluated in our schools. This brazen fact begs the question: "Whose knowledge do public schools produce, teach, and test?"

Without question, an ongoing discernable—and, I would argue, evil—political attempt to center life-draining knowledge and render the sacred invisible is occurring in our schools. Excuse me getting real for a moment, and please stick with me for just a few paragraphs. On the conservative side, a mixture of religion, principles and so on are somehow part of the claim-game, which denigrates what millions of people believe and use to improve their lives in a spiritual-religious-personal way. My claim here is that such manipulation leaves the genuine claim for education as a sacred human right behind, and douses the life-giving flame of the facts with cynicism. Religion is used/misused by conservatives as the base for impetuous claims used to shift policies and regulations in the name of educational amelioration.

So, then, I feel that it is fair to use the religious tools many use to back their political grabs for power to attempt to return the power of being to the people. Biblical knowledge indisputably aims to turn humankind towards a God who emanates knowledge, wisdom, grace, forgiveness, and freedom. Proverbs 2:6 says that "[t]he Lord gives wisdom that comes from His own mouth." Some political ideology with an anthropocentric interpretation stems from this verse, in that the push to "know" and "spread" the knowledge descending from God is amalgamated with corporate-driven politics and thereby prostituted, that is, involved in an activity for payment. It seems offensive, but it is embedded in the desire to commodify religion and its artifacts. To be sure, there are exceptions. But a superficial understanding of knowledge and wisdom denotes an absence of personal, practical knowledge. For Christians, knowledge implies a relationship with God, generally through Christ. While the few use God's wisdom for the wonderful connectedness and qualities detailed above, most use what they claim to "learn" from God for more nefarious ends.

There were many other pieces of the biblical "cake" that neoconservatives could have gone for, but this use of God's word to drive the neoliberal machine is the Achille's tendon of society. Within this context, almost anything can be redefined. The generator of the ever-growing desire to compete intellectually and economically surges from this specific political-philosophical approach. Here, the high-aimed desire to maintain the competitiveness of the party and related endeavors to return to higher—Eden-like?—standards act ceaselessly to revivify Western traditions. The excuse used is a "call for return," as Apple (2013) suggests, which, embedded in this attempt, cynically emphasizes "values" encompassing forms of morality and political purposes that insidiously erode religious traditions and culture. In other words, this endeavor identifies and then diminishes "non-knowledge" in the face of its self-aggrandizing "real" knowledge.

This mentality emerges from a sense of loss. Not what is actually being lost now (i.e., the "being"), but what the current era seems to lack in comparison to the past, such as certain aspects of morality, intellectual proficiency, military power, political domination and alliances, and so on. Why do I say that? Because neoconservatives preach these specifics to send *messages* and to *massage* the present needs that exist on both sides of neoconservatism. It is a way of aggregating power. I'm not calling neoliberals culpable for intentionally camouflaging and wrongly and subliminally impregnating the core message and political leadership in any specific case. I am arguing that neoconservatives essentially act as political undercover agents, themselves ordered—subconsciously or consciously—by a fully empowered neoliberal vision that, when involved in power relations and political alliances, depreciates the essence of the truth, knowledge, and even the biblical (or other scriptural) base religions claim to have.

The more money becomes the sole center of interest, the more one discovers that honor and conviction, talent and virtue, beauty and the salvation of the soul, are exchanged for financial elements. Over the course of this degeneration, a more and more mocking and frivolous attitude inevitably develops in relation to these higher values, since they are seemingly for sale with the same type of valuation as groceries or appliances or any available service or product, that is, also commanding a "market" price. The concept of a market price value for values, which, according to their nature, reject any evaluation except in terms of their own categories and ideals is the perfect objectivation of what cynicism presents in the form of a subjective reflex (Simmel, 1978, p. 256).

Many times, this subject is used to justify political-philosophical endeavors, when we know full well that the results of such pushes from the top are reflected in society and, by the end of the day, they all run towards capital; indeed, the latter can classify as hyperbolic capital, since it storms all spheres of society, not ameliorating but creating inequality (Lipman, 2004; Rizvi & Lingard, 2000 p. 420). Through textbooks, and by those who own the manufacturing apparatuses of knowledge and publishing, this ideology is disseminated and knowledge is slowly dissolved within the schools. For instance, history and geography books valorize the dominant power history and the "Baroque excess of the elites" more than any community's historical and local geographic structure. After 1990, it was common for Latin American schools to literally abandon the teaching of students' own culture (local social studies, geography, etc.) to slot in instruction in a new language, usually English. The message? It is much better to know about other cultures and languages and stop learning about your own.

When the original culture is not adequate or valued in the classroom, a new culture, wherein certain things are valid and others are not, takes precedence. Williams (1998) argues that such selective traditions come with an emphasis on what is adopted as valuable, while, clearly, "elements important to us [where "us" represents not just those who are currently or recently students, but also all of us] have been neglected" (p. 55). Somehow, the period we are living in is intellectually organized and ideologically aligned with initiatives involving practices that are not traditional to society but are nonetheless introduced/insinuated as cultural norms. This process is endlessly repeated:

> Within a given society, selection will be governed by many kinds of special interests, including class interests. Just as the actual social situation will largely govern contemporary selection, so the development of the society, the process of historical change, will largely determine the selective tradition. (Williams 1998, p. 55)

Similarly, Apple (1979, 2000), as deeply influenced by Williams, challenges how curriculum content has been repeatedly produced and legitimated based on a selective tradition. Thus, rather than debating and dissecting the Spencerian question of "What knowledge is of most worth?" Apple (1979, 2000) argues for the need to unpack *whose* knowledge is of most worth. Adding to the same argument (Paraskeva, 2011), raises similar question on whose knowledge, leaning towards the great question of who is behind of the very specifics of knowledge manipulation/fabrication. In so doing, Apple (1995; also see Apple & Bean, 1995) places curriculum within an intricate matrix of cultural politics. Needless to say, the absence of spirituality in the curriculum of our public schools needs to be seen as part of such a selective tradition, since the latter not only controls what is "in" and "out" of the curriculum, but also what constitutes reasoning, as well as, crucially, what does not. The importance of spirituality in education has been championed as well by Wringe (2002), who notes some of the challenges to its inclusion posed by this relentless engine of selection. In examining the British Reform Act, Wringe (2002) strongly advocates for language as a key mediator to help address spiritual issues in the educational realm. As we will see in the next chapter, this absence needs to be seen within the colonial matrix of power (Quijano, 1992).

Later on in life, I understood this process as a form of decolonization of the mind, as Thiong'o (2011) contends. Fueled by the globalized fear of being exceeded by the new and feeling obligated to abide by this vision of the future (disguised as a "better" world direction), schools across the world—especially those on the other side of the abyssal line—bought the curriculum (off the shelf), hired new teachers (English teachers), and promised a specific future for their current students. This promise had hidden messages. I need to point out that, although neoconservatives seem concerned with restoring society—a goal which seems benign when taken at face value—we need to be very, very careful. This so-called restoration cited by conservatives is used to back up their reformation claim, which leads quite naturally to notions of immigration reform, educational reform, healthcare reform, prison system reform, judiciary reform, and so on. In short, the reformation part of this pro-restoration argument could be a trap: What/who is being (re)formed? What is society being restored to—and from?

Neoconservatism laments the "decline of the traditional curriculum" and values, argues Levine (2001). Yet behind this worry is a set of assumptions about "tradition," about the existence of a social consensus over what should count as legitimate knowledge, and about "cultural superiority." And so the representations of other nationalities that we have in the U.S. are designed to reflect, instill, reify cultural and intellectual commonalities that to others are not comprehensive at all, because these commonalities exist only as judged by a certain, select set of U.S standards. The judgment and constant revision neoconservatives enforce throughout the educational process are not based on, or even taking into consideration, the effects of the global changes that force other countries to stay behind—largely due to their dependency on their colonizers. Conservativism and neoconservativism, by their friction of ideas and their "We do not have to learn from anyone" mindsets, fabricate their own absolute superiority. In such a system, how can I fairly and accurately measure the academic achievements of multicultural schools wherein students are still going through an adaptation process and situated in a language accommodation environment? Whose benchmarks should we compare such students to? The fight here is over whose knowledge is valued in teaching, testing, evaluating, and more. In our current era, the extant selected/valued knowledge has little or nothing to do with the students themselves.

Another point I would raise regards attempts to legitimize knowledge. I'm referring not just to who would be legitimizing said knowledge, or to the knowledge itself, but to the ways legitimization of knowledge gives control over the "correct" knowledge and teaching. Automatically, that control will claim rights around the determination of regulations in institutions and beyond, especially when it comes to the ways—how, where, why, what—knowledge is shared. This covers how teachers should teach and the specific qualifications required to do so, as well as which institutions are accredited to teach. "Acceptable" institutions have ties with corporations that validate the knowledge they deploy, forcing all participants (teachers, principals, administrators) in the distribution of this "knowledge" "curriculum" to possess certain credentials in order to validate that the knowledge is "correctly shared" in their school. This hyper-credentialized process is implicated in usurping teachers preparation terrain, sapping the time, energy, and resources that would otherwise be devoted to developing ways to truly reach and inspire students. Note that there are two ways it does so: (1) via the exigencies of the curriculum, and (2) via the requirements for "adequate" training (certain courses, qualifications, and degrees, offered only by certain institutions). Both can occur only with the political "go-ahead"—a reality applicable to both parties.

Dominant politics becomes epistemological when it is able to make a credible claim that the only valid knowledge available is the one that ratifies its own dominance. It makes sense, then, that in addition to this selective knowledge, the system also generates a selective culture that normalizes and popularizes the claim that such knowledge is valid. It seems to me that the way out of this impasse is premised upon the emergence of "a new epistemology that is explicitly political" (Santos, 2018, p. VII).

Let's keep in mind that the neoliberalism seeks to create an individual who is an enterprising and competitive entrepreneur. Apple (2013) has argued that such "legitimization" is leading to students "disliking" their teachers. Teachers need to abandon their students inner needs to comply with curriculum exigencies. In this arrangement, they are losing both "autonomy and respect" (Apple, 2013, p. 43). There is no democracy in the way that we learn nor in the way teachers choose their methods to teach in this multicultural terrain. Consequently, the knowledge that has been passed on is full of a false understanding of democracy.

As I have stated, there are elements of good and bad on both sides of the political spectrum. I do see conservatives boldly advocating for their philosophy more than they did before the influence of neoconservatism became so strong. Consequently, parents perceive formal education as a necessary developmental process for students. I myself also believe in the right to education, based on the fact that the family is the core of society and the commonly held agreement that parents have the sole prerogative to educate their children according to their will, whether that means religiously, spiritually, physically, secularly, etc. I mean to stress here that democracy as a right must be allowed first and foremost at home. Why? The moment a child and their parent(s) and/or caregiver(s) first encounter the educational system is the very moment that the family starts to lose its democratic rights. Parents almost inevitably have to send their kids to school—and, of course, by now we see the importance of doing so—but they also have to obey the codes imposed by the state. Parents have no voice without fighting for it, and very few have the necessary means, privilege, knowledge, and/or courage to do so. The curriculum is imposed. The testing system embodies an invisible contract that can fail kids and fire teachers for not successfully following the prescribed educational materials. Contradictory, right?

As I have mentioned before, many immigrant families praise schools and teachers for being academically tough on their children, forcing them to abandon their own linguocultural heritage because their understanding is that absorbing from the colonizer will provide their children with better opportunities. This manipulation of parents towards misunderstanding democracy begins, as Apple (2013) points out, in the teaching process, and unfolds in the ways students learn. Under the auspices of neoliberalism, democracy ensures that citizens have a basic education by supplying public education to disseminate its reconstructed ideology of democracy, preaching colonization, the guarantee of democracy through war, sanctions, and invasions, and the preservation of one language as valid, while non-validating all others. Guess what? Non-democratic countries use the same approach, offering free public education to all, and acknowledging that schooling is a right every child is entitled to. Indeed, the validation of each human being can almost exclusively happen only through education—though whether this happens for most students in most current systems is certainly in question. Furthermore, those who do not have access to education have no place in the job market. They become disposable, unworthy of democracy's benefits, non-beings (Santos, 2018).

More than ever before, the union between economy and culture has turned neoliberalism into an unstoppable beast. According to Nullmeier (2012), in the era of second-stage neoliberalism, with its omnipresent culture of enforcement, the risks of resentment and illiberalism are constantly on the rise. Neoliberalism has been "loaded up" by adding elements from conservative, nationalistic, or other right-wing viewpoints. For instance, let's take look into a relatively recent Facebook scandal. One of the minds that helped to orchestrate the corporative dominion of personal information, "Christopher Wylie" (who worked for the data firm Cambridge Analytica), explained how corporations work with the psychology of an entire nation in order to change politics, all of which, in the end, comes down to economic aims. He contends that "if you want to change politics, you must change culture" (Wylie, 2020) which is a concept extracted from his book, not a quote. In fact, the United States provides a vivid example of this very idea. In addition, if you want to change politics by changing culture, you must begin by changing people. The very unity of culture is the people. Hall (2014) claims that

> a national culture is not a folk-lore, nor an abstract populism that believes it can discover a people's true nature. A national culture is the whole body of efforts made by a people in the sphere of thought to describe, justify and praise the action through which that people has created itself and keeps itself in existence. (p. 237)

Giroux (2011) boldly claims that "the moral implications of pedagogy also suggest that our responsibility as public intellectuals cannot be separated from the consequences of the knowledge we produce, the social relations we legitimate, and the ideologies and identities we offer up to students" (p. 144). That is to say, teachers and intellectuals need to honor their moral responsibilities to students in their understanding and implementation of the pedagogy offered in class in order to wisely, pedagogically intervene. Intellectuals need to assume accountability for the democratization of schools. Democratization is not aimed and fought for just so students can conceive of the chance to choose between one thing and another. It is more than that. In *On Critical Pedagogy* (2019), Giroux claims that democracy doesn't merely entail attitudes towards free choice and a political standing. It is a force that never rests "until we accommodate the majority of the needs one's has in order to live a life with dignity" (Giroux, 2001, p. 144). Meanwhile, thousands are victimized by the current system as conservatives and neoliberals exchange power and interests, turning teaching into a negligent apparatus. Sontag (2003) urges teachers to assume responsibility for their actions within this apparatus—and to bring their teaching in line with moral principles that enable and exhort us to do something about human suffering.

I end this chapter with a declaration. As much as neoliberalism's agenda might arguably promote material and intellectual growth in certain ways, it has never been concerned with human suffering or even human being, only with profit. The forces behind what we are facing now—"our" selected tradition and popular norms—will resist the changes I am suggesting, especially since I am advocating for personal and interpersonal human gains, not financial ones. As well, given the many tentacles of the neoliberal-neoconservative machine, we must avoid promoting shifts that might be twisted to result in yet another kind of selective tradition that does not align with human relevance. Instead, in this battle for the educational terrain, we must seek to emphasize inclusion of the full "being," in part by keeping traditional traditions alive, as Williams (1998) claims. That is, we must always bear in mind that the lifeblood of every student, every human, deserves to be honored by sustaining and nurturing their individuality, identity and culture as integral to their state of "being."

Due to the compelling attractiveness of neoliberalism, it has become normal for conservatives to seek out neoliberal economic strategies and schemes and adopt them as instruments of wealth creation across the nation. And so, not so far from each other, but indeed under the same umbrella, each wing depends on the other's hunger for power. Exchanging six for a half dozen, conservatives and neoliberals depend on each other's agenda to build up both financial and political coalitions and power. One claims that our educational standards are low. The other approves policy changes and negotiates curriculum standardization. And then the former patches the social, financial, and spiritual gaps that curriculum refuses to acknowledge, and on and on, in an endless cycle of mutual reinforcement that traps students in a system that depletes their humanity, year after year.

In this chapter, I outlined the history of neoliberalism, identifying its strongest and most distinctive features, illuminating its overlaps with conservatism, and dissecting its connections with the absence of spirituality in public education. I also examined how the school curriculum is part of a selective tradition, and how that selectivity produces the invisibility of spirituality in schools. I explored how the widespread attack on the humanities and liberal arts provides solid ground for the consolidation of dangerous, so-called "neutral"—e.g., deterministic and objectivistic—educational reforms detached from the organic indeterminacy of the personal component and its inner spiritual self. Bearing in mind these destructive processes, I will next explore the role of coloniality in the repression of spirituality in schools, and outline some of the many ways in which neoliberalism has carried forward the goals and practices of colonialism.

### Note

1   The reason why I say liberal arts is because curriculum can, through liberal arts help to promote and unfold spirituality and subjects related to humanity.

CHAPTER 4

# Coloniality and the Pedagogies of Neoliberalism

In this chapter, I will contextualize the lack of spirituality in public schools' curriculum within the complex mantle of coloniality. In so doing, I will attempt to unpack the ways in which neoliberalism is the contemporary face of the matrix of coloniality. I will explore modernity's impacts on society, along with its pertinent ideologies. Further, I will look into how the changes modernity has imposed on the world reproduce and guarantee the colonial evolution matrix of society (Mignolo, 2011), which, among other things, paved (and paves) the path to sidelining spirituality in our public schools and curriculum. To do so, I will intentionally work on defining coloniality and modern rationality, bringing them to the surface in light of ideas advanced by decolonial thinkers such as Quijano (2007), Mignolo (2011), Dussel (2011, 2014), Walsh (2018), and others. I will also frame the lack of spirituality in schools within what Santos (2014) calls a sociology of absences. I will end the chapter by positing Paraskeva's (2011, 2014, 2016) itinerant curriculum theory (ITC) as an alternative way to think about the importance of and possibilities for spirituality in the public school curriculum.

Autobiographical accounts will jazz up my examination, as they are crucial to understanding the impact of *el patron colonial del poder* (Quijano, 2000) in colonial subjects, whether those subjects are human, cultural, or racial—or even academic or spiritual (Maldonado, 2007). I will also look into the intricacies of inequalities, and, finally, discuss the intention to decolonize coloniality (Quijano, 2000) and inspire and foster decoloniality (Grosfoguel, 2009).

When I took the Brazilian federal qualification test to be accepted into college, the essay question was "How important is globalization for third world countries?" Gosh, how I wish I knew the truth at the time. If I had, though, my response would have been misinterpreted and probably failed by the committee. Instead, my essay was chosen as college material. I didn't know why or how, but I passed. Now I understand that, at that time, globalization was presented to me and others as good and wanted by millions under political, spiritual, and educational oppression. So I, because of my own miseducation about globalization—received through my schooling, but also via the media—and still blind to its implications, not to mention the possibility of exploitation wearing the face of freedom, boldly exalted the need for globalization, modernity, and a free market. In my essay, I worshipfully discussed the importance of modernity, the inter-American exchange of goods and knowledge, the relationships we could develop with other countries and the ways we could benefit from their cultural values, all necessary to fulfilling our desire to "be like *them*." I perceived our roads, school system, economy, hospitals, and all the related state apparatuses from a new perspective. Hope, to be honest.

Motivated by the idea of "thinking critically," which for me is admittedly still an unsettled definition, modernity subtly pointed out to me that we need all new things, including our way of seeing the world and the word. This was a political, ideological, and economic matter (Mignolo & Escobar, 2013) for most Latin Americans. The horizon of my country felt very enticing; it called to me with the appeal of other countries, other universities, students from elsewhere crisscrossing the world delivering speeches, reframing "old knowledge" and bringing "new, better knowledge"…or so I thought. The advances once seen in the United States and European countries kept me, and millions of other Brazilians, dreaming about the so-called modern world. This modernity was propaganda, spread by TV commercials and other media, but also by our educational system. Any progress was good, so long as it went in the direction "given by Western civilization" (Mignolo & Escobar, 2013, p. 152). How transformative this idea was. And there I was, entrenched within the educational setting and unable to see what was going on, with no teacher or professor able to decolonize the idea of modernity. In my academic journey, I did not encounter a single adult who was willing and/or able to help we students to think on our own behalf.

In this chapter, I want to speak as someone who carries the scars of modernity and colonial sociability, as Santos (2018) would put it, as a "being" struggling with how colonialities operate and who has endured the non-validation of those who live on the other side, beyond the abyssal line (Santos, 2015). I do acknowledge that I can only speak for myself, but I do so for others to hear another voice beyond the loud and dominant assertions of Western modernity, so that they may think about their experiences, too.

1      **On Coloniality**

Paraskeva's (2011) *Conflicts in Curriculum Theory* introduces the coloniality armada in the field. Coloniality instead, refers to long-standing patterns of power that emerged as a result of colonialism, but that define culture, labor, intersubjective relations, and knowledge production…it emerges in a particular socio-historical setting (Mignolo & Escobar, 2013, p. 97). "Coloniality is a practice of domination which involves the subjugation of one people [by] another" (Mignolo, 2018, p. 116). Coloniality is *per se*—for itself—intrinsic and omnipresent in texts (whether written or streamed), altering knowledge production and the validation of knowledge, acting directly on academic performance, playing in cultural spheres, influencing how the self is defined by society and how the self in turn defines common sense and reason, redefining the truth and the aspirations one may aspire to, thereby radically and totally shaping the future: "Coloniality, in other words, is constitutive of modernity—there is no modernity without coloniality" (Mignolo, 2007, p. 39). The darker side of modernity is indeed coloniality, so much so that "without coloniality, there cannot be either global modernity without global colonialities" (Mignolo, 2007, p. 4).

Colonialism experienced its heyday in certain time periods and geographies. Spain, Portugal, France, the Netherlands, Germany, the United Kingdom, the U.S.—virtually all of the large, powerful countries were colonizers back in the day. Some or all still are, depending on how colonization is defined. For much of the colonial era, the concept of national advancement fit well with the perception of colonialism. It can be said to have reached its apex (or, more correctly, nadir) in the enormous endeavor of conquering the largest piece of land ever, the Americas (Mignolo, 2016), a process which in itself is intrinsic to the concept of modernity. Although the majority of colonizing countries conceived the process as consisting of taking over more and more territories while looking to advance their culture and production for the fulfillment of their own needs, the most direct, impactful truth related to coloniality was the modes[1] of modernity. What, then, is modernity? Modernity was and is a persuasive ideology of substitution, deployed when someone occupying an influential position starts using the conceit that what is old is no longer useful in order to create a disturbance consisting of the exchange of what is for what "should be," i.e., the new, the better, the modern. As a method of persuasion, modernity is highly effective. This is largely because, as Mignolo (2007) states, the rhetoric of modernity is a rhetoric of salvation (p. 24), which specifically started around 1600 in the form of salvation by conversion. Of course, at the time, the latter was (and, generally, still is) intrinsically connected to religion.

Coloniality began and then thrived for centuries by creating and stirring up conflict. From there, modernity stepped in to enact its exhausting takeover of gender, race, language, culture, the production of goods, medicine, education, etc., all the while attempting to redefine spirituality and de-subject the subjectivity of the "being." It remains the general form of domination today, now that overt colonialism has been substantially reduced on the grounds that it does not accommodate the aims of the form of democracy that currently permeates the majority of the world. According to Quijano (2007),

> [Euro-centered] colonialism, in the sense of domination has been defeated in the large majority of the cases…since the Second World War,

formal system of political domination by Western European societies over others seems a question of the past. (p. 1)

Rather than exercising its might over colonized nations now that it is running from the "imperial" label, coloniality articulates its power between social classes and ethnicities, especially in countries where inequality is rampant. These days, coloniality assumes its power with a different face, as modernity, and audaciously condemns slavery and explicit genocide, and yet does not see the *minimum wage* as a problem, nor does it recognize the citizens of the Global South, if not of European descent and aligned with Eurocentric values and knowledge. In this environment, the rejection of one's cultural knowledge becomes an act of superiority rather than of spiritual genocide. The knowledge of the colonized or subjugated individual is rendered unacceptable, thereby delinking people's cultural memories, language, and spirituality from their "being." As I've argued in Chapters 1 and 2, there is no genuine identity or citizenship if an individual's culture, which in many cases integrally involves spirituality and language, is forcibly and intentionally disengaged from a mandated, scientized learning process. This mode of education consists of the de facto denial of human rights via the insertion of "superior" ones, based on the notion that modernity requires rejection of/separation from the past in the interest of the sole "acceptable" goal of rebuilding a new future. Languages other than that of the colonizer are demonized, "modern" languages valorized; selected "rational" knowledge is framed as the only route to success, "non-valid" ideas are denigrated and/or rendered invisible. Such attempts are better understood as yet more tentacles of modernity acting in favor of the colonization of minds. This unfolds via a coloniality of knowledge that intends to colonize the "being" through "democratically"—yet with no other options—received information and "democratically"—again, also sole—enforced processes. Such knowledge is crucial in defining the individual value of each person.

> Science (knowledge and wisdom) cannot be detached from language; languages are not just "cultural" phenomena in which people find their "identity"; they are also the location where knowledge is inscribed. And, since languages are not something human beings have but rather something of what human beings are, coloniality of power and of knowledge engendered the coloniality of being. (Maldonado, 2007, p. 240)

This interdependent matrix of knowledge, "being," and power acts to redefine and change ideologies and ideas about what reality is—and what is disposable. There are two points I would like to raise in this regard. The first is that with the coloniality we see today (i.e., modernity), the necessities of modernity, such as modern schools with the latest technology and the most "modern" options ("modern" languages, sciences, and so on) built into the curriculum, are framed to students and their families as key factors in having power (in the form of "success") over those who don't have the same benefits. The mother languages spoken by immigrant students are completely denied, despite the fact that such languages in part carry who each one is, as well as where they are in the unfolding stages of their identity (as detailed in Chapter 2). My second point is that the exigencies of modernity (again, the new term for coloniality), are so diabolical that they are able to create in society and, moreover, in the individuals ensconced in that society, the desire to abandon those things that truly constitute the "being," such as culture, language, and beliefs, thereby creating a permanent and troubling stage of dissatisfaction. This inner turmoil can only be extinguished by fully emulating the colonizer. This can be achieved by simply becoming the perfect American family we see on the TV: light skin color, young dad, blond mom, two or three kids, and a white Labrador or golden retriever, speaking unaccented English in their pristine suburban home. In this model, all components are designated as facets of the principle of modernity, and, as Williams (1998) would argue, they thus represent the "correct" and selected culture. Such propaganda is deployed to bend students to accept what has been proposed academically. The teaching atmosphere and curriculum have been unequivocally dehumanized, while the liberal arts have been removed and supra-individual activities have been subbed in as replacements. All this, when what students really need is literally the opposite:

> So, we need to cultivate students' "inner eyes," and this means carefully crafted instruction in the arts and humanities—appropriate to the child's age and developmental level—that will bring students in contact with issues of gender, race, ethnicity, and cross-cultural experience and understanding. This artistic instruction can and should be linked to the citizen of the world instruction, since works of art are frequently an invaluable way of beginning to understand the achievements and sufferings of a culture different from one's own. (Nussbaum, 2010, p. 108)

Critical thinking is intrinsically related to the liberal arts (the arts themselves, plus the humanities). The modern curriculum, however, has been pushing aside the spaces where critical and genuine and democratic dialog about such subjects can occur.

Daily, students come to class and encounter a setting built to serve the needs of modernity and the future market. Computers, testing, memorization, regurgitation of information, pressure to complete activities.... Because of its fast pace, the standardized curriculum leaves no room for teachers to ask open questions or to address students' inner needs. In much the same way that the modern approach demands efficiency in economy and politics, coloniality (modernity) is able to—through the control of knowledge—make schools a corporative machine that produces only "graduates who are career ready" (Hursh, 2016, p. 29). Anywhere students and teachers look, there is no time for humanities. Both have their stories denied, their spirituality repressed, and their subjectivities asphyxiated.

Students come to class with emotional problems. Many don't have acceptable living conditions as a result of modernity's unceasing growth, others are emotionally unstable, lacking love, attention, a word of encouragement—again, consequences of modernity. Teachers do not have time to impact their students' lives in positive ways because modernity needs the students to join the labor or prison forces soon as possible. The rush alienates outer reality from students' and teachers' inner realities. The disparity between one world and the other is a deep canyon. In the process, schools act as a cowshed, where they count by the head, ignoring who individuals really are. The "innocent human beings" are deprived of their humanity (Fabricant & Fine, 2013). The neoliberal school, naturally presenting itself as a modern, democratic school, is engaged in weakening the minds and perspectives of the student and the teacher in order for all parties to give in to fatigue, in exchange for a sacrifice mixed with a little snack of hope. Coping with modernity is not feasible, but it is, indeed, profitable. For some, modernity has created a different kind of "being," new kinds of jobs and working and workers, new frictions between nationalities, ethnicities, the sexes, and more; in this context, true emotional strength is seen as emotional dysfunctionality. If we look clearly into the history of immigration, people have immigrated from all over the world to United States since its "discovery," but the idea most of the population now holds is that only Mexicans and some other Latin Americans continue to "invade" "our" country. What changed? The preference for one specific race—again a contested concept both scientifically and ethically—or type/group of people and the related depreciation of other sub-races or groups of people. Coloniality evolves and changes its face when it needs to, according to momentum and location. At the turn of the last century, for instance, it targeted Italian and Irish newcomers, among others. Our collective subconscious has already been induced and prompted to judge which race-nationality-ethnicity is "right," and very, very few are able to resist this pervasive, often subtle mindset. This rare form of defiance is all the more imperative, yet also perhaps especially challenging, for those in the "wrong" skin or from the "wrong" background.

It is thus clear that immigration is deeply informed by coloniality, but there are other phenomena that are also strongly influenced thereby. For instance, coloniality always exists in relation to class, which connection is starkly visible over the course of history. Its meritocratic, selective, alienating, separating, supplanting, and evolving ways of acting are stamped on schools today as traits of modern advancement. If the bold claims of modernity are to maintain its advancement, then the modern curriculum naturally becomes the main focus of its endeavor. However, year after year, the side effects of this enterprise have projected students into a stage of alienation from "who they really are" as "beings." This lack of humanity, this lack of sensitivity in dealing with the above-mentioned social and intrapersonal problems, this commodification of learning and students—all point to a stage of severe degeneration rather than the continual progress modernity markets. Modern curricula automatically numb students, and progressively detach them from their inner selves to the point that

> We do not automatically see another human being as spacious and deep, having thoughts, spiritual longings, and emotions. It is all too easy to see another person as just a body—which we might then think we can use for our ends, bad or good. It is an achievement to see a soul in that body, and this achievement is supported by poetry and the arts, which ask us to wonder about the inner world of that shape we see—and, too, to wonder about ourselves and our own depths. (Nussbaum, 2010, p. 102)

When confronted with what education has by and large become, we must ask ourselves how such atrocities can take place? From the educational setting itself to the destruction of students as unique "beings," this system perpetuates a hidden, subtle, yet no less destructive violence on our most vulnerable population, our children.

Going back to my personal experience, I never thought in my scariest dreams that one day I would have to face a tragic, unthinkable death while still a child myself. On a Sunday afternoon, after we had searched along the beach for hours, we sadly heard my mother and father screaming like someone was ripping their hearts out. My little brother Rui was found dead in one of the tributaries of the Amazon River, the Xingu. I still have the scars from losing him, in a place where only I can go, deep in my soul. I know what it takes to casually turn your back on someone you love, not knowing there will never be any more dialogues, hugs, companionship, and so on. Someone who had your promise that if they ever died, you would die with them. It took a long time to settle with the pain. No matter how much time goes by, nothing ever erases the horrible memory of such a tragedy. It seems to give you a thick skin and makes you look at life through a different lens. Although it can severely affect your behavior in a regressive or negative way, you can, if you are lucky, slowly recover, somehow accommodating the suffering.

Many kids become emotionally numb, as I did, in the wake of such a terrible loss. I was only able to focus on activities that would give me a sensation of happiness and gratitude. I had no other focus, no ability to concentrate, no interest in or goals for keeping up with my academic work. The only thing I felt was a fear of losing another family member. Losing my brother Rui did, however, trigger in me a sense of the value of life. Sometimes, pain introduces you to a new, different level of questioning. Indeed, some may question if the existence of another life is possible; others ask where the good and bad are in the current scenario; others may wonder why and how to live if we all eventually die. But I won't be delving into such questions here, however relevant and worthwhile they may be. Instead, I want to highlight my understanding of how this scenario played out throughout my life. For instance, when I looked closely at my experiences visiting and supporting patients at the hospital, I realized that, yes, they were about to die, but they were also about to be offered as a sacrifice to the empire. Forgive me for using such an ancient concept, but I want to refer to the brutality of a system that so completely dehumanizes young "beings" from the outset and throughout the schooling process that, even at the end of their lives, they have to admit that they only just barely existed over the course of their lives—and never truly, fully lived. Society, through modernity, redefined the meaning of success and the purpose of life, slowly changing the aims of humankind. My impression as I stayed with the dying in hospice was that so many had lived their lives to fulfill someone else's goals. By being with these individuals at the end, I perceived how we have all been part of the modernity/coloniality project. And those like me with fully or partially European backgrounds can call this wonderful "luck," as they may have had some tiny voice in the matter. Across the world, the everyday, cultural, personal, and other realities of indigenous populations, people of African descent, and most people with mixed ancestry, have been denied all value in the process of colonization, with such groups barred from any possible participation in decisions about social and political organization during the process of organizing the new state, often in lands where they themselves were the original inhabitants (Quijano, 2000, p. 564). Over the centuries and into the present, these colonized peoples directly experienced the devastating repercussions of global Eurocentric modernity:

> The globalization of the world is, in the first place, the culmination of a process that began with the constitution of America and world capitalism as a Euro-centered colonial/modern world power. One of the foundations

of that pattern of power was the social classification of the world population upon the base of the idea of race, a mental construct that expresses colonial experience and that pervades the most important dimensions of world power, including its specific rationality: Eurocentrism. (Quijano, 2000, p. 533)

Such imposed ontological differences between human beings themselves may spur us to ask questions about where we have been/are important to society, where we have the highest value, whether our culture made/makes sense and represented/represents who we really were or are. In moments like this, we come face to face with society's deluded priorities, and our hope and despair may bring us to reflect on our hardships. We are forced to give up ourselves in order to survive a little longer. So, Maldonado (2007) speaks wisely when he says that suffering does not allow hope to come in, does not allow the smallest thought of another way out. This is directly, and in some sense intentionally, caused by

the fact that the colonized person, who in this respect is like men in underdeveloped countries or the disinherited in all parts of the world, is perceiving life not as a flowering or a development of an essential productiveness, but as a permanent struggle against an omnipresent death. (Maldonado, 2007, p. 254)

My claim is that, even though we are deeply engaged with modernity, we appear to have no strength to confront its impositions, even when we have been charged with our loved one's lives. Although we struggled to accept the loss of my brother, my parents still used to say, in tears, "He's resting," meaning he does not have to fight this world anymore. How could that be so? I did not understand. Couldn't we join forces and help each other to overcome the challenges of life? No. The absence of any hope for the future is an undeniable facet of life for most "beings" subjected to the modernity machine. At the time, believe it or not, I already sensed the absence of hope, a lack of expectations for better days or the possibility of improvement as an individual. Can we not agree that someone who was mourning should at least have been able to expect a few small crumbs of hope to descend from a curriculum purporting to address students' fundamental needs? As much as lay people do not have the language or vocabulary to explain or deconstruct the ideology and dynamics that govern this terrain, these forces are sensed and understood.

Although coloniality of "being" primarily refers to the normalization of extraordinary events such as suffering, war, and death, its overall impact "makes the absence of being more acceptable" (Maldonado, 2007, p. 252). Because of decades, even centuries, of indoctrination, teachers themselves, as well as others who should know better (i.e., parents), act in favor of modernity's requirements, rushing mourning time, ignoring the unsettled soul or empty stomach, all so students will stop begging to be seen, in order to ensure that tests and exams will be completed. This is a snapshot of the coloniality matrix in which I lived. Indeed, in the classroom, I felt like an anonymous "being" beyond any imaginary expectations (Escobar, Mignolo, & Francis, 2013).

This non-stop impregnation of modernity into every aspect of our lives causes extreme discomfort and thus pushes us forward to cope with the required advances, most specifically, monetary requirements. As I grew older, I decided to move to the United States to pursue my education. I remember reading Williams' work—which had been suggested by my adviser—during my doctoral studies. Williams (2007) explicitly writes as a working class kid from Wales who went to an Ivy League-level university in the United Kingdom, and discusses how he faced the challenges of functioning in a different class context. However, he also speaks about how his Welsh cultural background had immense value in dealing with most of the hardships he encountered, and how his own working class matrix influenced certain class metamorphoses. With all due respect to Williams' unique life, I see many parallels between his experience and my move to the U.S. I did and do face blunt racism, xenophobia, and classism—in my doctoral program, in my daily life, etc.,—however, my tumultuous Brazilian cultural background is also an asset in navigating blurry social terrains. Although in a sense I became a half person (Macedo, 2015) when I came to the U.S, I also know full well that my cultural fabric, in which spirituality is a core component of my identity, helped me not only to resist, but also to re-exist (Walsh, 2018). And so, even though my live continues to entail a struggle to "be," I nonetheless exist as a whole person despite the constant battle I and others must wage against imperial modernity.

The laboratory of modernity ensures that the Global South (especially Latin America) has been denuded of power by its geopolitical and subcultural state of non-"being." By saying this, I am borrowing Mignolo's (2013) concept of how, in the absence of rationality in what constitutes the "being," (such as dreams, feelings, culture, knowledge, rituals, faith, beliefs, language, etc.) the "being" becomes anonymous, invisible, nonexistent, according to the dominant Eurocentric narrow model of thinking and imposing the idea of what and who constitute a "being." Although Mignolo (2013) avoids defining what "being" is, philosophically and as a whole, he does describe how this "being" stops existing in the eyes of modernity/coloniality. I again recall the patients I met at the hospital when I was a chaplain. Could it be that we, as emotional survivors, having given our life in exchange for our existence and having worked so much just to comply with modernity, in turn end up neglecting ourselves and thereby participating in our own erasure? Yet, I also saw that through the process of facing intense end-of-life struggles, people's minds often become more analytical and proactive at the same time that their hearts open to compassion. In truth, we often gain access to transcendence via our most devastating experiences. We do not waste time looking for answers, especially those that do not fulfill our critical needs. Instead, we immediately put superficial things—work, the high paycheck, disagreements, etc.—aside, and we see what is left. For those patients, poor health and no remaining expectations for abundance in this lifetime remained, along with many regrets. They are, we are, the casualties of this system. But the system itself surges ever onward.

Modernity capitalizes on the ease of human replacement: my dying patients knew another worker had filled their role long before their death. This new worker will work his or her shirt off in an attempt to keep his or her head above the water. S/he needs to give his or her life in exchange for his or her existence, spending that entire life trying to prove to herself/himself and society that s/he has value. We spend our whole lives being non-"beings," dispossessed of things and therefore denied the right to be a "being." In the search for the freedom to be, Santos (2018) states, "there is no individual freedom," since we are all inserted in a system that creates a false ideology that only by oppressing others is one free. As a result, these systems typically offer a few choices that generate a sensation or simulacrum of freedom that can be achieved by comparing one "superior" set of physical/material conditions to another "inferior," "oppressed" set. In this context, there is an underlying, carefully hidden truth: "You own nothing, not even your body" (Santos, 2018, p. 226).

When asked what he wanted for himself and his people, Gandhi responded, "I want freedom for full expression of my personality" (Santos, 2018, p. 226), a refuge where inner and outer needs could be met. The pursuit of spiritual satisfaction, the sentiment of freedom (even the freedom to simply be content within a context of social equality), the progress of the individual toward the fullness of their own "being"—all stand at odds with their opposite, the modern/Eurocentric idea of freedom in which the "one aim is material progress" (Santos, 2018, p. 226). I have three daughters and a wife. Daily, I go out to face the world, not just for me but for them as well. Knowing the price of pain, I myself tend to fight hard to keep my head above water, even as I try to promote a better life for my family. I did promise myself that I would live life and not just exist. However, when I sit on the couch to talk to my kids about school or life in general, I sense that there is a very real possibility that the prevailing social fabric tends to bring us invariably to the same enclosed definition of life as mere existence. The abyssal line scares individuals, especially those like me who came from the other side, the side closer to misery, the servile/*servant* side.

More precisely, over the last century or so, historians, sociologists, and others have registered the dissatisfaction of human beings over the social and political forces shaping the world. In fact, these feelings and the expression thereof picked up speed with the rise and proliferation of many new forms of communication and media. Human dissatisfaction has always existed (think the United States Revolution of 1776, just for starters). But the forces of coloniality are creating a common dissatisfaction in many aspects of life for many, many people. They can be seen in the exploitation, usurpation, and inequalities individuals, families, communities, and certain other groups (whether based on ethnicity, nationality, gender identity, class, cultural background, ability, sexual preference, and on and on) encounter daily.

If we look into the history of modernity, we cannot pinpoint the very moment it started. What we may discern is that the rhetoric or story of modernity began being told prior to the last few centuries' commodification of lives, massive genocides, and slavery. This has produced a certain banalization of life, according to Mignolo (2007), and,

> As a result, we are living in a world in which humans' lives are dispensable and the life of the planet is secondary. ...institutions come first, they should save the democracy, the state and the capitalism, etc. At the expense of life, of human beings, all living organism and the planet itself. (p. 12)

Today, modernity's rhetoric can no longer entirely hide these bleak truths. However, there are still those who are persuaded by it, and many of the latter possess significant power.

Given how entrenched these forces are, and how enduring their influence remains, how can we de-colonize modernity and eradicate coloniality? By engaging in this line of reasoning and questioning, we are already delving into decolonial thinking. Modernity is a monster, never uniform, never immediately identifiable if we are looking for an exact replica, because it presents under different guises in different times and locations. Yet make no mistake, Western modernity nonetheless created, controlled, and transformed Western power into certain ways of running the world under the auspices of certain groups and institutions. These spheres of social life do not operate independently, but are interwoven with one another, for they cannot exist in isolation. They form a complex, dynamic system "whose character is always historical and specific," constituting a "historical head of power" (Quijano, 2000, p. 22). As just one example, the Spanish and Portuguese conquests of America constituted a new head of power, or "nuevo patron." To challenge such "nuovo patron" Analzdúa (2002b, p. 540) advocates the need for "aja" or

> conocimiento, one that guides your feet along the path, gives you el ánimo to dedicate yourself to transforming perceptions of reality, and thus the conditions of life. Llevas la presencia de éste conocimiento contigo. You experience nature as ensouled, as sacred. Éste saber, this knowledge, urges you to cast una ofrenda of images and words across the page como granos de maíz, like kernels of corn. By redeeming your most painful experiences you transform them into something valuable, algo para com-partir or share with others so they too may be empowered.

As I've previously argued, by engaging in this discourse, we are already attempting and entering into a decolonizing process wherein our views and ideas are mutating and taking other points of view. We are acknowledging and calling out the existence of other forces dominating us through the arts, politics, and economy in order to enact counter-hegemonic attempts and foster a decolonizing process for our ideas and viewpoints, all of which—until we begin to think critically—are inevitably shaped through the exercise of the coloniality of knowledge. Looking at the immensity and comprehensiveness of coloniality, the idea of decolonization seems to me a bit too abstract. Yet the small steps we take as individuals do matter. Moreover, there is hope in the possibilities that could be embedded in the curriculum. We have, too, inspiring works on the pedagogy of decolonization and the theology of liberation, which for now are motivating people through critical readings of biblical texts. These situate the Christian population as a very powerful decolonizing ally, specifically via new theologies of liberation that are grounded in social justice and education and reassert the validity of other knowledges and ways of learning, especially indigenous ones, which have been denied and denigrated for hundreds of years in the name of modernization, as Mignolo (2018) notes. Academics are looking into new ways of decolonizing knowledge, breaking the power structure of knowledge by making education a local endeavor in order to empower the decolonial process; they are suggesting an inclusive, variable, participatory "itinerant curriculum" (Paraskeva, 2016). Surely, part of modernity's endeavor is to separate and classify society through gender, race, spiritual, linguistic, and other hierarchies, according to geographical necessity and whatever else the modern/colonial capitalist/patriarchal world-system requires. Let's not forget that modernity resides in the absolutization of particular cultural spheres and their characteristics (Dussel, 2009).

If we are looking to move on into decolonization mode, departing from specialist definitions and discussions of colonialism and modernity and shifting into the realm of action, then we do have to engage in sincere and comprehensive dialogue with curriculum theorists and the others who shape the educational realm. But we must also begin to experiment with finding ways to go back to who we are as people, to figure out how to genuinely serve human beings in the classroom. Gordon (2015) claims that education should invite learners in by taking questions of the human condition seriously and exploring their relevance to our understanding of recent social and political realities in order to deal with the antipathetic age of thinking we now are living in. In this way, students may become aware of the impossibility of being their full selves within this all-encompassing system. Yet who is not attached to the system? Possibly that individual who does not have the language to decolonize it. Coloniality requires a radical transformation of power, knowledge, and "being," leading to the coloniality of power, the coloniality of knowledge, and the coloniality of "being" (Gordon, 2015, p. 18); therefore, considering the opposite is in itself already a decolonizing attitude. Still, when we engage only in discourses of criticism, we leave mutual hope in a sort of intellectual prison—and thereby continue to uphold the goals of the coloniality that has imprisoned so many minds and bodies. In order to move on in the process of decolonizing Western epistemologies, we need to interrogate a subject that it is concomitant with keeping the status quo of modernity-coloniality-capitalism in charge of (cursing) the globe.

The abyssal line is indeed the motive for the millions who immigrate to the U.S, attempting to erase themselves as they endeavor to live a dignified life as human beings. Therefore, I will next delve deeper into aspects of coloniality/modernity using a lens that centers the abyssal line. Power and control emanate from both coloniality-modernity and abyssalism, leading to the destruction of the individual's realm and "being," with the destruction of our one and only planet as the ultimate apex. Having unpacked the matrix of coloniality and its impact on the lack of spirituality in our schools, I will now turn my attention to examine the spiritual void at the heart of the decolonial framework, what Santos (2017) calls the sociology of absences. My discussion of these topics will reveal all the more why spirituality is a human rights issue.

## 2   A Sociology of Absences

The sociology of absences (Santos, 2007) helps us to position ourselves at an epistemological angle that allows us to identify and critique the dominant epistemologies and structures of knowledge. It gives us a counter-facing framework to question how these forces present and want us to see the world, even as they directly render certain "other" people and forms of knowledge invisible, creating absences of such magnitude that many realities vanish and, with them, the human beings inhabiting them. This is directly connected to Eurocentric ideas of who is allowed to be a "being," whose knowledge is valid knowledge, whose identity matters, and so on. For so long, sociology has evolved and learned how to tell the world only what it wants the world to know. By the same token, this discipline has all along continued to deny the existence and struggle of many groups, delegitimizing their right to exist. For instance, indigenous people were not considered "beings" on the same level as Westerners, but instead relegated to a realm of study deeming them lesser creatures. Some tribes were nonexistent to civilization's eyes. None of their knowledges, struggles, or cultures were ever made visible; instead, absence and denial were imposed. Africans, for instance, were considered sub-human. How could slavery otherwise have taken place? The consequences still resound today—in the racism, class separation, language hierarchies, ethnic preferences, and minority marginalization of the abyssal line dividing these realms. They persist in the skepticism and denial waged by the insidious realities Eurocentrically whitening the South, implicating the existence and perpetuation of the transcontinental empire (Muthu, 2012) in all spheres of society, especially those colonized by the Spanish and Portuguese. To approach the matter with more clarity, let's work on defining what the abyssal line means, and the sociologies of the absences that are perpetuating these epistemicides.

In the previous chapters, I've used the term abyssal line several times, having in my introduction briefly defined it as the visible and imaginary lines that define where one's culture, knowledge, and "being" as a full human being vanish. Abyssalism is embedded in the current contexts we are inserted into, not just as nations, but in global financial power, knowledge, existence, identity, and social justice ghettos.

Initially, the abyssal line was a metaphorical topographical line that was created at a certain time between metropolitan and colonial societies. Consequently, this line became inter-personalized far more deeply than its original aims indicated. It became part of our human subconscious, embedded into our individual, cultural, and national perceptions of the world, of words, of geographies, and more. But the separation we are going to discuss is one that, yes, includes landmarks and other concrete elements, but it also entails a more radical sort of exclusion, involving—and devolving—the quality of human life to a concerning degree. We can all agree that every country offers ups and downs in its citizens' quality of life. These variations can depend in part on geography, location, natural resources, weather, and other naturally occurring factors that can secure or destabilize any country's economy. The quality of life I am referring to, however, is a general claim for the need for substantial amelioration in respect to people's existence, sense of belonging, respect, citizenship, and so on, all of which may be mutually correlated with the environment. The abyssal lines speak to how those within the Global South are living within a non-rationalized oppression that not only excludes science and its cognition but also excludes the "being" as human. In this context, no clear right or wrong can reign as the rule of law, instead, the right of the empire, the constructed rightful ways of everything—thinking, "being," knowing, appearing, existing, and doing—prevails. Because there is no intrinsic right to be right, because there is no full human to be the receptor of such rights, there is only one truth; thus, there is no need for human rights. And, therefore, the living creatures in such lands are not considered a real reality. This nonexistent reality (Santos, 2016) is hegemonically taught and lived in all the aspects of modernity, especially in the accumulation of capital. Note that Santos (2007) points to it as "realities radically excluded which lies beyond the realm of what the accepted conception of inclusion considers to be" (Santos, 2007, p. 2). If there is no knowledge that can be measured, then there is nothing to be validated. What is worthy of reflection is that, in many of these countries where abyssalism is strongly entrenched, the idea of democracy is certainly present—which, in itself, gives us goosebumps, if we dare to think critically. How can such abyssal orchestration within oneself coexist with a sense of democracy? It seems a dysfunction of the metaphysical terrain; but perhaps metaphysics, given its often unfeasible state of abstract truth, is classified as such for this very reason. So, the possibility of the abstract, too, is vanished. Transcendence or metaphysics are not valid concerns, but instead roadblocks that oppose the "normal" or "common" understanding of sociology.

Many times, we classify the countries of the Global South as "poor" or "third world" or "developing," assuming food, water, and other important resources are scarce, but this is not necessarily so. Such skeptical and dualistic assumptions are yet another part of what we call abyssalism. This force

> operates through radical lines that divide social reality into two realms, the realm of "this side of the line" and the realm of "the other side of the line." The division is such that "the other side of the line" vanishes as reality, becomes nonexistent, and is indeed produced as nonexistent. (Santos, 2007, p. 45)

One of the things I have experienced throughout life is an uncomfortable, vague, unsure sensation when sitting on the other side of the table as an immigrant during an academic conversation or a job interview. It took me a long time to understand that the sub-citizen (the immigrant, the citizen or child of the Global South, etc.) ceases to exist when it becomes a matter of choosing between one person and another. And, believe it or not, within coloniality-modernity-neoliberalism, even nonexistence has a hierarchy. Let's look at an example from Brazil. So much credit is given to the MST (a movement of those who are dispossessed of land), to such an extent that even the federal congress is shaken. But the country's indigenous people claiming their origins and fighting for a small share of the vast lands that used to be theirs alone, the media and lawmakers do not pay the same attention. Congress largely ignores the latter, and there is a shameful lack of space in the curriculum to include indigenous concerns, histories, and knowledge.

Such divisions intuitively and urgently force us to put on our critical and social justice lenses in order to see the unreasonable, unethical social discrepancies that alert us to the need for emancipation. The profound gaps between these worlds also beg the question of why this subject requires such attention and historical-theoretical clarification after all these years—and in which areas we should proceed. The answer to the latter question is: in everything! In this sense, an amalgamation of aspects and details come into play. Abyssalism is more than one thing or the denial of one aspect of social life. It is by no means just about race. Abyssalism moves around in both racialized and racially homogenous societies. For instance, in the late teens and early 20s of this century, we saw caravans of immigrants departing from much of Latin America, moving into Mexico, and marching towards the U.S. border, while immigrants from African and other countries surged into Europe. Two different continents, and a myriad of languages and cultural backgrounds, all in search of safety and security for themselves and their families. Even those who came from—or now live in—democratic societies still carry their skin color and/or language as a trait worthy of social and intellectual disqualification. Indeed, the imaginary lines of abyssalism are almost visible in the way languages play an important abyssal role.

As just one "proof," we can observe the quality of life of immigrants entering Europe. They are not truly considered citizens by the Western eye. Through this denial, their social and cultural attributes, the very sources of who they are, are dehumanized. Even if they went into a society consisting of people of the "same race," they would still endure an obscured reality.

> Human dignity is thus revealed as both a representation of the finitude of human reason and a bulwark against social and political injustice, rather than an affirmation of metaphysical essences or a nonexperimental world…European states are legitimate because they secure agreements and contracts that constitute the realm of acquired rights and that this

can be theorized form a social contract doctrine, but that they should also be roundly criticized for often failing to respect the one "innate value of humanity:" freedom, specifically the cultural agency that constitutes humanity itself. (Muthu, 2003, p. 125)

As in the past—but without the explicit physical cruelty of being beaten and tied to a pole as a slave—immigrants now enter a new country to serve the purposes of the labor market. They are forced to expose their families as non-"beings," with no dignity. Blinded by the dream that they will experience freedom, they instead obscure themselves, not knowing that they will in their own generation be deleted from their newfound realm. Such immigration is orchestrated by the same hand that in the past enslaved. Today, in general, society is more enlightened in regard to slavery, but there are manifold other ways of enslaving. Despite media exposure and the evolution of human rights in an increasingly democratic direction, people are still taking advantage of other human beings' language, ethnicity, and skin color. Slavery did not end with abolition in the 19th century, but it evolved in different forms. It is now less about people owning other people and more about a system owning entire nations. Such exploitation is democratic, legalized—coloniality in the form of "legitimate," "fair" abyssalism and slavery.

Returning to the above quote regarding cultural agency, let's just take a moment and think about whether people who live beyond the abyssal line could respond to the following questions with at once more scars and superior clarity than those who have lived above that invisible demarcation. How many of your school books taught you about your culture, your people, their social mores, cities and states, or even about their political systems and so on? How much of your classroom time focused on things that belonged to the common lifeblood and communities of you and your classmates? History, geography, language, social studies...in my schooling, all exalted the colonizers' culture and knowledge, but not my own. When I entered eighth grade, I knew more about Greek mythology than the common religions of my own country. Religion in Brazil is as ordinary as culture is, yet it was invisible in our curriculum. How can social studies depart entirely from local society and cultures? In my estimation and experience, Brazil's curriculum seems to be an ideal social contract through which Eurocentric knowledge is enabled to perpetuate both the imaginary abyssal line and its continued construction. As a representative result of just one function among many, it indoctrinated me (falsely!) to see the other side of the line as the only place I could finally exist.

As I have mentioned in my introduction and elsewhere above, it is possible to consider oneself a socially moral person but remain amoral when it comes to honest truths about how we perceive certain struggles and the absence of empowerment. When, as teachers, we somehow nurture in students the desire to be on the colonizer's side, we regularly deliver their own realms as non-valid. We teachers have freely indoctrinated our students in the name of ameliorating social discrepancies, not knowing that our actions actively perpetuate abyssalism, never realizing that our local realities are depleted and made invisible when a more "relevant" reality is presented.

In how modern western thinking operates, Santos (2016) states that "whatever is produced as nonexistent is radically excluded because it lies beyond the realm of what the accepted conception of inclusion considers valid." What most fundamentally characterizes abyssal thinking is thus the impossibility of the co-presence of the two sides of the line. To the extent that it prevails, this side of the line only prevails by exhausting the field of relevant reality. Beyond it, there is only nonexistence, invisibility, non-dialectical absence (Santos, 2016, p. 45) and whatever is produced, taught, or made therein does not have the legality, existence, legitimacy, or functionality established by Eurocentric rationality. Our theories of social emancipation have been very limited and restricted (Santos, 2016), because they have never expanded to address the real and vital practical concerns they refer to. My goal is not only to amplify and concretize questions about where invisibilities and absences of people occur and what their silences are trying to tell us, but to begin to propose human rights solutions, namely, to bring the "being" into the curriculum.

Many times, we citizens of the South persist in simultaneously fighting and condoning oppression, but how often do we actually delve into the process of liberation? For example, throughout Latin America, we see discount stores, such as Dollar Tree and Family Dollar, packed full of customers. The low prices in these stores naturally attract people. But if these products are so cheap, and the store chain makes an adequate profit on each product, how much does it actually cost to produce such below-market-value products? What kind of labor cost is involved? Who or what country in fact hosts such factories? In business, this is called product dumping for a reason. Another example involves the ways in which families move from rural areas into urban centers and metropolises looking for a more dignified life, as if the life they had been living was not worthwhile. But abyssalism follows the individual even when they run away from an "inferior" geographic location, because abyssalism is not a place. It is a condition, a state of life. It enacts a mobile form of transcontinental oppression (Muthu, 2003) that follows individuals wherever they go, forcing them to carry their own denial with them through language, color, nationality, theology, and more. When we acquire the colonizers' knowledge and language, we think we are finally becoming "right" and moving up in the

COLONIALITY AND THE PEDAGOGIES OF NEOLIBERALISM        207

world. In truth, we merely shift from a fully abyssal state to the colonial status quo, which renders us colonized, even as we believe we have become (and are seen by some as) citizens of power. This possession of "valid" knowledge and its products is yet another way of transposing abyssalism! Why on earth do we fall for this ruse? Santos (2018) tries to untangle the reasons why those below the abyssal line themselves have such biased attitudes:

> The social experiences of injustice and oppression caused by capitalism, colonialism, and patriarchy are always corporeal experiences; however, their main manifestation may involve physical, mental, emotional, spiritual, or religious dimensions. They tend to be lived with greater intensity once they include resistance and struggles against injustice and oppression. In very unequal and unjust society like ours, the greater the intensity of the oppression, the harder is for oppressed groups to communicate the suffering and the emotions that accompany their experience of oppression in such a way as to arouse active solidarity. (p. 79)

On the 22nd day of June, 2002, aiming for a better life, I immigrated to the United States. As I have mentioned, many facets of the world I grew up in, such as injustice, poverty, inequality, lack of opportunities, and locally short lifespans, motivated me to pursue my education in hope for a future different from what my parents had to endure. I vividly remembered where I came from, where I was born, raised, acculturated, and taught. But on that day, at New York City's John F. Kennedy airport, I sat on my luggage and looked around: Everything was so different. The language barrier scared and demoralized me. When anyone asked me anything, I would run away to avoid the conversation. I could neither speak nor understand. I barely knew how to count to ten, and could say little besides "Thank you" and "Please." My best friend told me that if I used those words well, I would survive. I came with two other friends, who had summer jobs doing construction work. I had nothing, just my best high school friend Zeti's (pseudonym) promise that I could stay in his apartment for little while, until I got on my feet. While sitting there on my luggage, I took an emotional look back, and contemplated what I was leaving: my life, my parents, my sister, uncles, grandparents, and my beloved little nephew. Not to mention my job. I had been accepted into an MBA program at an Ivy League-level university in Brazil called FGV (Fundação Getúlio Vargas) just a few months before my trip to the United States. But what difference would it have made? Like so many, I had been accepted, but I could not pay. I was just so sick of sitting around and watching inequality triumph over honesty. I was tired of the suffering, struggles, and pain I experienced and witnessed all around me. It was sad for me, as a young 25-year-old full of dreams, to get to the point of leaving everything I knew and loved behind and endeavor a new life in a new land. In Brazil, the patriotism that resonated every single time the Brazilian national anthem played was put into question by the realities around me. I felt my homeland was somehow denying me my rights. I was discontent with its political, economic, and social practices. The hegemony of neoliberalism had taught my people to accept oppression, which, for me, was the same as being hopeless. Leaving Brazil was, for me, an act of defiance and hope. As Freire (1970) writes, such

> struggle is possible only because dehumanization, although a concrete historical fact, is not a given destiny but the result of an unjust order that engenders violence in the oppressors, which in turn dehumanizes the oppressed. Because it is a distortion of being more fully human, sooner or later being less human leads the oppressed to struggle against those who made them so. In order for this struggle to have meaning, the oppressed must not, in seeking to regain their humanity (which is a way to create it), become in turn oppressors of the oppressors, but rather restorers of the humanity of both. (p. 44)

Fleeing from its imposed abyssal absences, I somehow sensed that my homeland saw me as something other than a "being." I felt like a citizen of an empire (Jensen, 2004), but one dispossessed of both capital and hope. I felt a bit like a prototype or a project in development. It seems odd for me to say that, especially after all of the critical reading and thinking I did in graduate school and while writing my dissertation, but this is the most honest truth. To be more precise, I only began to observe the words and world around me after paying attention to many of my friends, who (I now feel comfortable saying), like me, were asking themselves painful and necessary questions: Where is our humanity? Our sense of social interrelation? Where are our possibilities for the future, hope, recompense for overcoming struggles and greed? Santos (2017) argues that the "sociology of absences works to transform the impossible into possible objects" (p. 3). The curious fact is that hidden in the monoculture given to us throughout life is the urgent need for an ecology of knowledge, for the recognition of the existence of a plurality of knowledges beyond scientific knowledge (Santos, 2007, p. 31), which can act as an effective counter-epistemology. As Santos (2017) explains, "The ecology of knowledges is a destabilizing epistemology to the extent that it engages in a radical critique of the politics of the possible without yielding to an impossible politics" (p. 40). This stands in stark contrast to the dominant culture of scientific knowledge (Santos, 2004). As an added benefit, any system that takes a comprehensive, holistic perspective in some sense furthers the growth and sustenance of all types of ecologies, not just human, but environmental, planetary, and so on.

Absent such an inclusive ecology of knowledge, the individual but ubiquitous claim of 'I am not yet" reveals how one sees the world, as well as the ways in which one pursues self-erasure in order to merely "exist." In this sense, abyssalism plays a significant role in reconstructing social awareness of what "to be" means in a "to-exist" context, obligating the sense of "being" to be exploited by "I am not yet," and reflecting a sense of worthlessness or frustration with the self—all feelings I grew up with. Please allow me to claim once again that the absence of spirituality as a human right has, by its very own outcomes, shown us why spirituality in schools must be allowed: so that instead of "not yet" "being," students can "be." Such absences have created a terrible silence for way too long. So, for now, I want to use the sociology of absences to make a claim, one I believe can allow the themes, social conflicts, noisy silences and hegemonic epistemologies I explore to be questioned, dissected, and dialogued. The aim of the sociology of absences is to "identify and valorize social experiences available in the world, although declared nonexistent by hegemonic rationality and knowledge" (Santos, 2004, p. 180). Yet it is clear that we cannot achieve this goal via conventional critical analysis because the process/system/modernity keeps reinventing itself. Therefore, itinerant curriculum theory (ICT), in all its agility and specificity, becomes all the more useful. It addresses Huebner's (1962) claim of the need "to build an environment which structures educational activity means to, select content from the whole, wide, wonderful world and to make it available for students" (p. 109). Many scholars, such as Paraskeva (2011, 2016), Santos (2006), Maldonado (2018), Mignolo (2013), Nkrumah (1965), Cabral (1979), Escobar (1995), Frank (1969), Grosfoguel (2000), Dussel (1995), and Andreotti (2013), have suggested reinventing social emancipation through new lenses. Some claim that counter-hegemonic movements should put a significant amount of energy into decolonization and anti-colonization so that new sociologies can freely take form and place, based especially on the principles of equality and the recognition of differences, In such sociologies, wherein the absent is made present by the very individuals and groups impacted, space is created in which those silenced by subhuman conditions could in fact have life and voice.

In more simple terms, students are looking to make sense of life in education—and they are not being helped to do so by current curricula. Santos (2009) argues that we need a new critical theory in order to exercise a new praxis

> contrary to their predecessors, [such] theory and practices must start from the premise that the epistemological diversity of the world is immense,

> as its cultural diversity, and that the recognition of such diversity must be at the core of global resistance against capitalism and of alternative forms of sociability. (p. 12)

As I have argued before, the fierce and demonic power of coloniality, as metamorphized into modernity, exercises an omnipresent and direct attack on our social and academic fabrics, and it has forced education into a mode of dependency, complete with passive moral, political, and social discouragement. This force re-educates student's minds and shapes their actions, pouring challenges into their daily lives. If it truly aims to help, society needs to find its way back to a point of sanity. I believe that, academically speaking, a curriculum that reduces the spaces in which coloniality/modernity can exercise its power would entail a more individualized and local curriculum, in which the reforming parties (teachers, administrators) and institutions would have more ground to re-educate students around conscience, consciousness, and the subconscious. According to Paraskeva (2016), "the struggle against the epistemicides and the curriculum epistemicides is difficult, but it needs to be done" (p. 10). Our theory, Paraskeva (2022) argues, in its dominant and counter-dominant Eurocentric forms, faces a deadlock and reduces curriculum praxis to an involution, an egregious regression. It is crucial to aim at a theory that can respond to the world's epistemological difference and diversity. In what follows, echoing Paraskeva's (2011, 2014, 2016) ICT approach, I argue that another curriculum is possible—one that respects the spiritual dynamics of each and every self.

## 3   The Decolonial Turn: Towards an Itinerant Curriculum Theory

I have long sympathized with the idea of ICT as a decolonizing force in education. More than simply a decolonizing and anti-imperialist theory, ICT

> Is also a human rights issue, a challenge to the dichotomy ethics and chaos since it is the ethic of the (needed) chaos. ICT praises the consistency of inconsistencies and foster a reckless philosophy of praxis above and beyond the rumble "being-non-being"; it is a eulogy of "being." ICT is à la Marti, "an infinite labor of love" one that perceives that the act of thinking is not just theoretical. ICT works in a never-ending matrix determined and determine by sensations, forces, fluxes, and "happenings," all of which are linked and reacting against the modes and conditions of production of the capitalist system. (Paraskeva, 2016, p. 9)

COLONIALITY AND THE PEDAGOGIES OF NEOLIBERALISM 211

The yoke of modernity placed on students' lives continues to bend them, and those educators who serve them, towards chaos, desperation, and failure. Students are literally pushed into prisons, teachers are losing their jobs for not coping with the exigencies of modernity.... This utter distortion of learning, identity, spirituality, and socialization necessitates an emancipatory cognitive rupture from colonial epistemologies and praxis. The rejection of hegemonic dogmas can become a liberating political force, able to transform our current social and material conditions, as Darder (2016a) claims. Epistemological totalitarianism cannot completely stamp out the possibility of resistance, nor can it prevent our rising above the neoliberal devastation by which we all have been victimized. When humans start to understand their own humanity, post-abyssal thinking emerges—and emancipation begins.

Generally speaking, though, it seems that the more common state—even for those who seek to liberate themselves and others—primarily involves a river of con fusion, rampant misunderstandings about the philosophy and principles of education, and an incomplete grasp of the theory and praxis of pedagogy. ICT then

> is meant to guide us in transforming our labor into a living praxis of global cognitive justice. This entails curriculum driven by emancipatory epistemologies of difference and resounding otherness that provide us the space in which to (re) imagine and transform the rigid, disembodied, fractured, and reductive ideologies that plague our teaching and our lives...it is a curriculum driven by emancipatory epistemologies. (Darder, 2016b, p. XVI)

Note that it is important to understand what modernity is and how it is attached to knowledge, power, and social fabrics in order to identify where power is centralized. For Dussel (2013), modernity is the fruit of management of the centrality of the first world system. Needless to say, it is, as Mignolo (2008) explains, infused in public pedagogy and formal academic curricula:

> modernity is associated with literature, philosophy, and history of ideas, whereas the modern world system is associated with the vocabulary of the social sciences. Second, this first characterization is important if we remember that since 1970 both concepts have occupied defined spaces in academic as well as public discourse. Third, modernity (and, obviously, post-modernity) maintained the imaginary view of Western civilization as a pristine development from ancient Greece to eighth-century Europe, where the basis of modernity was laid out. In contrast, the

conceptualization of modern world system does not locate its beginning in Greece. It underlies a special articulation of power rather than a linear succession of events. (p. 228)

Here, Mignolo (2008) underscores some of the developments that have led to the need to ignite a whole new set of curricula, one that can generate spaces for other epistemologies and integrate a holistic ecology of knowledges—a system that can effectively eliminate the rule of dominating sources of knowledge that eliminate possibilities for change and ceaselessly perpetuate wrongdoing.

Many intellectuals, such as Darder (2012), Jupp (2017), Süssekind (2017), Oliveira (2017), Moreira (2017), Janson (2017), Price (2017), Pinar (2013) and Schubert (2017), seem to agree that the modern curricular approach has exhausted its capacity to propose or bring about freedom, emancipation, and humanity. The modern curriculum is rotten with the pain, tears, and oppression caused by greed. It has not cooperated in the formation of people who are free to think and live—quite the contrary. Social absences find the perfect place to evolve and perpetuate their unjust existence in a curriculum and society that deny the tears, struggles, and suffering of the people they serve. It is far past time to bring about changes, before the human race becomes ineluctably entrenched in its ignorance of its own freedom, enslaved forever in its own denials. The field of curriculum theory is one area of hope, offering ideas for transforming social absences into forms of liberation. For instance, Moreira (2017) argues that while ICT does not automatically turn the discourses of linguistic minorities, or of given social, professional, or other groups, into something intrinsically good, it should nonetheless be part of our constant surveillance of these discourses because it makes them visible, present, full of potential. Further, engaging in academic critique through an ICT lens will bring an eye-opening perspective to the fields of curriculum studies and teacher education. Indigenous and local knowledge should not be *a*critically glorified or romanticized: we still need to ask the crucial questions—*Whose knowledge? Who benefits? How is this information classed? How is it gendered? How democratic is it?*—while also bearing in mind another key line of interrogation: *Who speaks and who is heard? Who will listen?* In other words, we must still act as a vigilante framework (Moreira, 2017, pp. 10–11), to ensure that no one way of knowing comes to dominate and oppress again. Schubert (2017), similarly, sees ICT as an embodied theory that we need to imagine, pursue, and live—a continuously evolving, never ending curriculum which enables us all to seek, create, be, and share. I see it as a shape-shifting theory that lives within us and is recreated in each situation encountered, according to which we strive to do and be what is worthwhile and just. Similar to Dewey's (1934) *common* *faith*, a continuously growing faith in humanity and its capacity to form and reform participatory democracy, refine its philosophical imagination, attend to consequences, re-envision, and move onward, seeking growth (p. 13). Furthermore, Price (2017) raises an interesting point. Noting Paraskeva's (2016) view of ICT as giving a positive signal of something feasible, he encourages us to be bold, and—gelling in the imagination, forming a cascading hermeneutic theory—a sort of thinking and doing, calls for us to make meaning, not only through curricular study, but via tapping the reservoir of life itself. Life will save education…life *is* education. ICT is a *poesis* that itinerantly throws the subject against the infinitude of representation to grasp the omnitude of the real(ity) and the rational(ity), thus mastering the transcendent (Price, 2017, p. 1). ICT calls for a radical rethinking of all pedagogical relationships, not only between curricularists and teacher education or between students and teachers, but within our respective curricular fields in this, education's season of great discontent.

Moreover, ICT proactively intervenes in the formation and expression of what comes to be called "teacher education" (Price, 2017, p. 5). Price (2017, p. 11) saw in ICT a factor not observed by other scholars: ICT could be the educational protein needed to nourish and sustain our strength and vigor as we pick ourselves back up and move forward decisively and with resolve. ICT helps "us as curricularists to take the road less traveled, a clarion call that we dare not ignore" (Price, 2017, p. 2). On the other hand, Janson and Silva (2017), intellectuals who deal daily with minoritized youth, concluded that ICT becomes a way for rearguard intellectuals to challenge dominant knowledge paradigms and to resist epistemicides. ICTtheorists, are sentient of the need to be responsive to the world's epistemological differences and diversity (Paraskeva, 2011, 2016, 2018, 2021a, 2022). They know full well that

> All of man's knowledge, wisdom, and skill is required to build a just educational environment. The study of curriculum can be and should be a great liberal and liberating study, for through it the specialist must come to grips with the great social and intellectual problems of today. The study of curriculum need not be the search for curriculum theory, although eventually a theory or theories may emerge. The study of curriculum need not be labeled as a profession, for prestige follows from work, not labels. Is it possible, now that we are partially freed from the vision-hindering busy work, that we can begin to make efforts to grasp the overall design of curriculum and to see how man's evolving techniques can be made subservient to man's evolving spirit? Educational environment and activity in the schools are symbolic of what man is today and what he

wants to be tomorrow. The design of these symbols is a great art. The study of curriculum should be a preparation for this artistry. (Huebner, 1962, p. 111)

ICT empowers us to see beyond the abyssal line, and thus to challenge the Western epistemological framework's position as the only legitimate one; ICT refuses to let epistemicides go silently, unnoticed, and instead wrestles with the complexities and power of educational policies (Janson & Silva, 2017, p. 14). Furthermore, ICT requires us to challenge the rhetoric of scientific supremacy in U.S. public education, to analyze other epistemologies, and to craft other ways of educating and knowing through dialectical teaching and learning. In the same terrain, Oliveira (2017) argues that ICT provides a way to think about curriculum from perspectives encompassing ecologies of knowledge and South-North dialogue, and considers ICT to be a daily knowledge practice, contributing both to the curriculum and everyday school-life studies (p. 15). Paraskeva (2016) develops his own branch of the sociology of absences by recognizing and centering the ideas of underrepresented African philosophers, even as he demonstrates the validity of his own arguments and, at the same time, implicitly points to some possibilities for curriculum theory to advance a South-North curriculum dialogue very different from previous versions of curriculum internationalization (Paraskeva, 2015a, 2015b). This amounts to a curriculum theory that is both itinerant and de-territorialized. Jupp (2017) boldly contends that adopting an ICT approach can paradoxically provide loving, yet mercilessly hard-hitting, critiques of curriculum studies as a field, and possibly shift its admittedly mixed legacy towards serious, meaningful, and activist scholarship in the present moment. Süssekind (2017) believes that ICT has arrived at a crucial moment in curriculum studies and promotes ICT as the "best answer" to the discipline's profound paradigmatic crisis. Finally, I myself contend that implementing ICT may well be the most effective and humanitarian way to nurture and truly educate the whole "being"—as they exist in the moment, have been shaped by their past, and dream toward their future. By definition, this will include a spiritual dimension, as I have described it above. ICT allows me "a camiñar con el mi saber," "mi conocimiento,"—within and beyond the immanent and the transcendent—which is "skeptical of reason and rationality, and questions conventional knowledge's current categories, classifications, and contents (Anzaldúa, 2002b, p. 541). ICT respects and responds to the pragmatism of my intimacy, my critical conscienciousness. ICT is the autochthonous riverbed of spiritual reason. ICT is the critical inquiry and praxis of "consciencism" (Nkrumah, 1964) and "conscientização" (Freire,

1973); ICT certifies the spiritual as a political act to better grasp the human being's temporality within the finitude of the transcendent.

I thus propose the integration of ICT into all relevant aspects of education, from the discipline of curriculum studies and the various academic and institutional levels of administration to teacher education and the classroom. This inclusive theory presents a powerful force against the epistemicides, silences, absences, abyssalism, and sub-humanization of modernity-coloniality-neoliberalism. It seeks to add diversity, delve into many ways of "being" and knowing, ask questions, share freely, and liberate education from its longtime hegemonic dependency and the intellectual pandemic of oppression it imposes. In so doing, ICT still grants spaces for differences to be settled, humanity to be cultivated, pain to be acknowledged, tears to be understood and addressed, spirituality to be acknowledged, cultivated, and supported, metaphysics to be respected as unmeasurable but valid, knowledge to be free of frontiers while allowing the local to hold its cultural value, freedom to be dreamed of as a constant aim, diversity to exist as genuinely diverse, not forced to be unified, and, finally, for "beings" to cease to exist, and instead fully live. In sum, ICT will allow the educational system to serve our students in such a way that their individual sovereignty will be restored and they will regain the right to be.

### Note

1  By using the word "modes," I am referring to the definition of given by Saltman (2014). The aim, the hidden will of modernity was not to modernize the world starting from the west, but rather to create implications that potentially would lead to governance of social structure as a whole throughout the entire world.

CHAPTER 5

# A Conclusion

*Spirituality as a Counter-Hegemonic Human Right*

A large majority of the world's inhabitants, Santos (2015) argues, "are not subjects of human rights" (p. 1). I would complexify his statement by adding that a high proportion of spiritual people are, likewise, not full subjects when it comes to human rights. Like so many of their fellow human beings, "they are rather the objects of human rights discourses" (Santos, 2015, p. 1). To complicate my claim, echoing Santos' (2015) insightful arguments, I hold that the dominant notions and praxis of human rights exclude spirituality. Spirituality is thus a stark absence within the hegemonic human rights framed by the colonial power matrix (Mignolo, 2018; Quijano, 2008; Dussel, 2009). In this regard, and along with Santos (2015), I also argue that the current human rights hegemony is a fragile one, lacking as it does any genuine regard for what most humans need most. The (related) insensitivity of the current modern Western Eurocentric matrix towards spirituality is not innocent; to be more precise, it is both evolving and intelligent. It is, as I have demonstrated, eugenic. If spirituality is, as I claim, a human rights issue, it becomes crucial to understand, along with Santos (2015, p. 63), how we can edify counter-hegemonic forms of human rights in which spirituality stands as an uplifting and powerful principle.

Needless to say, I am not claiming that there is no such thing as human rights. In fact, some of the great accomplishments of oppressed groups throughout history are related to human rights battles, as with, for example, the civil rights movement, women's rights, children's rights. My claim is that despite such indisputable historical accomplishments, it is undeniable that extant hegemonic forms of human rights have been historically silencing not just religion, but also spirituality, as an integral component of human rights struggles. Granted, large swathes of the civil rights movement had a religious base. As hooks (2001) argues, it is impossible to accurately comprehend Malcom X—and other African American intellectual historical and contemporary figures—political struggle out of spirituality. The political dynamic of the civil rights movement, hooks (2001) maintains, cannot be grasped out of the forces of the divine spirit. The racial question in the U.S. cannot be fully addressed out the spiritual matrix (West, 1988).

In such context, I argue that it is crucial to develop a counter-hegemonic platform of human rights (Santos, 2015) that explicitly positions spirituality at its very core. In doing so, we will be able to question the real epistemological colors (Mignolo, 2018) of the current hegemony of human rights that, in so many ways, produces specific visibilities at the expense of the invisibilities it creates (Santos, 2014). The resulting paradoxes are entirely and overtly irrefutable. Why, then, is the alternative so frightening to so many? Is it because spirituality allows the mind to be set free? I would answer with a resounding "Yes!"

And so we continue to take one step forward and two steps back. Talking about women's rights or liberation is all well and good, but we are nowhere near achieving wage equality. Is there some sort of "machismo" that defends woman's rights while contradicting this stance in the financial realm? The same could be said about children's rights. Despite being sanctioned by the United Nations—in its Declaration of the Rights of the Child and elsewhere—the fact is that our society violates children's purportedly universally agreed-upon rights daily, even denying very basic rights, such as access to education and health care. We still have a racialized, genderized, and class-laden school system that functions as a sorting machine, advocating for specific groups while condemning others (Spring, 1989). As a consequence of this systemic violation, oppressed groups do, in their desperation, attempt to act counter-hegemonically to counter the manifold forms of oppression they experience. But such oppression virtually eliminates the possibility of critical thinking, and it destroys the necessary and liberating hope all "beings" need.

With de Certeau (1984), I argue that hegemonic forms of human rights have cracks, and that it is vital to work counter-hegemonically within those fissures if we want to truly promote change. We do have some examples of counter-hegemonic moves expanding the tenets of hegemonic platforms of human rights (Santos, 2007). One such case comes from the great advances produced by liberation theology (Boff, 1987). However, there is much sense in the nomenclature per se. Although my argument here is not religion-based, credit needs to be given to the liberation theologists and other religious thinkers who stood counter-hegemonically with those facing social struggles, seeing such a stance as a matter of honesty and morality:

> For such theologies, turning to God amounts to turning to a neighbor when in need. In doing so, they opened the possibility of releasing in society a new energy, "infusing" social struggles with the motivational strength contained in spirituality. This explains in part why in the last forty years so many human rights activists who paid with their lives for their commitment to struggles for social justice were disciples of liberation theology in one of its many versions. (Santos, 2015, p. 81)

Liberation theology and related movements were in part the result of critical observation and questioning of the praxis and practice of theology. Such theologies inevitably had to position themselves on either the side of the oppressor or on the side of the oppressed, as Santos (2015) claims.

I guess the central question in my argument is one that yet again echoes Santos' (2015) reasoning: Can human rights genuinely be used in a counter-hegemonic way? It is a tough question to ponder, but I would—carefully—respond in the affirmative. This stance, however, simultaneously situates the spiritual "being" in two different yet intertwined positions, i.e., the individual and the collective. While, individually, the spiritual "being" always thinks and acts counter-hegemonically, s/he needs to work collectively to be able to translate their way of reading the word and the world (Freire & Macedo, 1987) into a collective counter-hegemonic battle.

This is the challenge with which individuals must contend, and that spirituality itself faces; navigating it adeptly and with strength will help to edify collective, non-discursive, alternative forms of human rights. This imperative process will substantiate spirituality as a human rights issue, while also fortifying the "side" of human beings in the battle to generate a counter-hegemonic form of human rights that does not silence spirituality as a human right. In this sense, it is a social justice issue (Purpel, 1989), too. Needless to say, this implies a drastic reconceptualization of the very field of curriculum studies, as well as the infusion of spiritual ways of thinking and living into the disciplines (Zajonc, 2003). The curriculum needs to reflect more than just the real material conditions of our lives, it needs to address the endless "immaterial dynamics at the heart of liberal education" (Zajonc, 2003, p. 51); at present, it does neither.

In the end, the democratically imposed moral blindness caused by the absence of knowledge and wisdom leads to an ambivalence of feelings that "permeates everything" (Balman, 2016), causing unambiguous discourse, fear of the truth, worldwide misery, ignorance, prejudice, countless forms of inequality, and, in Henry David Thoreau's words, "lives of quiet desperation." In contrast, spirituality as I have defined it allows people to think freely, inhabiting and honoring inclusive ecologies of knowledge; it enables them to thrive as individuals and in communities, and exercise their purpose in life. When imbued into the educational system and curriculum, spirituality will feed the inner development of children as full and flourishing "beings" from the very start and over the course of their learning—and teachers and others in their lives will profit as well.

So again I ask: Why has spirituality been denied if it is a positive, restorative, life-enhancing, constructive, reflective, and internally fulfilling element of life? Do the neoliberal modern-colonial matrix and its minions fear facing fully self-realized, whole "beings" so deeply that they will prevent genuine human development at any cost? Are teachers and professors themselves content to teach and perpetuate generations of personally unfulfilled and intellectually undeveloped automatons? While my life has held serious challenges and hardships, I refuse to believe that the apparent answers to these questions, as manifested in the status quo, reflect the best of humanity. After all, isn't a truly beneficial, life-affirming education what we, as human beings, should aim to offer our students?

# References

Abrahão, B. (2012). Autobiographical research: Memory, time and narratives in the first person. *European Journal for Research on the Education and Learning of Adults*, *3*(1), 29–41. doi:10.3384/rela.2000-7426.rela0051

Adorno, T., & Horkheimer, M. (2016). *Dialectic of enlightenment*. Verso.

Agamben, G. (2005). *The state of exception*. Chicago University Press.

Amin, S. (2008). *The world we wish to see: Revolutionary objectives for the twenty-first century*. Monthly Review Press.

Anderson, L. (2009). *Advocacy leadership toward a post-reform agenda in education*. Routledge.

Andreotti, V. (2011). *Actionable postcolonial theory in education*. Palgrave Macmillan.

Andreotti, V. (2014, October 10). *Actionable curriculum theory*. Retrieved March 20, 2019, from https://ojs.library.ubc.ca/index.php/jaaacs/article/view/187728/185833

Anyon, J. (1997). *Ghetto schooling: A political economy of urban education*. Teachers College Press.

Anzaldúa, G. (2002a). (Un)natural bridges. (Un)safe places. In G. Anzaldúa & A. Keating (Eds.), *This bridge we call home* (pp. 1–6). Routledge.

Anzaldúa, G. (2002b). Now let us shift...the path of conocimiento...inner work, public acts. In G. Anzaldúa & A. Keating (Eds.), *This bridge we call home* (pp. 540–578). Routledge.

Appiah, A. (2005). *The ethics of identity*. Princeton University Press.

Apple, M. (1979). *Ideology and curriculum* (1st ed.). Routledge and Kegan Paul.

Apple, M. (1982). *Education and power*. Routledge.

Apple, M. (1995). *Cultural politics and education*. Teachers College Press.

Apple, M. (2000). *Knowledge, power, and education*. Routledge.

Apple, M. (2001). Education and new hegemonic blocs: Doing policy the "right" way, *International Studies in Sociology of Education*, *8*(2), 181–202, doi:10.1080/0962021980020021

Apple, M. (2004). Away with all teachers: The cultural politics of home schooling. *International Studies in Sociology of Education*, *10*(1), 61–80. doi:10.1080/09620210000200049

Apple, M. (2013). *Education and power*. Routledge.

Apple, M. (2014). *Official knowledge: Democratic education in a conservative age*. Routledge.

Apple, M., & Beane, J. (1995). *Democratic schools*. Association for Supervision and Curriculum Development (ASCD).

Arrighi, G. (2005). *The long twentieth century*. Verso.

Arya, A. (1997). Emotional maturity and values of superior children in family. In *Fourth survey of research in education* (Vol. 11). NCERT.

Babbage, F. (2004). *Augusto boal*. Routledge/Taylor & Francis.
Baker, B. (2009). *New curriculum history*. Sense Publishers.
Bardin, L. (1999). *Análise de conteúdo*. Edições 70.
Bauman, Z. (1998). *Globalization: the human consequences*. Polity Press.
Bauman, Z. (2008). *Consuming life*. Polity Press.
Bauman, Z. (2018). *Liquid modernity*. Polity Press.
Bauman, Z., & Donskis, L. (2016). *Moral blindness: The loss of sensitivity in liquid modernity*. Polity Press.
Benedict, R. (2005). *Patterns of culture*. Routledge and Kegan Paul.
Bennett, L. (2012). The personalization of politics. *The Annals of the American Academy of Political and Social Science, 644*(1), 20–39. doi:10.1177/0002716212451428
Berger, L., Berger, B., & Kellner, H. (1981). *The homeless mind: Modernization and consciousness*. Vintage Books.
Bhabha, H. (1994). Culture's in-between. In S. Hall & P. du Gay (Eds.), *Questions of cultural identity* (pp. 53–60). Sage.
Boal, A. (2019). *Theatre of the oppressed*. Pluto Press.
Boff, L. (1987). *Introducing liberation theology*. Orbis Books.
Boni, A., & Walker, M. (2018). *Universities and global human development: Theoretical and empirical insights for social change*. Routledge.
Boyd, D. D. (2012). The critical spirituality of Paulo Freire. *International Journal of Lifelong Education, 31*(6), 759–778.
Bowles, S., & Gintis, H. (2011). *Schooling in capitalist America; Educational reform and the contradictions of economic life*. BASIC.
Brummelen, H. V., Koole, R., & Franklin, K. (2004). Transcending the commonplace: Spirituality in the curriculum. *Journal of Educational Thought, 38*(3), 237–254.
Cabral, A. (1973). *Return to the source: Selected speeches*. Monthly Review Press.
Cabral, A. (1979). *Unity and struggle: Speeches and writings*. Monthly Review Press.
Camões, L. de, Barreto, F. J. V., & Monteiro, J. G. (1843). *Obras completas de Luis de Camões*. Livraria Europa de Baudry.
Carr, D. (2008). Music, spirituality, and education. *Journal of Aesthetic Education, 42*(1), 16–29.
Carrington, V., Rowsell, J., Priyadharshini, E., & Westrup, R. (2016). *Generation Z: Zombies, popular culture and educating youth*. Springer.
Césaire, A. (1977). *Discourse on colonialism*. Monthly Review Press.
Chomsky, N. (2002). *Chronicles of dissent*. New Star Books.
Chomsky, N., & McChesney, R. (2006). *Profit over people: Neoliberalism and global order*. Seven Stories Press.
Cronk, L., & Wasielewski, H. (2008). An unfamiliar social norm rapidly produces framing effects in an economic game. *Journal of Evolutionary Psychology, 6*(4), 283–308. doi:10.1556/jep.6.2008.4.3

Crouch, C. (2011). *The strange non-death of neoliberalism*. Polity Press.
da Cunha, E. (1902). *Os Sertões*. Laemmert & C. Editores.
da Cunha, E. (1947). *Revolt in the backlands*. The University of Chicago Press.
Dantley, E. (2005a). The power of critical spirituality to act and to reform. *Journal of School Leadership, 15*(5), 500–518. doi:10.1177/105268460501500502
Dantley, M. (2005b). African American spirituality and Cornell West Notions of prophetic pragmatism. *Education Administration Quarterly, 41*(4), 651–674.
Darder, A. (1991). *Culture and power in the classroom: A critical foundation for bicultural education*. Bergin & Garvey.
Darder, A. (1996). *The critical pedagogy reader* (2nd ed.). Routledge.
Darder, A. (2012). *Culture and power in the classroom: Educational foundations for the schooling of bicultural students*. Routledge.
Darder, A. (2014). Cultural hegemony, language, and the culture of forgetting: Interrogating restrictive language policies. In P. Orelus (Ed.), *Affirming language diversity in schools and society: Beyond linguistic apartheid*. Routledge.
Darder, A. (2016a). Latinos, education, and the church: Toward a culturally democratic future. *Journal of Catholic Education, 19*(2), 18–53. doi:10.15365/joce.1902032016
Darder, A. (2016b). Foreword. In *Curriculum: Decanonizing the field* (p. XVI). Peter Lang.
Darder, A. (2019). *Decolonizing interpretative research*. Routledge.
Darder, A., & Giroux, H. A. (2011). *Culture and difference: Critical perspectives on the bicultural experience in the United States*. Bergin & Garvey.
Darder, A., Torres, R., & Baltodano, M. (2017). *The critical pedagogy reader*. Routledge.
de Certeau, M. (1984). *The practice of everyday life*. University of California Press.
De Lissovoy, N. Means, A., & Saltman, K. (2014). *Toward a new common school movement*. Routledge.
Denzin, N., & Lincoln, Y. S. (Eds.). (2000). *Handbook of qualitative research*. Sage.
Deutsch, M. (1979). Education and distributive justice: Some reflections on grading systems. *American Psychologist, 34*(5), 391–401. doi:10.1037//0003-066x.34.5.391
Dewey, J. (1897, January 16). Declaration concerning education. *The School Journal, LIV*(3), 77–80.
Dewey, J. (1916). *Democracy and education*. SMK Books.
Dewey, J. (1934). *A common faith*. Yale University Press.
Drisko, M. (2017). *On power and dominance: Cultural politics in the opioid crisis in Massachusetts* [Unpublished master's thesis]. University of Massachusetts-Dartmouth.
Drucker, P. (1995). *Managing in a time of great change*. Routledge.
Drucker, P. (2002). They're not employees, they're people. *Harvard Business Review, 80*(2), 70–77.
Dussel, E (1995). *The Invention of the Americas: Eclipse of "the other" and the myth of modernity* (M. D. Barber, Trans.). Continuum.
Dussel, E. (2008). *Coloniality at large: Latin America and the postcolonial debate*. Duke University Press.

Dussel, E. (2011). *Politics of liberation: A critical global history*. SCM Press.

Dussel, E. (2014). *Ethics of liberation in the age of globalization and exclusion*. Duke University Press.

Eagleton, T. (1991). *Ideology: An introduction*. Verso.

Elias, J. (2006). Paulo Freire: Religious educator. *Religious Education, LXXI*(1), 40–56. doi:10.1080/0034408760710106

Elliott, M., & Weaver, J. (1998). That the people might live: Native American literatures and Native American community. *American Literature, 70*(4), 900. doi:10.2307/2902396

Escobar, A. (2008). *Territories of difference: Place, movements, life, redes*. Duke University Press.

Escobar, A. (2013). *Globalization and the decolonial option*. Routledge/Taylor & Francis.

Fabricant, M., & Fine, M. (2013). *The changing politics of education: Privatization and the dispossessed lives left behind*. Routledge/Taylor & Francis.

Fairclough, N. (2003). *Analysing discourse: Textual analysis for social research*. Routledge.

Fanon, F. (1961). *The wretched of the earth*. Penguin.

Fiennes, S. (2012). *Slavoj Žižek: The pervert's guide to ideology* [Film]. Zeitgeist Films.

Fine, M. (1991). *Framing dropouts: Notes on the politics of an urban high school*. State University of New York Press.

Fine, M. (2003). *Silenced voices and extraordinary conversations: Re-imagining schools*. Teachers College Press.

Foucault, M. (1980). *Power/knowledge: Selected interviews and other writings* (C. Gordon, Trans.). Harvester Press.

Foucault, M. (1984). *The Foucault reader*. Vintage.

Foucault, M. (1990). *The archaeology of knowledge*. Routledge.

Foucault, M., Fruchaud, H.-P., Lorenzini, D., & Luxon, N. (2019). *Discourse & truth and Parrēsia*. The University of Chicago Press.

Foucault, M., Gros, F., Ewald, F., & Fontana, A. (2006). *The hermeneutics of the subject: Lectures at the Collège de France, 1981–1982*. Picador.

Foucault, M., & Pearson, J. (2001). *Fearless speech*. Semiotext(e).

Fowler, J. W. (1995). *Stages of faith: The psychology of human development and the quest for meaning*. HarperOne.

Frank, A. (2009). *Latin America: Underdevelopment or revolution. Essays on the development of underdevelopment and the immediate enemy*. Monthly Review Press.

Fraser, N. (2000). Rethinking recognition. *New Left Review, 3*, 107–120.

Freire, P. (1970). Cultural action for freedom. *Harvard Educational Review (U.A.)*.

Freire, P. (1972). *Pedagogy of the oppressed* (M. B. Ramos, Trans.). Penguin Education.

Freire, P. (1973). *Conscientização: Teoria e prática da libertação, uma introdução ao pensamento de Paulo Freire*. Cortez & Moraes.

Freire, P. (1974). *Education for critical consciousness* (M. B. Ramos, Trans.). Bloomsburry.
Freire, P. (1979). *Conscientização. Teoria e Prática da Libertação*. Cortez e Moraes.
Freire, P. (1991). *Pedagogy of hope* (R. R. Barr, Trans.). Continuum.
Freire, P. (1994). *Pedagogy of hope* (R. R. Barr, Trans.). Continuum.
Freire, P. (1995). *Pedagogy of the oppressed*. Penguin Education.
Freire, P. (2017). *Pedagogy of hope: Reliving pedagogy of the oppressed*. Bloomsbury.
Freire, P., & Macedo, D. (1987). *Literacy: Reading the word and the world*. Bergin & Garvey.
Friedman, M. (1964). *Capitalism and freedom: Problems and prospects: Proceedings of a conference in honor of Milton Friedman*. University Press of Chicago Press.
Gay, P. (1996). *Questions of cultural identity*. Sage.
Geary III, J. (2013). *Questions of spirituality in education* [Dissertation]. University of Illinois at Urbana-Champaign.
Geo-JaJa, M., & Majhanovich, S. (Eds.). (2016). *Effects of globalization on education systems and development debates and issues*. Sense Publishers.
Giddens, A. (1990). *The consequences of modernity*. Polity Press.
Giroux, H. (1981). *Ideology, culture and the process of schooling*. Temple University Press.
Giroux, H. (1988). *Teachers as intellectuals: Toward a critical pedagogy of learning*. Bergin & Garvey.
Giroux, H. (1998). *Teachers as intellectuals: Toward a critical pedagogy of learning*. Bergin & Garvey.
Giroux, H. (2009). *Market-driven hysteria and the politics of death*. Retrieved January 12, 2017, from https://truthout.org/articles/marketdriven-hysteria-and-the-politics-of-death/
Giroux, H. (2012). *Disposable youth: Racialized memories, and the culture of cruelty*. Routledge.
Giroux, H. (2015). *Zombie politics in the age of casino capitalism*. Peter Lang.
Giroux, H. (2018). *The terror of neoliberalism: Authoritarianism and the eclipse of democracy*. Routledge.
Giroux, H. (2019). *On critical pedagogy*. Bloomsbury.
Goodson, I. (2006). The rise of life narrative. *Teaching Education Quarterly*, Fall, 7–21.
Goodson, I. (2012). *Developing narrative theory: Life histories and personal representation*. Routledge.
Goody, J. (2008). *Capitalism and modernity: The great debate*. Polity Press.
Goody, J. (2011). *The domestication of the savage mind*. Cambridge University Press.
Gordon, L. (2015). *Disciplinary decadence: Living thought in trying times*. Routledge. doi:10.4324/9781315635163
Greene, M. (1978). *Landscapes of learning*. Teachers College Press.
Greene, M. (1988). *The dialectic of freedom*. Teachers College Press.

Greene, M. (1995). *Releasing the imagination: Essays on education, the arts, and social change*. Jossey-Bass Publishers.

Griffin, D. (1988). *Spirituality and society: Postmodern visions*. State University of New York Press.

Grosfoguel, R., & Georas, C. S. (2000). "Coloniality of power" and racial dynamics: Notes toward a reinterpretation of Latino Caribbeans in New York City. *Identities*, 7(1), 85–125. doi:10.1080/1070289x.2000.9962660

Grumet, M., & McCoy, K. (1997). *Education: Discipline analysis*. Towson State University National Center for Curriculum Transformation Resources on Women.

Gula, R. (2002). *Nonsense: A handbook of logical fallacies*. Axios Press.

Guy, T. (1999). *Providing culturally relevant adult education: A challenge for the twenty-first century*. Jossey-Bass Publishers.

Hall, S. (1996). *Questions of cultural identity*. Sage.

Hall, S. (2000). *Representation: Cultural representations and signifying practices*. Sage.

Hall, S. (2011). *Modernity: An introduction to modern societies*. Blackwell Publishing.

Hall, S., & Gay, P. D. (2013). *Questions of cultural identity*. Sage.

Han, B., & Butler, E. (2015). *The burnout society*. Stanford University Press-Stanford Briefs.

Harmon, W. E. G. (1952). *Education*. Pacific Press Publishing Association.

Harvey, D. (1989). *The condition of postmodernity*. Blackwell Publishing.

Harvey, D. (2011). *A brief history of neoliberalism*. Oxford University Press.

Hirsch, E. (2016). *Why knowledge matters: Rescuing our children from failed educational theories*. Harvard Education Press.

hooks, b. (1999). *Remembered rapture: The writer at work*. Holt Paperbacks.

hooks, b. (2000). *Teaching to transgress: Education as the practice of freedom*. Routledge.

hooks, b. (2001). *All about love*. William Morrow.

hooks, b. (2003). *Teaching community: A pedagogy of hope*. Routledge.

hooks, b. (2009a). *Where we stand: Class matters*. Routledge.

hooks, b. (2009b). *Teaching critical thinking*. Routledge.

hooks, b. (2014). *Yearning, race, gender, and cultural politics*. Routledge.

hooks, b. (2017). *Teaching to transgress: Education as the practice of freedom* (new ed.). Routledge.

hooks, b. (2018). *All about love: New visions*. William Morrow.

Huebner, D. (n.d.). *Appropriating belief systems* [Unpublished paper].

Huebner, D. (1976). The moribund curriculum field: Its wake and our work. *Curriculum Inquiry*, 6(2), 153–67.

Huebner, D. (1962). Politics and curriculum. In H. Passow (Ed.), *Curriculum crossroads* (pp. 87–95). Teachers College Press.

Huebner, D. (1966). Curricular language and classroom meanings. In J. Macdonald & R. Leeper (Eds.), *Language and meaning*. ASCD.

Huebner, D. (1975). Curriculum as concern for man's temporality. *Theory into Practice, 6*(4), 172–179.

Huebner, D. (1976). The Moribund curriculum field: Its wake and our work. *Curriculum Inquiry, 6*(2), 153–167. doi:10.1080/03626784.1976.11075527

Huebner, D. (1985a). Education and spirituality. In *The lure of the transcendent: Collected essays by Dwayne E. Huebner* (pp. 401–416). Routledge.

Huebner, D. (1985b). An educator's perspective on language about God. In *The lure of the transcendent: Collected essays by Dwayne E. Huebner* (pp. 257–284). Routledge.

Huebner, D. (1985c). Babel: A reflection in confounded speech. In *The lure of the transcendent: Collected essays by Dwayne E. Huebner* (pp. 312–320). Routledge.

Huebner, D. (1985d). *The lure of the transcendent: Collected essays by Dwayne E. Huebner*. Routledge.

Huebner, D. (1999). The tasks of the curricular theorist. In W. Pinar (Ed.), *The lure of the transcendent: Collected essays by Dwayne E. Huebner* (pp. 212–230). Lawrence Erlbaum.

Hursh, D. (2007). Assessing no child left behind and the rise of neoliberal education policies. *American Educational Research Journal, 44*(3), 493–518. doi:10.3102/0002831207306764

Hursh, D. (2008). *High-stakes testing and the decline of teaching and learning: The real crisis in education*. Rowman and Littlefield.

Hursh, D. (2016). *The end of public schools: The corporate reform agenda to privatize education*. Routledge.

Hursh, J. (2012). Advancing women's rights through Islamic law. *Berkeley Journal of Gender, Law & Justice, 27*(2), 1–55. https://ssrn.com/abstract=2173872

Iannone, R., & Obenauf, P. (1999). Toward spirituality in curriculum and teaching. *Education, 119*(4), 737. https://link.gale.com/apps/doc/A55410000/AONE?u=mlin_oweb&sid=googleScholar&xid=813039a7

Idleman, S. (1993). The role of religious values in judicial decision making. *Indiana Law Journal, 68*(2), Article 3.

Janson, E., & Paraskeva, J. (2015). Curriculum counter-strokes and strokes: Swimming in non-existent epistemological rivers. *Policy Futures in Education, 13*(8), 949–967. doi:10.1177/1478210315579981

Jensen, R. (2004). *Citizens of the empire: The struggle to claim our humanity*. City Lights Books.

Jones, L. (2005). *The big ones: How natural disasters have shaped us (and what we can do about them)*. Anchor Books.

Jupp, J. (2017). Decolonizing and de-canonizing curriculum studies: An engaged discussion organized around João M. Paraskeva's recent books. *American Association for the Advancement of Curriculum Studies, 12*(1), 1–16. https://doi.org/10.14288/jaaacs.v12i1

Keating, A. (2002). Charting pathways, marking thresholds...a warning. An introduction. In G. Anzaldúa & A. Keating (Eds.), *This bridge we call home* (pp. 6–20). Routledge.

Kirylo, J. D., Boyd, D., & Araújo, F. A. M. (2017). *Paulo Freire: His faith, spirituality, and theology*. Sense Publishers.

Kliebard, H. (1995). *The struggle for the American curriculum, 1893–1958*. Routledge.

Kohm, L. (2008). A Christian perspective on gender equality. *Duke Journal of Gender Law & Policy, 15*, 339–364. https://ssrn.com/abstract=2112419

Krug, E. (1969). *The shaping of the American High School, 1880–1920*. The University of Wisconsin Press.

Laclau, E. (1990). *New reflections on the revolution of our times*. Verso.

Ladson-Billings, G. (1994). *The dreamkeepers: Successful teachers of African American children*. Jossey-Bass Publishers.

Lamont, C. (1990). *The philosophy of humanism*. Humanist Press.

Lazzarato, M. (2011). *The making of the indebted man: An essay on the neoliberal condition*. Semiotext(e).

Leonardo, Z., & Grubb, W. (2019). *Education and racism: A primer on issues and dilemmas*. Routledge.

Levine, L. (2001). *The opening of the American mind: Canons, culture, and history*. Beacon Press.

Lipman, P. (1998). *Race, class, and power in school restructuring*. State University of New York Press.

Loewen, J. (1995). *Lies my teacher told me: Everything American history textbooks get wrong*. The New Press.

Lorde, A. (2007) *Sister outsider*. Crossing Press.

Macdonald, J. B. (1974). *Theory as a prayerful act: The collected essays of James B. Macdonald*. Peter Lang.

Macdonald, J. B., & Zaret, E. (1975). *Schools in search of meaning: Prepared by the ASCD 1975 Yearbook Committee*. ASCD.

Macedo, D., Dendrinos, B., & Gounari, P. (2003). *The hegemony of English*. Routledge.

Maldonado, N. (2007). On the coloniality of being. *Cultural Studies, 21*(2–3), 240–270. doi:10.1080/09502380601162548

Maldonado, N. (2018). *Decolonialidade E pensamento afrodiaspórico*. Autêntica.

Marcuse, H. (1974). *The aesthetic dimension: Toward a critique of Marxist aesthetics*. Beacon Press.

Marti, I. (2009). Entrepreneurship in and around institutional voids: A case study from Bangladesh. *Journal of Business Venturing, 24*(5), 419–435. doi:10.1016/j.jbusvent.2008.04.006

Martins, P. (1991). *A reinvenção do sertão: Organização social e governança do bello monte (1893–1897)*. Hucitec Editora.

McCarthy, M. (1991). *Discourse analysis for language teachers.* Cambridge University Press.

McKee, A. (2003). *Textual analysis: A beginner's guide.* Sage.

McLaren, P. (2015). *Life in schools: An introduction to critical pedagogy in the foundations of education.* Taylor & Francis.

McNamara, P. (2007). *Where God and science meet: How brain and evolutionary studies alter our understanding of religion.* International Society for Science and Religion.

Mignolo, W. (2005). *The idea of Latin America.* Blackwell Publishing.

Mignolo, W. (2007). Delinking. *Cultural Studies, 21*(2–3), 449–514. doi:10.1080/09502380601162647

Mignolo, W. (2011). *The darker side of Western modernity: Global futures, decolonial options.* Duke University Press. doi:10.1215/9780822394501-001

Mignolo, W. (2012). *Local histories/global designs: Coloniality, subaltern knowledges, and border thinking.* Princeton University Press.

Mignolo, W., & Escobar, A. (2013). *Globalization and the decolonial option.* Taylor and Francis.

Mignolo, W., & Walsh, C. (2018). *On decoloniality: Concepts, analytics, praxis.* Duke University Press. doi:10.1215/9780822371779

Moreira, M. (2017). And the linguistic minorities suffer what they must? A review of conflicts in curriculum theory through the lenses of language teacher education. *Journal of the American Association for the Advancement of Curriculum Studies, 12*(1), 1–17.

Muthu, S. (2003). *Enlightenment against empire.* Princeton University Press.

Muthu, S. (2012). *Empire and modern political thought.* Cambridge University Press.

Nkrumah, K. (1964). *Consciencism.* Monthly Review Press.

Nkrumah, K. (1965). *Neo-colonialism: The last stage of imperialism.* International Publishers.

Nussbaum, M. (1997). *Cultivating humanity: A classical defense of reform in liberal education.* Harvard University Press.

Nussbaum, M. (2010). *Not for profit: Why democracy needs the humanities.* Princeton University Press.

Oliveira, I. (2017). Itinerant curriculum theory against epistemicides: A dialogue between the thinking of Santos and Paraskeva. *American Association for the Advancement of Curriculum Studies, 12*(1), 1–16. https://doi.org/10.14288/jaaacs.v12i1

Palmer, P. (1997). *The courage to teach: Exploring the inner landscape of a teacher's life.* Jossey-Bass Publishers.

Palmer, P. (1999). *Let your life speak: Listening for the voice of vocation.* Jossey-Bass Publishers.

Palmer, P. (2003a). Education as spiritual formation. *Educational Horizons, 82*(1), 55–67.

Palmer, P. (2003b). Teaching with heart and soul. *Journal of Teacher Education*, 54(5), 376–385. doi:10.1177/0022487103257359

Paraskeva, J. M. (2007). Kidnapping public schooling: Perversion and normalization of the discursive bases within the epicenter of new right educational policies. *Policy Futures in Education*, 5(2), 137–159. http://dx.doi.org/10.2304/pfie.2007.5.2.137

Paraskeva, J. M. (Ed.). (2010). *Unaccomplished Utopia: neoconservative dismantling of public higher education in the European Union*. Sense.

Paraskeva, J. M. (2011). *Conflicts in curriculum theory: Challenging hegemonic epistemologies* (1st ed.). Palgrave.

Paraskeva, J. M. (2012). Challenging the neoliberal global Minotaur. *Policy Futures in Education*, 6(12), 700–716.

Paraskeva, J. M. (2015a). *Curriculum: Whose internationalization?* Peter Lang.

Paraskeva, J. M. (2015b). Opening up the curriculum canon to democratize democracy. In J. M. Paraskeva & S. Steinberg (Eds.), *Curriculum: Decanonizing the field* (pp. 3–38). Peter Lang.

Paraskeva, J. M. (2016). *Curriculum epistemicide: Towards an itinerant curriculum theory*. Routledge/Taylor & Francis.

Paraskeva. J. M. (Ed.). (2018). *Towards a just curriculum theory: The epistemicide*. Routledge.

Paraskeva, J. M. (2021a). *Curriculum and the generation of Utopia*. Routledge.

Paraskeva, J. M. (2021b). Did Covid-19 exist before the scientists? Towards curriculum theory now. *Educational Philosophy and Theory*, 54(2), 2–13. doi:10.1080/00131857.2021.1888288

Paraskeva, J. M. (2022). *Conflicts in curriculum theory* (2nd ed.). Palgrave.

Paraskeva, J. M. (Ed.). (2023). *The curriculum. A new comprehensive reader*. Peter Lang.

Paraskeva, J. M., & Janson, E. (2018). *Voicing the silences of social and cognitive justice: Dartmouth dialogues*. Sense Publishers.

Paraskeva, J. M., & Macrine, S. (2015). Neoliberal pedagogy of debt vs debtor pedagogy. In M. Peters, J. Paraskeva, & T. Besley (Eds.), *Global financial crisis and education restructuring*. Peter Lang.

Parrella, F. (1995). *Paul Tillich's theological legacy: Spirit and community*. Walter De Gruyter.

Pear, T. (1944). The concept of mental maturity. *Bulletin of the John Rylands Library*, 28(2), 404–421. https://doi.org/10.7227/bjrl.28.2.7

Pinar, W. (1975). *Curriculum theorizing: The reconceptualists*. McCutchan.

Pinar, W. (1994). The method of *currere*. In W. Pinar (Ed.), *Autobiography, politics and sexuality: Essays in curriculum theory 1972–1992* (pp. 20–27). Peter Lang. (Original work published 1975)

Pinar, W., Reynolds, W., Slattery, P., & Taubman, P. (1995). *Understanding curriculum: An introduction to the study of historical and contemporary curriculum discourses*. Peter Lang.

Pinar, W. (Ed.). (1998). *The passionate mind of Maxine Greene: "I am...not yet."* Falmer Press.

Pinar, W. (2004). *What is curriculum theory?* Routledge.

Pinar, W. (2015). *Educational experience as lived: Knowledge, history, alterity.* Routledge.

Pinar, W. (2019). *Moving images of eternity: George Grant's critique of time, teaching, and technology.* University of Ottawa Press.

Popkewitz, T. (1976). Myths of social science in curriculum. *The Educational Forum, 40*(3), 317–328.

Postman, N. (2008). *The end of education: Redefining the value of school.* Vintage.

Price, T. (2017). Welcome to the new Taylorism! Teacher education meets itinerant curriculum theory. *American Association for the Advancement of Curriculum Studies, 12*(1), 1–16. https://doi.org/10.14288/jaaacs.v12i1

Quijano, A. (1991). Colonialidad y modernidad/racionalidad. *Perú Indígena, 29*(1), 11–21.

Quijano, A. (2000). Coloniality of power and Eurocentrism in Latin America. *International Sociology, 15*(2), 215–232. doi:10.1177/0268580900015002005

Quijano, A. (2007). Coloniality and modernity/rationality. *Cultural Studies, 21*(2), 168–178. http:www.campusdemocracy.org/wtoed.html/

Reis, P. (2017). *The real colors of coloniality: The open veins of the achievement gap* [Dissertation]. University of Massachusetts.

Richardson, L. (2000). Writing: A method of inquiry. In N. K. Denzin & Y. S. Lincoln (Eds.), *Handbook of qualitative research* (2nd ed., pp. 923–948). Sage.

Rizvi, F., & Lingard, B. (2000). Globalization and education: Complexities and contingencies. *Educational Theory, 50*(4), 419–426. doi:10.1111/j.1741-5446.2000.00419.x

Rorty, R. (2003). *Education, philosophy, and politics.* Rowman & Littlefield.

Saad-Filho, A., & Johnston, D. (2005). *Neoliberalism a critical reader.* Pluto Press.

Saltman, K. (2003). The securitized student. *University of Louisville, Workplace, 10,* 47–63.

Saltman, K. (2009). Putting the public back in public schooling: Public schools beyond the corporate model. *DePaul Journal for Social Justice, 3*(1), 8–32. https://via.library.depaul.edu/cgi/viewcontent.cgi?referer=https://www.google.com/&httpsredir=1&article=1051&context=jsj

Saltman, K. (2015). *The failure of corporate school reform.* Routledge.

Saltman, K. (2014). *The politics of education: A critical introduction.* Routledge.

Santos, B. (2004, March 27). *The world social forum.* Transnational Institute. Retrieved September 24, 2021, from https://www.tni.org/en/article/the-world-social-forum

Santos, B. (2006). Globalizations. *Theory, Culture & Society, 23*(2–3), 393–399. https://doi.org/10.1177/0263276406023000268

Santos, B. (2007). *Another knowledge is possible.* Verso.

Santos, B. (2014). *Epistemologies of the south: Justice against epistemicide.* Routledge/Taylor & Francis.

Santos, B. (2016). *Epistemologies of the South and the future.* http://www.boaventuradesousasantos.pt

Santos, B. (2018). *Epistemologies of the South: Justice against epistemicide.* Routledge/Taylor&Francis.

Santos, B., Galanter, M., Komesar, N., Thome, J., Couso, J., Webber, J., & Johnson, R. (2007). Beyond abyssal thinking: From global lines to ecologies of knowledges. *Review (Fernand Braudel Center), 30*(1), 45–89. http://www.jstor.org/stable/40241677

Sarmiento, D. (1961). *Life in the Argentine republic in the days of the tyrants; Or, civilization and barbarism.* Collier McMillan Publishers.

Schubert, W. (1986). *Curriculum: Perspective, paradigm, and possibility.* Macmillan.

Schubert, W. (2010). Journeys of expansion and synopsis: Tensions in books that shaped curriculum inquiry, 1968–present. *Curriculum Inquiry, 40*(1), 17–94. https://www.jstor.org/stable/40602915

Schubert, W. (2017). Growing curriculum studies. *Journal of the American Association for the Advancement of Curriculum Studies, 12*(1), 1–21.

Selden, S. (1999). *Inheriting shame: The story of eugenics and racism in America.* Teachers College Press.

Shaw, C. (1966). *The jack-roller: A delinquent boy's own story.* Chicago University Press.

Sheldrake, P. (2011). *A brief history of spirituality.* Blackwell Publishing.

Shields, C. (2006). *Transformative leadership primer.* Peter Lang.

Simmel, G. (1978). *The philosophy of money.* Routledge.

Sleeter, C. (2011). *Turning on learning: Five approaches for multicultural teaching plans for race, class, gender and disability.* Wiley.

Smith, D. (2004). *Zygmunt Bauman: Prophet of postmodernity.* Polity Press.

Smith, L. T. (2012). *Decolonizing methodologies: Research and indigenous peoples, by Linda Tuhiwai Smith* (1st ed.). Zed Books.

Solgi, M., & Safara, M. (2018). Philosophical-psychological's recognition of concept of spirituality. *Advances in Language and Literary Studies, 9*(2), 84–90.

Sontag, S. (2003). *Regarding the pain of others.* Farrar, Straus and Giroux/Picador.

Spring, J. (1989). *The sorting machine revisited.* Pearson Longman.

Süssekind, M. (2017). Against epistemological fascism: The (self) critique of the criticals—A reading of Paraskeva's itinerant curriculum theory. *American Association for the Advancement of Curriculum Studies, 12*(1), 1–16. https://doi.org/10.14288/jaaacs.v12i1.189707

Thiong'o, N. (2011). *Decolonizing the mind: The politics of language in African literature.* James Currey Ltd.

Tierney, W. (2000). Undaunted courage: Life history and the postmodern challenge. In N. K. Denzin & Y. S. Lincoln (Eds.), *Handbook of qualitative research* (pp. 537–553). Sage Publications.

Tillich, P. (1952). *The courage to be.* Yale University Press.

Tillich. P. (2000). *The courage to be* (2nd ed.). Yale University Press.

Tillich, P. (2011). *The shaking of the foundations*. Wipf and Stock.

Tinker, G. E. (2008). *American Indian liberation: A theology of sovereignty*. Orbis Books.

Tisdell, E. J. (2005). *Exploring spirituality and culture in adult and higher education*. Jossey-Bass Publishers.

Tlostanova, M., & Mignolo, W. (2012) *Learning to unlearn. Decolonial reflections from Eurasia and the America*. The Ohio State University Press.

Trousdale, A. (2005). Intersections of spirituality, religion and gender in children's literature. *International Journal of Children's Spirituality, 10*(1), 61–79. doi:10.1080/13644360500039709

Tyack, D. (1974). *The one best system: A history of American urban education*. Harvard University Press.

Valenzuela, A. (1999). *Subtractive schooling: U.S.-Mexican youth and the politics of caring*. State University of New York Press.

Vygotsky, L. (1997). *The collected works of L. S. Vygotsky Vol. 4. The history of the development of higher mental functions* (M. Hall, Trans.; R. W. Rieber, Ed.). Plenum Press. (Original work published in 1931)

Waaijman, K., & Vriend, J. (2002). *Spirituality: Forms, foundations, methods*. Peeters.

Watson, V. (2012). *Learning to liberate: Community-based solutions to the crisis in urban education*. Routledge.

West, C., & Ritz, D. (2010). *Brother West: Living and loving out loud*. Smiley Books.

Williams, R. (1966). *Modern tragedy*. Verso Editions.

Williams, R. (1989). *Resources of hope*. Verso Books.

Williams, R. (1998). *Cultural theory and popular culture: A reader*. University of Georgia Press.

Williams, R. (2005). *Culture and materialism: Selected essays*. Verso Books.

Williams, R., Blackburn, R., & Gable, R. (2007). *Resources of hope: Culture, democracy, socialism*. Verso Books.

West, C. (1988) *Keeping faith: Philosophy and race in America*. Routledge.

Wright, A. (2000). *Spirituality and education*. Routledge.

Wringe, C. (2002). Is there spirituality? Can it be part of education? *Journal of Philosophy of Education, 36*(1), 157–170.

Wylie, C. (2020). *Mindf*ck: Cambridge analytica and the plot to break America*. Random House.

Zinn, H. (1999). *A people's history of the United States: 1492–present*. HarperCollins.

Printed in the United States
by Baker & Taylor Publisher Services